The Frame of the Century?

Pulpless.Com™ Books by J. Neil Schulman

Novels
Alongside Night (trade edition forthcoming)
The Rainbow Cadenza (trade edition forthcoming)

Nonfiction
The Robert Heinlein Interview and Other Heinleiniana
The Frame of the Century?
Stopping Power: Why 70 Million Americans Own Guns
    (trade edition forthcoming)
Book Publishing in the 21st Century, Volumes One and Two

Short Stories
Nasty, Brutish, and Short Stories (trade edition forthcoming)

Omnibus Collection
Self Control Not Gun Control

Collected Screenwritings
Profile in Silver and Other Screenwritings
    (trade edition forthcoming)

The Frame of the Century?

J. Neil Schulman

PULPLESS.com, inc.
775 East Blithedale Ave., Suite 508
Mill Valley, CA 94941, USA.
Voice & Fax: (500) 367-7353
Home Page: http://www.pulpless.com/
Business inquiries to info@pulpless.com
Editorial inquiries & submissions to
editors@pulpless.com

Sections of this book were first published between 1997 and 1998 on the
World Wide Web as a paperless book™ from Pulpless.Com™.

First Pulpless.Com™, Inc. Edition June, 1999.
Library of Congress Catalog Card Number: 99-60515
Trade Paperback Edition ISBN: 1-58445-060-6
Adobe Acrobat Edition ISBN: 1-58445-061-4
HTML Edition ISBN: 1-58445-062-2

Book and Cover designed by CaliPer, Inc.
Cover Illustration by Billy Tackett, Arcadia Studios
© 1999 by Billy Tackett

Author's Note

This book is a highly personal account of the author's journalistic investigation of a crime. While the author has documented his subjective personal beliefs regarding the individuals referred to by name in the book, drawn from his knowledge of the facts, and has constructed speculative scenarios regarding these individuals based on inferences from those facts, it is in no way the author's intent that anyone should regard this book or any scenario within it as an accusation against any real individual. In those instances where the author does make statements regarding a real individual's possibly criminal activities or possible personal misconduct, the reader is cautioned that such statements are not based on any personal knowledge of the author but only on representations made to the author by sources whose credibility must be judged by weighing their statements against other known facts. It is the author's intent that this book's publication attempt to stimulate a threshhold of probable cause sufficient for further official investigation of the Brown-Goldman murders on June 12, 1994, to explore and either falsify or verify the crime scenarios in this book. Any defamatory statement within this book with respect to any real individual is unintended, and the author retracts it herewith.

To Barbara Branden
Who Taught Me That Logic and Feelings
Are Both Tools of Cognition

Table of Contents

A Revelation

Everything is different than I thought.
What I thought was my cage
was the nest I'd built for myself.
What I thought was my life
was just my basic training.

We really don't know what's going on
right next to us.
The universe is so strange,
so surprising,
so dramatic.

Life can be exactly like
the most exciting novel
and for the writer,
how could I not jump in
to play one of the roles?

Shakespeare, after all,
used to play his characters.

But it's different
when your character suddenly is *You*,
and you find out
that you're not what you thought you were.

What had just been glimpses
through a dark glass
before
became an open window
for a few hours.

Do you know how long a few hours is
and what you can see
if you look around?
I wanted a glimpse
my curiosity was boundless
and be careful what you pray for
because the guy who answers
"Thy will be done"
has a real rough sense of humor.

The thing is, he climbed inside with me
and let me share the joke.

Unbefuckingleivable.

The game's afoot!
Heinlein was right.
Yoda was right.

The universe is not what it seems
and,
the amazing thing is

Neither are *You*.

February 18, 1997

Author's Introduction

I first published *The Frame of the Century?* on the World Wide Web almost two years ago.

The main essay in Part One, with the two postscripts, was published on my personal website on May 21, 1997, and a series of my answers to letters I received as a consequence of publishing it was placed on my website, and finally published May 31, 1997 as "Part Two, Additional Questions."

On June 21, 1997 I added an addendum to the book called "Ron Shipp's Alibi."

Ron Shipp, the focus of my investigation into the framing of O.J. Simpson for the Brown-Goldman murders, had made an appearance on *Larry King Live*, June 12, 1997, the third anniversary of the Bundy Drive murders. For the first time I was able to find, Ron Shipp was publicly representing that he had been at home the night of the murders. During that program, Shipp made a slip of the tongue that might possibly be interpreted as a confession that he'd been to Simpson's Rockingham estate the night of the murders.

I added "Part Three—New Allegations" on May 27, 1998.

During *The Frame of the Century?*'s almost two years as a free download from my website, close to 20,000 readers downloaded it. Without being available in any bookstore, the book was recommended as summer reading by a major American newspaper. I received perhaps two or three emails a week asking whether I had made any progress in my project to prove or disprove my theory. My answers to those inquiries were always vague optimism. The fact is, World Wide Web publication of my book opened up several sources to me who were intimately involved with O.J. Simpson, Nicole Brown Simpson, their friends and families, and the murder investigations themselves.

Much of the information I have been made privy to is material I still cannot publish, some because it is the result of the investigations of other writers who intend to publish it eventually themselves, and some because it involves sources who wish to remain nameless and would be compromised if I were to publish the information. But for some of this new information, my sources have allowed me to publish it, so long as I don't identify them. This is a common demand made to investigative journalists seeking information, regardless of the skepticism it is bound to raise.

My personal source for the allegation that Ron Shipp knew about Nicole's murder five hours before the time to which Shipp testified in the Simpson criminal trial—a source also pseudonymized by Dominick Dunne as "Charles McCracken" in his memoir *Another City, Not My Own*—is a man who was a close friend of both O.J. Simpson and Nicole Brown Simpson for many years.

Another of my sources, also close to the Simpson family, may yet write his own book someday, and is not yet ready to go on the record.

Both of these men think that while Ron Shipp may have been an accomplice to the murder of Nicole, they are convinced that the murders were carried out by O.J. Simpson himself. Yet, in extensive discussions with both of them, neither one has been able to give me a single reason, beyond alternative interpretations of facts that we both know, why they think O.J. Simpson is guilty.

When all is said and done, it comes down to their having lost faith in O.J. because he was unable to convince them of his innocence against a heavy weight of incriminating evidence. Both of them have, in their own minds, placed the burden of proof on O.J. Simpson to prove his innocence to them.

O.J. Simpson, a man of pride if nothing else—whether you choose to use the synonyms "conceit" or "egotism"—has declined to do so.

The third part of *The Frame of the Century?* updated the book with information I obtained in the first year following the book's web publication. I included a section on my call-in to KABC's *Larry Elder Show*—which resulted in the first and only response Ron Shipp has ever made to my investigation—and a meeting and subsequent correspondence I had with Larry; two more recent articles, an unanswered email I wrote to Fred Goldman's attorney in the civil suit against O.J. Simpson, Daniel Petrocelli, and my replies to comments made on my more-recent articles from Internet readers.

When I first wrote *The Frame of the Century?* I followed the principle of Occam's Razor that I would not make the theory more complex than necessary by bringing in elements that were not required by the theory and known facts. Since my book's first publication on the World Wide Web, the allegations of William Benson Wasz that on January 14, 1994 Robert Kardashian hired him to murder Nicole Brown Simpson have been made public.

The investigation of Wasz's allegations first and most completely by true-crime author, Joseph Bosco, and later by journalist David Bresnahan, and their impact on my own investigation, are the subjects of the chapter, "Wasz There A Conspiracy?" Wasz's allegations constituted a new element which required me to examine a more complex theory of why Nicole Brown Simpson might have been killed and why Ron Shipp, if he was even to be considered as a still-possible participant in the crime, would have had to be considered as one of several perpetrators rather than as a solo perpetrator.

Nonetheless, I am not eliminating my original theory of a one-man murder and frame-up (with a few unwitting accomplices before the fact and possibly some help well afterwards) as still possible. I have done no investigation whatsoever of William Benson Wasz and his allegations, and I don't see it as my job to lend or not lend any particular weight of credibility to them. I find it odd only that the Wasz allegations—well known to all principals in the Simpson criminal, civil, and child custody cases and common knowledge on the Internet—are still entirely unreported in all major U.S. media including newspapers, national magazines, and broadcast news. Apparently, nowadays, it's possible to keep a closely held secret among hundreds of thousands of people, just so long as it doesn't appear on the evening news.

The Frame of the Century? is not unique for suggesting that someone other than O.J. Simpson murdered Ronald Goldman and Nicole Brown Simpson and framed O.J. Simpson for them.

A book by Christopher Springer, *Solving the Simpson Murder Mystery*, presents the theory that not only did Mark Fuhrman plant evidence against O.J. Simpson, but that Fuhrman was the actual murderer.

The book *Blood Oath* by "Steven Worth" (now identified by David Bresnahan as an alias for software millionaire Charles Cass) posits that the Brown-Goldman murders and frame-up of O.J. Simpson were part of a long-standing conspiracy, motivated by a desire for interracial strife, not unlike the "Helter Skelter" of the Manson family cases.

A persistent email correspondent of mine uses the physics of sound and a deconstruction of his criminal-trial testimony to challenge Kato Kaelin's alibi and argues that Kato was the actual murderer.

I trust it's more than "not invented here" syndrome that causes me to reject these other theories out of hand. Not one of any other theory brought to my attention—Mafia hits, L.A.P.D.-C.I.A. plots, drugselling connections—meets the test of the Venn Diagram—the overlapping circles of personal access and motives, professional law-enforcement skills, perjured testimony, and premature knowledge—which has been the basis for my own investigation.

After a lengthy trial, a jury of twelve men and women quickly acquitted O.J. Simpson of the murders that took place at 875 South Bundy Drive in West Los Angeles, the night of June 12, 1994. This leaves the official police inquiry into who murdered Nicole Brown Simpson and Ronald Goldman still open. The Los Angeles Police Department's Robbery-Homicide Division still has a detective, Vic Pietrantoni the last time I checked, officially assigned to the case. Regardless of proclamations by attorney Daniel Petrocelli, a jury verdict in a civil suit does not change the fact that as far as the criminal justice system is concerned, reasonable suspicion—the corollary of reasonable doubt—exists that someone other than Orenthal James Simpson committed those murders.

Los Angeles County District Attorney, Gil Garcetti, whose office prosecuted O.J. Simpson, is terrified of the prospect that they not only blew the Trial of the Century but actually might have pursued a wild goose. There are reasonable grounds to conclude that the investigation of the Brown-Goldman murders has been, since before the Simpson trial, hampered by instances of obstruction of justice, and the corporate-owned major media, using the excuse that "if it ain't official, it ain't news," has been complicit in this inaction.

Other pundits declare further investigation passé, the case merely an artifact of celebrity with no social overtones, ignoring the obvious fact that five years after the murders you still can't escape the late-night TV monologues with their snide references to Simpson's guilt, or the ongoing statist attacks on the jury system premised on its presumed failure to convict Simpson.

It has been up to radical alternative journalists to conduct our own investigations until a threshold is reached where the public officials no longer have any choice but to do their job and investigate, and the major media to do *their* job and report.

Our standards of propriety today have fallen so far that they allow radio and television broadcasters to use their microphones to harangue their listeners with an assertion that a criminal jury was mistaken and that a man declared "not guilty" got away with murder. Two disagreeing jury verdicts, one criminal, one civil, establish reasonable doubt as a fact of public policy, if nothing else.

But these reasonable doubts are self-righteously ignored by these oracles of omniscience who justify their pronouncements of unquestionable guilt with cult worship of a failed prosecution's "mountain of evidence" that, upon close inspection, is revealed to be a plaster volcano suitable for a third-grader's science fair entry. These Orwellian Duckspeakers get away with their outrages against the dignity of due process without anyone punishing them for this arrogant irresponsibility.

Yet, if a writer like myself—with major credits—chooses to investigate the possibility that the first jury was right and someone else with means and opportunity *might have* committed these murders, *that* writer is subject to being called irresponsible by these media rabble rousers merely for demanding that a theory with supporting circumstance be investigated for its truth or falsity; and that writer must subject himself to public ridicule for refusing to kiss the ring of pundit-class wisdom.

With a media establishment like this, that has only *ad hominem* attack for its most worthy dissenters, no wonder Los Angeles has been set on fire twice in the last three decades.

In light of the current state of the evidence, I believe that questions and suspicions about who other than O.J. Simpson might have murdered Nicole Brown Simpson and Ronald Goldman on the night of June 12, 1994 are more reasonable than ever.

I will continue pursuing my investigation until either emerging facts prove the theory of my investigation false—in which case I will make a public apology to Mr. Ronald Shipp and his family for any emotional distress my investigation has caused them—or until facts emerge which prove my theory viable, in which case my energy and logic will have been vindicated, and Mr. Shipp will be subject to a more serious investigation than a lone writer is able to mount.

J. Neil Schulman,
January 18, 1999

Part One

Was O.J. Simpson Framed for Murder by his Biggest Fan?

> "When you have eliminated the impossible, whatever remains, however improbable, must be the truth."
> —Sir Arthur Conan Doyle, "The Sign of Four"

This is the story of a speculative theory I've been pursuing regarding the murders of Nicole Brown Simpson and Ronald Goldman, a double homicide for which O.J. Simpson was tried and acquitted for murder, then tried and found liable for civil damages.

But let me admit now that this story I am about to tell you is as much about what I am and the way my mind works as it is about anything I may or may not have found.

The very second sentence of this story—the one in the paragraph just prior to this one—has an assumption in it which may not be true: that what I have been doing has been a process of investigation leading to discovery, rather than a process of fictional invention.

I've been a writer now for about 27 years. During those years I've written both fiction and non-fiction.

I've written short stories and novels that I knew were completely made up: both the characters and the events of the story were fictitious.

I've written a fictional screen treatment about the pending divorce of the Prince and Princess of Wales—written when they were actually just barely home from their honeymoon—and an episode of the *Twilight Zone* TV series, in which I had the assassination of JFK interrupted by a time-traveling Kennedy descendant. In these particular stories for the screen, I freely mixed together real persons and fictional characters into fictitious, even outright fantasy, situations.

I've written brutally honest poetry about my own feelings after my divorce. I've written dry theoretical essays and cool op-ed pieces and straight journalistic reportage and sarcastic articles and passionate polemics and half of an unproduced stageplay in which the characters are closely modeled on myself and several of my friends, but the situations and dialogue are deliberately farcical.

Throughout all these years of writing, I've always known exactly where the dividing line was between that which was real and that which existed only as artifacts of my imagination.

But not this time.

This time, I've either discovered something which practically nobody else can possibly believe—they can't believe it just because it's just so damned improbable—or else the fiction writer in me has imagined a story so compelling that it's fooled even its author into thinking that it might be true.

I need to be very precise here, because I'm going to be relating a theory regarding a murder case that involves real people and real events, and I will be using real names, including the name of a real-life person I will be casting into the role of a sociopathic criminal.

I must emphasize as strongly as I can that I am *not* accusing this person of the crimes I will be attaching to his name because I can not offer any evidence to support the events I attribute to him.

But I believe that if O.J. Simpson did *not* commit the murders at 875 South Bundy, this individual is the only one I know of who possibly could have framed O.J. for them.

The particular real individual whose name I will be using is merely a person who, given my knowledge of the evidence, I am unable to eliminate as the murderer of Nicole Brown Simpson and Ronald Goldman.

The particular real individual whose name I will be using is merely a person who, in the mind of this particular writer of fact, fiction, and fantasy, *might* have committed the crimes in the manner that I am speculating.

But this individual has *never* been a suspect in the Brown-Goldman murder investigation by the Los Angeles Police Department, the police agency which investigated these murders. I know this from a direct statement to me by a detective in the Robbery/Homicide Division of the L.A.P.D..

In fact, this statement is so important I will repeat it again, in boldface: **The particular real individual whose name I will be using has *never* been a suspect in the Brown-Goldman murder investigation by the Los Angeles Police Department.**

This individual is fully entitled to continue living his life unbothered by the suspicions of a writer such as myself, a writer who may be guilty of allowing his imagination to run away with him.

This individual is cloaked in a presumption of innocence that is the cornerstone of the American system of jurisprudence. He has no legal obligation whatsoever to respond to, or explain the reality of, or refute anything I am outlining. He, and his family, should be able to live unmolested by *Hard Copy* and the *Enquirer* and *People* magazine unless, at some future time, it should come to pass that evidence should be discovered that makes my speculation more than idle.

Were I, in fact, to publicly assert, as a matter of established fact, that my theory is true, I think this individual would be entitled to sue me, as well as any publication that were to publish such an assertion, for libel ... and win.

So I cannot state strongly enough: what you are reading is

speculation, not fact. But it's speculation that is based on and consistent with known facts.

The only reason why, in good conscience, I feel that I'm justified in using the real name of this individual is that he has willingly made himself a public figure in the aftermath of the Brown-Goldman murders. It is not because he was a witness in the criminal trial of O.J. Simpson. That appearance, even though on television, was compelled by subpoena. But he has since that compelled television appearance willingly appeared on national television shows such as *Charles Grodin* and *Larry King Live*, and even allowed a photograph of himself and his family to accompany an interview with him in *People* magazine.

That willing and affirmative abandonment of his right to privacy, in a legal sense, makes him a public figure, with all that implies under our civil legal system. Still, let me make clear: I do not know this individual personally, and I bear him no malice. The only reason he is the centerpiece of this story is that either by providence, or chance, or his own acts, or some unknown combination of these, he fits into the puzzle I have been working on, and makes the other pieces come together.

Even though he has no legal obligation to respond, I provided an earlier draft manuscript of this story to this individual. A cover letter, and a subsequent telephone conversation I initiated with his attorney, has promised that I would not publish this if he provided me convincing proof that my theory is wrong. I made that offer because of journalistic ethics. I did not and do not bear him any malice and have no desire to subject him causelessly to public scrutiny and suspicion, if he can simply prove me to be wrong. If you are reading this other than in manuscript, that means that he failed to provide me such convincing proof. I will add a postscript to the published version of this story including his response, if any.

Early on, I brought my theory to the Robbery/Homicide Division of the City of Los Angeles Police Department, and to the office of Los Angeles County District Attorney Gil Garcetti, requesting that they re-open the currently closed investigation of this crime on the basis of my theory. I have never been told that they ever did anything about it, so I assume that they have not.

I don't blame them.

My speculations defy common sense and strain the credulity of anyone who's in the business of investigating crimes, because my speculations suggest that the *corpus delicti* found in the Brown-Goldman murder investigation—the body of evidence that led police and prosecutors to investigate, indict, and try O.J. Simpson for these murders—did not come about the way any professional investigator should assume it did, but that a "reality" was deliberately created by an obsessed individual with professional skills, for the specific purpose of leading police and prosecutors in the false direction of O.J. Simpson.

I'm going to suggest that those who argue that O.J. Simpson could not have been framed for the murders, and those who suggested that he was framed by Mark Fuhrman for racial motives, are both wrong.

I'm going to argue that a possible motive for a frame-up of O.J. Simpson had nothing to do with the color of his skin, but everything to do with his being a celebrity.

I'm going to suggest as a speculative theory that Nicole Brown Simpson was murdered by an individual who had the specific intent of framing O.J. Simpson for her murder. I speculate that the intended primary victim of this double murder was, in fact, O.J. Simpson, and that the murderer wanted to forever ruin O.J. Simpson's celebrated reputation and take away from him the woman he was obsessively in love with. I speculate that Nicole's murder was a means to this end ... and that Ron Goldman just showed up to drop off a pair of lost eyeglasses to Nicole's condo at 875 South Bundy at the tragically wrong time, and might have died trying to defend her.

My theory suggests that not only an innocent man was framed

for a double murder he did not commit, by an obsessed fan whom a celebrity had allowed into his life, but that the evidentiary frame up—including blood identifiable in the laboratory as the celebrity's—was in place before the first police officer arrived at 875 South Bundy at midnight June 13, 1994, and at O.J. Simpson's estate at 360 North Rockingham five-and-a-half hours later.

My theory suggests that not only the celebrity was framed, but the detectives investigating the case were framed, the accused man's lawyers were framed, the prosecutors were framed, the families of both the victims and the celebrity were framed, and—when the case was put on TV and made into the Trial of the Century—anyone who watched the unfolding of the evidence of this case was framed.

My theory may be dead wrong. I have found no evidence to convince me that it is right.

But I have been unable to discover any evidence in my careful study of the evidence brought out regarding these murders that convinces me that my speculative theory is wrong, either. The evidence I have found which has been presented against O.J. Simpson is as compatible with my theory as the theory that O.J. Simpson committed these murders.

If two explanations of the evidence can exist simultaneously, I acknowledge that there are still two good reasons to prefer the explanation that O.J. Simpson is the murderer. The first is that this explanation is simpler: the tool of logic called Occam's Razor suggests that the explanation requiring the fewest elements is the one to be preferred. The second reason is that the explanation of the evidence that points to O.J. Simpson is more ordinary.

One could combine these two reasons into the old aphorism: common sense tells us that if it looks like a duck and walks like a duck and quacks like a duck, then it *is* a duck.

My speculation is that in this case, common sense fails us, the wildly improbable can happen, and that what we have had presented to us is what duck hunters call a *decoy*.

This "decoy" has never been investigated with any tenacity. The Los Angeles Police Department thought they were investigating only a murder, not a frame-up. To the extent that O.J. Simpson's defense team seriously contemplated that their client had been framed, their only theory was that the frame was by detectives investigating the case.

Yet, if O.J. Simpson was, in fact, framed, then there is a *corpus delicti*—a body of evidence—for a *second* crime.

Follow the reasoning, please.

L.A.P.D. detectives investigating the Brown-Goldman murders found a body of evidence leading to O.J. Simpson as the murderer. These pieces of evidence are the *corpus delicti* of that crime, the murders. This is the only crime that has been investigated so far.

But if O.J. Simpson did not commit those murders, then there is a second crime to be investigated: the framing of O.J. Simpson for the murders with those pieces of evidence which appear to be the *corpus delicti* which were found by the L.A.P.D. detectives.

The O.J. Simpson defense team only investigated the scenario that the frame-up of O.J. was done by the L.A.P.D. after the murders were committed, and their suspicions led them in the directions of Detectives Mark Fuhrman and Philip Vannatter, the "twin devils of deception," as Johnnie Cochran called them in his summation.

What I did at a certain point was to eliminate as a possibility that the Los Angeles Police Department would frame O.J. Simpson for the Brown-Goldman murders. Consequently, any frame-up—the crime of creating a false *corpus delicti* for the murders—must have been committed before the L.A.P.D. arrived on the scene.

Whoever did the frame-up has to be either the murderer or an accomplice of the murderer. Whoever did the frame-up would have had to be able to know that O.J. Simpson had no alibi at the time of the murders, as well as being able to create the *corpus delicti* of the murders that frames O.J. for the murders. Whoever did the frame-up has to be able to bring to the crime scene evidence of O.J. Simpson being the murderer—including such possible items as O.J.'s blood, shoes, gloves, a watch cap, and O.J.'s white Bronco—in order to accomplish the *corpus delicti* of the frame-up.

Any investigation I've done was premised on the idea that following the *corpus delicti* of a frame-up would lead to the murderers of Nicole Brown Simpson and Ronald Goldman.

I have pursued an investigation of my theory for several obvious motives, and two inobvious ones. Some of these motives are mundane; but two are not. Some are not particularly noble, and two are.

So let's get my crass motives for this investigation out of the way, first.

Ego. If my theory were to turn out to be right, then I'm smarter than Sherlock Holmes, and reprints of the classic works by Arthur Conan Doyle should, in honor of my feat of ratiocination, correct the spelling to "Scherlock." If I am right, then what even I thought was my megalomaniacal ego may, in fact, be too small for the overfed and underexercised body it's in. The satisfactions of being able to say "I told you so" to people richer than I am, more celebrated than I am, and generally regarded as more accomplished than I am would be enormous.

Money. This case has already generated almost fifty books, many of them bestsellers, with the largest advance of the lot coming in at around four million bucks. As a freelance writer, I'm in chronic debt. I would be kidding myself if I didn't admit that the prospect of not only getting out of debt but being set up for life hasn't been enormously appealing to me.

Fame. I wasn't particularly popular as a child. As a matter of fact, most of my schoolmates despised me. I was a fat smartass with a big vocabulary. I don't know that anyone ever totally gets over the psychic wounds one suffers as a child, but becoming world famous for accomplishing something worthwhile and sensational is certainly not a bad analgesic for the pain. It also gets your phone calls to your agent returned, and gets you good seats in restaurants.

Good regard. This isn't the same thing as fame. This is having people you already know and respect know and respect you, too. It starts with one's own family. There's nothing like having your parents tell you, "You did good." This is also true of one's offspring, and friends.

And now, the noble, and perhaps inobvious, motivations for me to have pursued this.

A Love of Truth. As long as I can remember, I have feared the counterfeit. Because of that, paradoxes and contradictions have always bothered me, and created that state of mind called cognitive dissonance.

As soon as I heard that O.J. Simpson was a suspect in the murders of Nicole Brown Simpson and Ronald Goldman, I paid close attention not only to the facts of the case as they were brought out first in the media, then later in the trials, but also to how O.J. Simpson was observed reacting. You will notice that I did not say "acting." Acting can be faked, or we would not have a movie industry. Reacting can also be faked, but it requires a much better thespian than anyone who has worked with him professionally has suggested O.J. Simpson is.

Irrespective of the evidence that has tended to incriminate O.J. Simpson for these murders, I have always believed that his demeanor has been predominantly exculpatory in moments when I do not believe he would have been capable of faking his reactions.

One moment in Simpson's trial is I think indicative. For most of the prosecution's case, O.J. Simpson appeared tense, scribbling notes on a pad. Finally, it was the defense's turn, and O.J.'s mother, Eunice, took the stand. For the first time during the trial, the TV cameras showed O.J. Simpson as relaxed, and he smiled at her as he watched his mother's testimony.

I do not know what sort of person you would have to be to be able to smile at your mother when you are on trial for butchering two human beings. No doubt Marcia Clark and Christopher Darden could have argued that only a sociopath could smile under those circumstances.

Of course there is another explanation, which we must at least place on the table.

A man with a clear conscience, because he is innocent of the crime for which he is on trial, could smile at his mother under those circumstances.

Regardless of prosecution spin, the simple fact is that when O.J. Simpson was telephoned in a Chicago hotel room by L.A.P.D. Detective Ron Phillips phoning Simpson from his own home, to tell him that Nicole had been killed, Simpson immediately made plans to return home and did so as fast as he could—so, abruptly, according to one hotel employee, Caroline Gobern, that she considered him rude about it. It is true that Simpson telephoned his lawyer from the airliner going home, and prosecutor Marcia Clark suggests this as evidence of a guilty demeanor. But wouldn't you call your attorney if you learned in previous phone calls that a search warrant in a murder investigation had been granted for your estate?

When Simpson arrives home, he finds his home swarming with police and a media circus. He's immediately handcuffed, which lets him know that he is indeed a suspect. Even so, when L.A.P.D. detectives ask him to accompany them to police headquarters to be interviewed about the murders, he agrees immediately, even though grief and exhaustion would be perfectly reasonable grounds for his attorney, Howard Weitzman, to delay the interview for a day or so. Instead, after consulting with Weitzman for a half hour, Simpson agrees to talk to the detectives *without* his attorney present. Any licensed criminal attorney, especially one who knew or suspected that his client might be guilty, would never have allowed this if there were anything on earth he could do to prevent it. Instead, Weitzman goes to lunch and just asks the detectives to read Simpson his rights and record the interview. This request from Simpson's attorney does nothing to protect Simpson; but it would have protected the detectives from any confession being thrown out of court for a violation of Simpson's *Miranda* rights.

During the interview with L.A.P.D. robbery-homicide detectives Tom Lange and Philip Vannatter, while Simpson is quite possibly still in the "denial" stage of grief, in shock, and exhausted from almost no sleep in thirty hours (combined with two air flights and, at minimum, a high-profile family crisis), Simpson is tentative and imprecise in his answers to the detectives' questions. He can't account for blood evidence the detectives found, and appears to be making guesses about where it might have come from. He makes no glaring admissions which lead to guilt, but he does speak as if he assumes that a gun was the murder weapon, inviting the detectives to inspect his gun collection.

Whatever else he might be thinking, Simpson reacts as if he expects facts will clear him of suspicion. When Vannatter says to him, "We've got some blood on and in your car, we've got some blood at your house, and sort of a problem," Simpson's *immediate* response is, "Well, take my blood test." Simpson not only has *agreed* to a blood test, he has suggested it, first, *himself.* And when Lange asks about the possibility of a polygraph exam, Simpson asks "Does it work for elimination?"

Why would a guilty man who—regardless of anything else—is stressed to the max and exhausted, have thought to ask if a lie detector could *clear* a man? Are we to believe that even under these circumstances, Simpson is capable of not just giving a per-

formance from a memorized film script, which is his only professional acting experience, but of improvising a convincing dramatic performance on the spot while maximally stressed and
exhausted?

I keep on hearing rumors that Simpson confessed. Each time
I have tried to track down one of these rumors, I find it has been
denied. Rosie Grier denied to a Simpson investigator that Simpson
had confessed to him in his jail cell during a bible-reading ses-
sion. Simpson attorney, Robert Shapiro, denies that Simpson ever
confessed either to him or to Weitzman, whom Shapiro replaced—and emphasizes that Simpson declared his innocence
upon their first meeting and never wavered.

And, an L.A.P.D. detective asserted to me, after Simpson's loss
in the civil suit against him for liability in the murders, that
Simpson had long-before confessed to his criminal attorneys,
and that Simpson was planning to confess publicly, soon. I had
earlier spoken to two of Simpson's civil attorneys, who spoke as
if they still believed him innocent. Further, two days after this
detective's assertion to me, Simpson once again publicly asserted
his innocence—as he had consistently done since June 13, 1994.

The transcript of O.J.'s cell phone conversation with Detective Lange, during Simpson's famous June 17, 1994 Bronco ride
from Orange County back to Simpson's Rockingham house, has
Lange trying to talk Simpson out of suicide, when O.J. is sitting
in the back of Al Cowlings' Bronco with a Smith & Wesson .357
magnum revolver pointed at his head. Earlier in that Bronco
ride, according to Lawrence Schiller and James Willwerth in their
book, *American Tragedy*, O.J. Simpson made a cell phone call to
his friend Robert Kardashian, and Simpson had told Kardashian
that he had pointed the gun at his head and pulled the trigger
but it hadn't gone off.

During the cell-phone calls Simpson made to others from
Cowling's Bronco, including a call to Nicole's father, Lou Brown,
and his own mother, Simpson is crying, declaring his innocence,

and telling anyone who will listen that he has been framed. But he is definitely depressed and suicidal, and many observers have taken this to be an indication of guilt for the murders.

Those who observe Simpson feeling guilty about *something* in the aftermath of the murders are not without their clues.

In the book *Outrage*, by former prosecutor and famed author Vincent Bugliosi, Bugliosi relates how, in a cell-phone call to his mother from Cowling's Bronco, Simpson told his mother, "It was all her fault, Ma." Bugliosi interprets that Simpson means Nicole must have said something to make him mad enough to take a knife and nearly decapitate her, and is blaming the victim for instigating her own death.

But is there another possible explanation for Simpson's statement to his mother? Could he think Nicole caused her own death because he thought she was promiscuous since their divorce, that he believed Nicole tried seducing the wrong man and was killed for it? That explanation is consistent with Simpson being aware that Nicole had taken many lovers since their split-up.

Schiller and Willwerth include an excerpt from a microcassette tape recording Simpson made at Kardashian's house the day of the Bronco chase, just before his attempted suicide. In that tape, Simpson is asking himself how he got where he is, about to be arrested. "Everybody loved me, but I don't know why I was feeling so alone all the time." Those who think Simpson guilty can picture Simpson feeling lonely after Paula Barbieri left a phone message breaking up with him for refusing to take her to Sydney Simpson's dance recital, so he phones Nicole to ask for one more reconciliation, and when she tells him in graphic language what he can do to himself, he decides to drive over and murder her in a fit of rage. Or, "And there was things that caught up with me. Uhhhhh, I don't even know what I'm saying here.... Look where I am. I'm the Juice, whatever that means. But I felt at times like I was—ahhh!—I felt goodness in myself. I don't feel any goodness in myself right now. I feel emptiness.... I don't even know what I'm saying here! I don't even know what this tape is for."

A statement that one feels empty of goodness could certainly be interpreted as the beginning of a confession.

But the confession is never made.

Alternatively, for a man who's addicted to the adulation of his fans, the abandonment by his "public" might indeed make him feel empty. As an indication of that theory of his utter dependence on others for his self-esteem, Simpson's low spirits didn't rise after his jailing until he started reading the many thousands of supportive letters that were being written to him. After he saw that, he was a man restored.

That is why someone who wanted to utterly destroy O.J. Simpson—a fan who worshipped him and felt humiliated and rejected—might decide the best way to punish O.J. Simpson would be to utterly ruin his reputation, take his fans away from him. What better revenge than to drive a man into his own despairing suicide? No villain out of an Edgar Allan Poe story could dream up a better revenge.

Lange and Vannatter's book, *Evidence Dismissed*, contains the transcript of Lange's cell-phone call to Simpson in Cowling's Bronco. Lange is trying to talk Simpson out of committing suicide and tells Simpson just to throw his gun out the window so "nobody's gonna get hurt."

The transcript has Simpson answering, "I'm the only one who deserves—" and Lange cuts in, "No you don't deserve that."

Several writers have interpreted this as Simpson saying that he's the only one who deserves to get hurt because he started all this by murdering his ex-wife and Ron Goldman.

But surely, O.J. Simpson had plenty of other things to feel guilty about in what he saw as the last moments of his life? Perhaps it was his periodic abuse of Nicole over the course of their many-years love affair—abuse he could no longer apologize to her for? Or, perhaps, O.J. Simpson's guilt—as he replayed his life over and over in his mind—might have been caused by old regrets about not having been able to prevent the swimming-pool drowning death of the two-year-old daughter from his first marriage, right when Nicole and he had first moved into the Rockingham house together?

All these bits and pieces have been interpreted as evidence of a guilty demeanor. But none of this must necessarily be interpreted as O.J. Simpson's guilt for having committed the murders at Bundy.

But I am not the only person who considers O.J. Simpson's demeanor mostly consistent with innocence.

Attorney F. Lee Bailey knows how an innocent man reacts when charged with murdering his wife. Many years before he agreed to join Simpson's defense team, Bailey had been the defense lawyer who'd exonerated Dr. Sam Sheppard for murdering *his* wife, the famous case that was the basis for the TV series and movie *The Fugitive*. Years after his death, Sheppard has now been proved, by a recent DNA analysis, to indeed have been innocent. Upon Bailey's first meeting with Simpson in jail, Simpson once against asserted his innocence, as he had done consistently, and Bailey is reported by Schiller and Willwerth in *American Tragedy* to have remarked to Simpson's friend, Robert Kardashian, "There is no way this man could have committed those murders. He is innocent."

Renowned criminal-defense attorney Gerry Spence, whom O.J. Simpson had considered hiring early on, had an opportunity to observe Simpson intimately during the criminal trial, and his comment was that if O.J. Simpson committed these murders, then he did not *know* he committed them. Schiller and Willwerth report Simpson's reaction, upon being told of Spence's comment: "I know what I did, and I didn't do *this*."

Simpson is constantly ridiculed for never hiring detectives to look for the actual killers. But during his trial, Simpson had three private investigators following leads: former L.A.P.D. cop Bill Pavelic, former New York police detective, John McNally, and former law-enforcement officer and now a private investigator, Pat McKenna.

Of Simpson's investigators, Pat McKenna is the most emphatic in his belief in Simpson's innocence. Schiller and Willwerth report McKenna as accompanying forensic expert Dr. Henry Lee to visit Simpson in jail, where Lee brought up the subject of DNA.

In an account of the meeting in *American Tragedy*, McKenna describes Simpson's reactions. "[Simpson] starts the woe-is-me and I-would-never-hurt-Nicole routine. So what? McKenna has seen crocodile tears in jails from Miami to Chicago. Now Lee tells Simpson about possible DNA tests and other things that show his blood in all the wrong places. Suddenly it gets interesting: McKenna sees O.J. doesn't have that look on his face he knows so well, that geez-I'm-gonna-get-caught look. This is different. Like: How could this be? What does this mean?... On the way home... McKenna tells Lee about what he learned in Chicago. How absolutely regular Simpson seemed. Witness after witness described somebody who sounded like no actor."

Simpson's lawyers brought in two psychological professionals to evaluate Simpson during the trial.

Dr. Bernard Yoduwitz, a forensic psychiatrist, spent time evaluating Simpson in jail during the trial. According to *American Tragedy*, "Simpson had no obvious mental illness... no sign of the constant criminal aggression that marks criminal insanity ... He did not appear to be a psychopath, uninvolved with other human beings.... Psychopaths were almost always misfits.... He had, of course, reviewed Simpson's history of battering, but it did not measure up to that of the killers he knew. In seventeen years of stormy marriage, O.J. and Nicole had resolved any number of conflicts peacefully. Yes, there were incidents of violence, but there was not, by the doctor's standards, a pattern."

Dr. Lenore Walker, perhaps the top expert on domestic violence and spousal abuse (it was her work that defined the "batterer's syndrome" that would later be testified about in the prosecution's case), had been brought in by Simpson's defense team to interview Simpson and issue a report. When the prosecution decided to cut short its domestic-violence case and concentrate on forensic issues more, Dr. Walker was dropped from the defense witness list. But her opinions were made available to Lawrence Schiller to be used in *American Tragedy*, after the criminal trial.

According to Schiller and Willwerth, "Walker had administered a battery of tests: the Minnesota Multiphasic Personality Inventory, the Rorschach test, the Wechsler Scale of Intelligence test. Simpson's cognitive functioning was normal. His intelligence was in the superior range. His social skills were remarkable."

According to Walker's report, O.J. Simpson "did not fit the profile of a batterer who murders." "'He has good control over his impulses,'" Walker had said. "'He appears to control his emotions well.'"

Perhaps this is hard to believe for anyone who's heard Nicole's (highly edited) 911 calls to the police of October 25, 1993, where we hear O.J. Simpson obscenely ranting at Nicole. But then again, aside from shouting, all O.J. Simpson had done on that occasion was break a door that had already been broken and repaired once. O.J. never even entered the same room with Nicole on that occasion—and Nicole had later apologized to O.J. for calling the police.

According to Lenore Walker's report, "Simpson could control his anger. He had a bad temper, but he yelled and left, or just left."

These two professional opinions, had they been presented in court, would not have been consistent with the speculations Marcia Clark and Christopher Darden made during the trial, about O.J. Simpson's motivations, and his formation of an intent, to murder Nicole by slashing her to death.

At least I'm admitting that I'm speculating.

Prosecutors never do.

The contradiction between the physical evidence and O.J. Simpson's demeanor of innocence was the source of the cognitive dissonance that has led me on this quest for the truth—or a reasonable facsimile thereof.

A Passion for Justice. Simply stated: since I believe O.J. Simpson is innocent, for reasons that have nothing to do with the physical evidence, I would wish to clear his name if I can establish his innocence factually.

You don't have to believe me acting upon these two noble motives if you don't want to. Nobody nowadays wants to imagine that anyone has any motivations that aren't crass and self-serving.

But the twin passions for truth and justice means that one's view of the rightness and wrongness of things impacts upon one's life. If one can not distinguish the truth, then how can one know good from evil?

And as for justice: perhaps the race is not *always* to the swift, but if it's *never* to the swift, then why bother running? If the innocent can be punished for the crimes of the guilty, and the guilty man reaps the rewards of the innocent, then why, aside from a crass fear of getting caught, should anyone strive to do good and not do evil? It seems obvious to me that a world in which justice is something real is far too important in its effect on our daily lives, and our hopes for the future, to be regarded as not being a practical motive for an investigation.

Prior to this, I've written two articles on the O.J. Simpson case, that were published as chapters of my book *Self Control Not Gun Control*. In those articles, written in 1994 and 1995, I first expressed doubt about O.J. Simpson's guilt, then an outright belief in his innocence. I think it will be useful to the reader to establish my state of mind entering into the investigation I will be relating, so I will reproduce them here.

Is This A Case For Perry Mason?

1994

We've all seen the classic 60's show so much that we know the plot structure by heart. First, a dramatic murder of an ex-wife occurs where the suspect is obvious: a prominent ex-husband with a history of losing his temper violently. Second, damning circumstantial evidence provides the basis for the suspect being charged. Third, the suspect runs, and clinches his guilt in everyone's mind.

"You've just made your case twice as hard," says Perry Mason to his new client.

We all know that the actual murderer, someone we've given no attention until then, will confess under Perry's relentless cross examination at the end of Act Four, just before the final commercial.

The events surrounding the O.J. Simpson case have followed the Perry Mason scenario so closely to this point that it is irresistible for a scenarist such as myself to speculate on what everyone else seems to be avoiding: what if O.J. really didn't do it?

The dramatist is concerned with how long-term character will direct a person in their ultimate crisis. That's why it's hard to accept O.J. Simpson, a middle-aged family man regarded by most as a person seriously concerned with moral behavior, as laying in wait for his ex-wife just a few hours after attending their daughter's dance recital, then cold-bloodedly committing a brutal double murder more characteristic of a Ted Bundy or a Jeffrey Dahmer. The fiction writer couldn't get away with this: if someone can commit this savage a crime at the middle of their life, then where's the trail of bodies leading up to it?

There's also the problem of what our suspect actually did while he was AWOL from the police with his best friend. If there was "consciousness of guilt," why weren't they stealing a car and heading for Tijuana, instead of cruising aimlessly nearby with every cop for a hundred miles looking for them?

But the fiction writer would have a greater problem here. The suspect writes a despair-filled suicide note, proclaiming his innocence to the world, then heads for the grave of the victim whom he says he's always loved. He had a gun and planned to kill himself on his ex-wife's grave.

Here's the motivational problem: if our suspect actually committed the murder and is going to kill himself next then he *must* confess his guilt to his best friend, and the friend will show him the kindness of assisting his suicide to save him from the impending humiliations of arrest, public exposure, and possible execution.

But if the best friend instead does everything he can to keep our suspect from killing himself, then the suspect's soul-baring must never have happened and his continued protests of innocent despair are what motivated the friend to risk felony charges of abetting a fugitive in order to save him.

Perry Mason has his work cut out for him: an ambitious D.A. who sees this prosecution not only as the ticket to national fame, book deals, and higher political office, but a media circus that, like the tribal corn kings, proclaims a man a hero then sacrifices him on the public altar.

Everyone has something to gain from the harvesting of the Corn King. Pundits use him as an object lesson of what happens when social workers don't get to intervene early enough in domestic violence. Arbiters of culture declare that society has no use for heroes. Snobs condemn the unwashed masses who cheered their hero as he rode his chariot past them on the way to his sacrificial altar. And everywhere—everywhere—a people fighting off the boredom of their own colorless despair find a moment's brilliance when real life imitates drama.

O.J. Simpson may, in fact, be guilty. The detectives of the L.A.P.D. are not dummies, and neither are prosecutors who are resting their careers on a man who until now has been an exemplar of successful achievement.

Yet, prosecutor Hamilton Burger was back every week with an ironclad case, and if it had not been for Perry Mason's pursuit of the truth above all other agendas, justice would have gone awry week after week.

That was, after all, just make-believe. But when it comes to analyzing character, maybe fiction has more to teach us than history. Aristotle thought so.

We say that a man is innocent until proved guilty, so let's at least ask the question: If O.J. Simpson even *conceivably* might not have done these murders, who among us will search for who did?

O. J.

1995

I do not believe Orenthal James Simpson is guilty of the murders of Nicole Brown Simpson and Ronald Goldman.

In this opinion, I am joined by a majority of African Americans and a minority of my fellow Anglo Americans. I also seem to be alone in this view among every opinion-maker I know, from one end of the political spectrum to the other.

Everyone has an agenda they want served by the trial of O.J. Simpson.

The news, gossip, and talk media have a field day: a case such as this is their bread and butter for years. As Jimmy Durante used to say, "Everybody wants to get inta the act!"

The Los Angeles Police Department and the Los Angeles District Attorney's office both have a motivation to have tried O.J. Simpson for these murders because trying a celebrity brings vast publicity to them, both as individuals and as government entities. Personal publicity leads to career advancement for detectives and prosecutors; departmental publicity leads to increased funding opportunities.

Once having charged O.J. Simpson with this crime, convicting O.J. Simpson of the charges is a high-stakes game, in which the careers of detectives and prosecutors—and of the Los Angeles District Attorney, himself—will rise or fall according to whether or not O.J. Simpson is convicted. The trial of a more-ordinary defendant does not create incentives to falsify incriminatory evidence or suppress exculpatory evidence: both incentives exist in this case—and these extraordinary incentives have nothing to do with racism and everything to do with celebrity.

For the families of the victims, O.J. Simpson is a desirable person to believe committed these murders, because if their loved ones were murdered by some faceless, ordinary criminal, then these crimes lend no special grace to their loved one's memories.

If O.J. Simpson, a spousal abuser, did not murder Nicole Brown Simpson, then there is no grand cause to which her death can be dedicated as an example, and her death may seem unexplainable.

And even for the family of Ronald Goldman, having him murdered by a celebrity lends an explanation for his death in a way that having him murdered in an ordinary crime would not. According to Viktor Frankl in his book *Man's Search For Meaning*, the need to find an explanation or meaning in the death of a loved one is a necessary part of the healing of grief.

Without O.J. Simpson as murderer, such explanations are unknown, meaning is much harder to find, and solace is elusive.

Political conservatives, bent on seeing a restoration of tough treatment of criminals in this country, want O.J. Simpson convicted as proof that the criminal justice system can work.

Political liberals, who hate self-made millionaires, secretly want O.J. Simpson convicted as proof of their class-envy-derived feelings that anyone who fulfills the American Dream must be corrupt.

Radical feminists, bent on proving that men are beasts who first beat women then kill them, want O.J. Simpson convicted as proof that women need more legal protection against men.

The African American community is divided between those who feel O.J. Simpson should be punished because he married a white woman and lived the lifestyle of a rich white man, and those who want him exonerated because a white racist power structure is incapable of bringing true facts to light in a case involving an African American defendant who was married to a white woman.

Now let me reveal my agenda. I once personally encountered O.J. Simpson for all of ten seconds, and what I saw of him in that short a time left an indelible impression of him on my mind.

It was at a studio publicity screening of *The Empire Strikes Back* in 1980. O.J. Simpson and his then-young son, Jason, sat in the row in front of me. After the movie, as O.J. walked out of the screening room with his son, O.J. told him to pay close attention to Yoda's advice, "Do, or do not—but there is no try." I was left with the strong impression of a caring father who was concerned about seeing his son raised with strong values.

I was *not* left with the impression of a man who could cold-bloodedly murder his wife with their children asleep a few feet away.

I think O.J. Simpson, in spite of his having gotten drunk on occasion and maltreated his wife, is a man who when sober was extremely unlikely to have committed the brutal double murder with which he is charged, because the crimes do not logically follow from well-known facts about O.J. Simpson's character.

I am a writer by profession. I've written novels, screenplays, short stories, and journalism. Part of my craft is the study of character and motivation. The elements of character which are used to plot a story are based on our general knowledge of how people act in real life. A story in which individuals are shown doing things that don't follow from the established facts of their background fails to establish a "willing suspension of disbelief" in the reader, and fails the test of good writing.

My belief in O.J. Simpson's innocence is based on the known facts having failed to "suspend my disbelief." There are three main elements that give me reason to believe he is unlikely to be the murderer in this case.

First, I do not believe O.J. Simpson had sufficient motivation to want to kill his wife. He was not a loser without a life, was not sexually or romantically needy, and was not financially desperate. He was not destroying his life with drugs or alcohol. O.J. Simpson is a wealthy, attractive celebrity with charm and sex appeal who could have almost any woman he wanted. He was spending much of his life traveling, and his current girlfriend, Paula Barbieri is one of the most beautiful women alive. He had a prenuptial agreement with Nicole Brown Simpson that protected him from being financially drained by her.

No rational motive for premeditated murder can be derived from these facts.

Second, I believe that the circumstance of O.J. Simpson's activities on the day of the murders do not provide an adequate explanation for the formation of an intent for him to commit murder on that day. He had an obligation to attend his daughter's dance recital. He may have been in physical discomfort during the performance because of a flare-up of rheumatoid arthritis; this—aside from having to be present in a room with his ex-wife in stressful circumstances—would account for his seeming in a sullen mood during the performance. Yet, he seemed in a better mood by the end of the performance. Maybe he was just bored by the recital.

After the recital, he went home. We are told that he went out for some McDonald's fast food with Kato Kaelin and ate indifferently. Then there is some time—possibly as long as an hour—in which he seems to have been alone, without an alibi; except that we know that he called Paula Barbieri from his cellular phone during this period. This provides an indication that his focus during that unaccounted-for time was on his current girl-friend, not his ex-wife.

If he had been at home the previous week, stalking his ex-wife, his murdering her the night of June 12, 1994 would be easier to believe. If he had been drinking or doing cocaine during that afternoon or evening, uncharacteristic behavior would be easier to explain. There is no evidence to suggest that O.J. Simpson was engaging in obsessive or destructive behavior on the after-noon or early evening of June 12, 1994. Instead, even with a period of missing time, his known activities are consistent with a father who finds time to honor his daughter in the middle of a busy travel schedule. To my mind, this does not create a likeli-hood of the formation of an intent to commit murder.

Third, I do not believe that the method of the murder is one O.J. Simpson would have chosen, even if he had been inclined to kill Nicole Brown Simpson or Ronald Goldman. O.J. Simpson owned guns. A gun is a weapon which can be used from a dis-tance, making it less likely that one will be splattered with the victim's blood. O.J. Simpson has been repeatedly described as a man obsessed with cleanliness and neatness. He wouldn't allow smoking in his house. He has been described as folding his clothes neatly rather than just tossing them over furniture. He has been described as not even wanting to park his car under a tree because sap or leaves might dirty it. A bloody knifing is not the likely murder method for a man as compulsive about neat-ness as O.J. Simpson is described as being.

We have a murder with no witnesses, no murder weapon, and no fingerprints.

There is some blood, hair and fiber evidence linking O.J. Simpson to the murder scene; and a bloody glove on O.J.'s estate which matches one found at the murder scene.

There is knowledge that O.J. Simpson, when drunk, beat up Nicole Brown Simpson several times, the last known time several years ago; and more recently frightened her by busting into her house and shouting at her—an occasion on which he was not drinking and did *not* employ physical violence against her.

On what, then, are we to convict O.J. Simpson of these murders?

The negative proof that he can't provide an alibi for those exact minutes the murders were committed?

The fact that he was a spousal abuser, which provides less than a one-percent likelihood that this would lead to murder?

O.J. Simpson's despair about being charged with a double murder he may know he is innocent of, and a confused and panicked attempt to escape, knowing that a lifetime's worth of achievement and reputation had just been flushed down the drain?

Forensic evidence from police and prosecutors who have every incentive to convict O.J. Simpson for these murders and no incentive whatsoever to investigate the possibility that someone else may have committed them?

The physical evidence is not enough for me to convict him, given the exculpatory issues of character, motive, and formation of intent.

I think that there are so many people with agendas in this case, that the search for truth has been a casualty. If O.J. Simpson has been framed, it was not necessarily because of racist motives. It may well be that implicating O.J. Simpson was merely a convenient diversion by the actual murderer or murderers with their own unknown agendas.

We may never know, because by now, the actual murderers have had so long to cover their trail, no evidence will ever link them to their crimes.

It may be that even the "Dream Team" of lawyers defending O.J. Simpson believe their client guilty, and that in the absence of a solid alibi or evidence pointing to another culprit are simply doing the best they can to undermine the prosecution's case by the remaining means available.

Which leaves us with O.J. Simpson, a man already convicted in the media; a largely black jury which, if they acquit O.J. Simpson, will not be believed if they say it was because of lack of sufficient evidence; and a celebrity who—if innocent as seems at least possible—will never again regain his good name.

It's enough to make you wish Perry Mason was real.

That was how I thought about this case before I had any notion about how O.J. Simpson might have been framed for the Brown-Goldman murders.

After having researched this case in much more detail, I state my arguments why I believe him innocent differently, but my conclusions are the same. I don't see him as the sociopath that those who have decided he is guilty of these murders conclude that he must have been. I believe their conclusion of his guilt starts with the physical evidence, and then they project backwards onto O.J. Simpson the character of a person who must have been capable of committing the murders.

Jesus Himself would look guilty, merely by sitting at the defendant's table in a criminal trial. That's why the legal presumption of innocence is so important.

As a libertarian, I was also naturally inclined to view government with suspicion, and when I wrote these articles I had not yet eliminated in my mind the possibility that a police conspiracy was at work.

Today, as I write this, I must say I do not believe it would have been possible for any police officer to frame O.J. Simpson. I must agree on this point with those who think O.J. Simpson is guilty. Regardless of any possible racism by Mark Fuhrman—actual or merely invented by him to impress an attractive female screenwriter—I find it snaps even my elastic credulity to believe that Mark Fuhrman had anything to do with the murders of Nicole

Brown Simpson and Ronald Goldman—which is the only way he could have planted an Aris glove at the Bundy crime scene before L.A.P.D. patrolman Robert Riske discovered it there.

If O.J. Simpson was framed, I must conclude that the frame-up would have had to be in place before the first police officer arrived at the Bundy crime scene, two hours before Mark Fuhrman was called there.

Interestingly enough, the man whose name I will be using as my suspect in this case agrees with me.

I have one additional motivation for my persistent investigation: a purely subjective motivation. But I'll reserve discussing that for the second part of this book.

Vincent Bugliosi's book *Outrage* asserts as an incontestable fact that O.J. Simpson murdered Nicole Brown Simpson and Ronald Goldman. To make this assertion, Mr. Bugliosi must deny the intelligence and competence of anyone who disagrees with his assertion. This he does in copious detail.

I can understand the emotional force with which Mr. Bugliosi writes, and the passion for justice that makes him excoriate a man he thinks a smirking murderer, ridicule prosecutors he believes didn't do their job the way he thought it should be done, and dismiss the verdict of a jury that he believes was prejudiced, sloppy, and logically impaired.

In reading Mr. Bugliosi's book on the Simpson case, what seems to bother Mr. Bugliosi more than anything else is that O.J. Simpson appears totally unrepentant. If O.J. Simpson is, in fact, guilty, then Mr. Bugliosi's contempt for Simpson's demeanor is completely justified. But I believe Mr. Bugliosi makes a mistake in thinking that a man's demeanor is not evidence as worthy of being tested as physical evidence found at a crime scene, and if the two are in contradiction, one does not automatically veto the other. Mr. Bugliosi does assert that Simpson's demeanor is guilty;

but the instances he uses in his book are open to alternative interpretations—interpretations that you can find in the books on the case by Schiller & Willwerth or Joseph Bosco.

Mr. Bugliosi must rely on the same cognitive limitations as the rest of the human race. He is not omniscient. He just looks at the physical evidence that exists and assigns, in his own mind, a set of probabilities that this evidence compels certain conclusions. Those conclusions convince Mr. Bugliosi of O.J. Simpson's guilt, so therefore O.J. Simpson's demeanor, in Mr. Bugliosi's view, must be a devilish facade.

But the theory I present here wasn't figured by Mr. Bugliosi into his calculation of probabilities. Since Mr. Bugliosi seems married to common sense, I doubt very much that it would make any difference in his reading of the evidence anyway.

Marcia Clark, in her book, *Without A Doubt*, is as certain of O.J. Simpson's guilt, and as repelled by Simpson's demeanor of innocence, as is Vincent Bugliosi. But I find it less offensive coming from Marcia Clark. I admit, that may be my hormones talking.

I do find it amusing, however, that the only "abuse excuse" that appears in the trial of O.J. Simpson was Marcia Clark's accusations in her book that Judge Lance Ito's treatment of her contributed to her losing the case.

Some women are just unlucky with men.

If by some odd set of circumstances, my theory is ever proven to be true—if the dice Mr. Bugliosi has been rolling to calculate his odds were, unknown to him, loaded—then perhaps I may have some small lesson to teach him, and Marcia Clark, and others who think that there can be no reasonable doubt about O.J. Simpson's guilt.

After all, I have personally paid a visit to the *Twilight Zone.*

And that's always been good for a lesson or two.

Let me state an obvious fact. Nobody has been convicted of the murders of Nicole Brown Simpson and Ronald Goldman. Regardless of why you think the jury voted to acquit O.J. Simpson of the criminal charges brought against him, that acquittal legally leaves the case open and officially unsolved. There is no legal impediment to criminal charges being brought against some other individual for these murders, if evidence were brought to light which was compelling enough to be presented before a jury.

Neither does Mr. Simpson having been found liable for these murders in a civil trial prevent the prevailing plaintiffs in that lawsuit from deciding to release him from their claims of damages, if they ever found reason to do so.

In fact, Ronald Goldman's father, Fred Goldman, publicly told O.J. Simpson that he would willingly give up all winnings if O.J. Simpson were to confess to the murders. O.J. refused to do so, once again asserting his innocence as the reason he would not. Shortly thereafter, a moving van showed up at O.J. Simpson's house to cart off most of his valuables. And the house, itself, is in foreclosure. Surely, if Simpson is innocent, his willingness to sacrifice his property before admitting to a crime he did not commit is a signature of virtue?

But enough of preambles and covering my ass. It is time to tell my story, to offer my theory.

When we eliminate, from our consideration, O.J. Simpson's demeanor as evidence either of his guilt or innocence, and his history with his ex-wife, we are left with the *corpus delicti* of the crime: that body of evidence that led to his arrest, indictment, and criminal trial. The main elements of that *corpus delicti* are as follows:

1) At the approximate time that the murders of Nicole Brown Simpson and Ronald Goldman must have occurred, nobody who does not have a motive to slant the truth has been able to testify to O.J. Simpson's exact whereabouts. By O.J. Simpson's own ac-

count, he was no more than a five-minute drive from the scene of the murders while they were occurring. Brian "Kato" Kaelin has not been able to place O.J. Simpson's whereabouts at the approximate times of the murders. O.J. Simpson made no telephone calls from his home telephone at the time of the murders. Limousine driver Allan Park's observation of the number 360 on the curb where O.J.'s Ford Bronco would have been parked on Rockingham strongly suggests that the Bronco was missing when Park arrived at 10:25 P.M. to pick Simpson up for his flight to Chicago.

This leaves O.J. Simpson with no alibi for the time of the murders.

2) A left-hand brown Aris glove of a style that O.J. Simpson has been photographed wearing, and of a style that Nicole Brown Simpson is known to have purchased, was found at the Bundy crime scene. An apparently matching Aris glove for the right hand was found on O.J. Simpson's Rockingham estate, in a location that Kato Kaelin reported hearing three banging noises against a wall of his guest room—bangs that were so loud that they shifted a painting on the wall and made Kaelin think it might be an earthquake. The Rockingham glove contains blood evidence that links O.J. Simpson to the Bundy crime scene: the victims' blood mixed with O.J.'s own blood on the glove found at Rockingham. There is also some hair and fiber evidence attached to the gloves that is indicative but not as conclusive.

3) Drops of blood positively identified as Simpson's were found at the Bundy crime scene. Blood identified as Nicole Brown Simpson's and Ronald Goldman's, as well as O.J.'s own blood, were found in O.J.'s Bronco. A trail of blood drops identified as O.J.'s picks up from where the Bronco was found parked at O.J. Simpson's Rockingham estate and leads from the Bronco, across O.J.'s driveway, into the foyer of Simpson's house. Blood identified as Nicole Brown Simpson's was found on a sock found on the floor in O.J. Simpson's bedroom. There are additional loca-

tions of substances at O.J. Simpson's estate that are presumptively blood, but cannot be used to link him to the crime because they are unidentifiable and we also don't know when they were left.

4) Fibers matching the carpet of O.J. Simpson's Bronco were found on Ronald Goldman's shirt. Fibers matching a dark suit of a type that Kato Kaelin says O.J. Simpson was wearing the evening of the murders were found at the Bundy crime scene.

5) Hairs of a type consistent with O.J. Simpson's were found on a watch cap found at the Bundy crime scene.

6) Bloody shoeprints of size 12 shoes, the size O.J. Simpson wears, and identified by an FBI expert as rare Bruno Magli loafers sold at a store O.J. Simpson was known to frequent, and which some photographs which may or may not have been faked show O.J. Simpson wearing, were found in the victim's blood at the Bundy crime scene, leading to the alley. The footprints also, apparently, reverse, as if the killer returned momentarily for some reason. There are apparently no other confirmed footprints at the Bundy crime scene, leading us to conclude that whoever made those bloody footprints committed the murders.

In summary, the evidence links Simpson's blood and clothing to the Bundy crime scene, to the vehicle thought to have been used to transport him from his home to the crime scene and back again, and links the victims blood, hair, and fiber, to the Bronco and back to O.J. Simpson's home.

I believe that is it, as far as physical evidence goes. There are some additional DNA, fiber, and hair links between Bundy and Rockingham, with the Bronco as carrier, but nothing more. There are no fingerprints linking O.J. Simpson to the murders, though nine unidentified fingerprints were found at the Bundy crime scene.

No knife identified as a murder weapon was ever found. The Bruno Magli shoes were never found. There were extensive searches for both.

The black sweat suit Kato saw was apparently found by L.A.P.D. criminalist Dennis Fung in O.J. Simpson's hamper, but the criminalist, finding no evidence of it having been at a crime scene—no obvious blood—did not collect it. One can assume, as Marcia Clark did, that the criminalist was incompetent for not collecting it, if one wishes to believe that O.J. Simpson is guilty. (Or, one can consider that if the criminalist knew what his visual examination had failed to find, that this is exculpatory evidence that the clothes O.J. Simpson was wearing that night were not at the crime scene.)

If, even as a speculative exercise such as I am now conducting, we are to say that this *corpus delicti* of evidence could have artificially been created for the purposes of framing O.J. Simpson for these murders, then we already know certain important things about the framer/murderer.

1) The murderer is mentally capable of planning a murder and a frame-up of evidence in pathological detail.

2) The murderer is physically, mentally, and emotionally capable of then actually committing a brutal double murder with the intent of framing a third party. He would also have to have some life experience at conducting himself in risky and stressful situations.

3) The murderer has to at sometime in his life have obtained a body of knowledge which includes stealth, surveillance techniques (including possibly electronic surveillance), a knowledge of police, detective, and criminalistic procedures, and how to overcome impediments to entry such as locks and electronic alarm systems.

4) The murderer would have to have intimate knowledge of both O.J. Simpson and Nicole Brown Simpson, and be familiar with the layout of their homes.

5) The murderer would have to have access to O.J. Simpson's home in order to obtain clothing to be used in the frame-up.

6) The murderer would have to be approximately the same

physical type as O.J. Simpson and he would have to be able to wear some of this clothing, including O.J. Simpson's size 12 shoes. His stride while walking would have to bear close approximation to O.J. Simpson's stride. If he is seen near the murder scene, it is necessary that he can be physically confused for O.J. Simpson.

7) And, most importantly, the murderer would have to be able to obtain, prior to the murders, approximately forty or fifty drops of blood with genetic markers consistent with the blood of O.J. Simpson's. This blood would be the most convincing part of the frame-up, and would be indispensable. It would also require considerable resourcefulness, and access to an expert on the biochemistry of blood and its use in criminalistics, in order to obtain the blood and successfully use it in a frame-up.

Now, if there is any part of this that is impossible, we're done with this theory. Our speculation can account for the improbable or the merely difficult. We cannot account for the impossible.

Furthermore, if we know of no person in the real world who fits into those categories—a person who fulfills the known conditions necessary to commit the murders and the frame-up—we are also done.

If we have found such an individual and he has been investigated in relation to these crimes and a reason found to have eliminated him as a suspect (such as his having presented an ironclad alibi for the time of the murders), then we are also done.

On February 12, 1997, at approximately 8:30 in the morning, I awoke with a startling thought.

An individual related to the Simpson case had come to my attention, about a week earlier, at the close of the civil trial, because something he had done had created cognitive dissonance in me. He had been a friend of O.J. Simpson's for 26 years. He had, under subpoena in the criminal trial, testified to incriminating statements made by O.J. Simpson—testimony that others close to Simpson said had to have been perjurious, because he was never alone with Simpson when he claimed the statements had been made. Now, this individual, at the conclusion of the civil trial, was seen on TV news physically embracing the man who had sued O.J. Simpson for murdering his son: Fred Goldman.

What on earth, I'd wondered February 4, 1997 when the civil verdict against Simpson came in, was Ron Shipp doing hugging Fred Goldman?

I first saw Ron Shipp at the same time as did most everyone else in the world, on television, when he sat down in the blue witness chair during O.J. Simpson's criminal trial.

During the direct examination by Chris Darden, Ron Shipp appeared honest and forthright, but *very* uncomfortable. He had good reason to feel uncomfortable. As a black man testifying for the prosecution, and a friend of O.J. Simpson's to boot, Ron Shipp was alienating himself even more from the black community that now supported Simpson than he had done by becoming a L.A.P.D. officer. If O.J. Simpson had theoretically abandoned his African-American roots by moving to Brentwood and marrying the blonde Nicole, Shipp had done the same in the early 1980's by marrying a white Jewish woman and buying a house in the division of almost-all-white Santa Clarita called Canyon Country.

This alienation from the black community caused by his testimony against Simpson would later bring Ron Shipp death threats.

That is something I've had to keep in mind when contemplating going public with my theory.

Ron Shipp was called as a witness right at the beginning of the prosecution's case because in January 1989, after the one fully-documented incident of domestic violence between O.J. and Nicole Simpson, Shipp's current L.A.P.D. assignment had been teaching domestic violence at the L.A.P.D.'s police academy. As a friend of both, he could testify to both Nicole's and O.J.'s states of mind, including O.J.'s admission that his excessive jealousy of Nicole might have fit the pattern of "batterer" that Shipp's course materials outlined. (This was the "batterer profile" that had, in fact, been authored by none other than Dr. Lenore Walker, whose trial testimony, had she been called, would have been that O.J. Simpson didn't fit into it.)

In the beginning of his direct examination by Darden, Shipp was asked if he and O.J. Simpson remained friends. Shipp replied, "I still love the guy But—um—I don't know. This is a weird situation I'm sitting here in."

(*Very* weird, if what I now suspect him of has any truth to it.)

Shipp testified that on the night after Simpson's return from Chicago and his interrogation by the L.A.P.D. detectives, O.J. had supposedly invited Shipp alone into his bedroom to talk forensics. Shipp said that while O.J. got undressed for bed, O.J. had asked him how long it took DNA. to come back. (Shipp had also said that O.J. asked about a polygraph test—but this part couldn't be brought out in testimony because of California law forbidding mention of polygraphs.) And then, according to Shipp, O.J. Simpson had "kind of jokingly just said, you know, 'To be honest, Shipp ... I've had some dreams of killing her.'"

Later, under cross examination by Simpson attorney, Carl Douglas, Shipp was confronted with the question, "Isn't it true that you were never alone with O.J. Simpson that night at Rockingham? Isn't it true that the defendant's sister, Shirley, was the one who accompanied him upstairs alone that night?"

Shipp denied it.

The problem here, is that when O.J. Simpson got back from his interrogation, he was so depressed that O.J.'s old friend, Robert Kardashian, according to *American Tragedy*, had conspired with O.J.'s sisters, and O.J.'s brother-in-law Benny Baker, to make sure they stayed with him all night, because they were all concerned that O.J. might attempt suicide. There was a couch in O.J.'s bedroom where they have said one of them slept all that night. In Shirley's testimony during the defense's case, she testified that Shipp could never have been alone with her brother to have the conversation about DNA, polygraphs, and homicidal dreams referred to jokingly, because O.J. had never been left alone by his family.

In O.J. Simpson's deposition for the civil suit against him brought by the parents of Ron Goldman and Nicole, Simpson himself swore that he'd wished he *could* have been left alone that night, because the constant familial companionship, as he tried to finally get some sleep after almost two sleepless days, was bothering him.

Furthermore, O.J.'s grown daughter, Arnelle, testified for her father that Ron Shipp had never left his bar stool in the downstairs living room the entire time he was at the Rockingham house that Monday night.

So the first question was, for anyone who believed that O.J.'s sister, Shirley, and his daughter, Arnelle, were not perjuring themselves for him (and if they were inclined to, couldn't they have come up with an alibi for 10:30 P.M. June 12th?): what possible motivation could Ron Shipp have had to lie about a conversation with O.J. Simpson that implicated his friend in the Bundy murders?

This was the first cognitive dissonance I'd had regarding Ron Shipp.

The second was his hug of Fred Goldman.

The cognitive dissonance, brought about by Ron Shipp's having moved so far away from his almost-three-decade-long worship of O.J. Simpson that he would literally embrace his worst enemy, was working in me right away.

On February 5, 1997, KABC radio talk host, Dennis Prager, had been on the air, taking calls about the verdict against Simpson, a verdict of which Dennis mightily approved. Like Marcia Clark and Vincent Bugliosi, Dennis is so convinced of Simpson's guilt that the only theory he has been willing to express why anyone would believe in Simpson's innocence is self-delusion, usually among African American listeners of his who think Simpson was the victim of a police conspiracy.

Dennis, his wife Fran, and Fran's daughter, Anya, are friends of mine. I first met Dennis in January, 1992 when Fran, at that time booking guests for Dennis's Sunday evening KABC show, invited me at Dennis's request onto his show to discuss the first published of four op-ed pieces I eventually wrote for the *Los Angeles Times* on gun control. Dennis had been opposed to private ownership of handguns. My op-ed piece, relating a recent incident where a customer with a gun had saved a restaurant full of people from armed robbers, had been the final straw in his changing his mind.

Let me tell you. Dennis Prager doesn't change his mind lightly. He agonizes over every point.

Sometime after the first Simpson trial, I tried to interest a magazine editor I knew into letting me do an interview with Dennis. The interview was never sold, but in one of two taped sessions, which covered Dennis's views on a number of topics, I asked Dennis why he was so certain Simpson was guilty. Dennis's answer was, in essence, that everything he knew about how the world worked convinced him, and if at some future time he discovered that Simpson was innocent, it would be a major blow to his confidence in his reasoning processes.

I didn't think I had a chance of changing Dennis's mind on this one. But I did, at least, want to convince him that I might *not* be crazy.

On February 5, 1997, I faxed Dennis the following letter.

Dennis,
   From our conversation, I know you hang your entire concept of how things work on your belief that no reasonable person can look at the evidence and conclude that O.J. Simpson did not commit the double

murder. You make it quite clear that you think his acquittal in the criminal trial is an artifact of an imperfect jury system.

Since I still believe O.J. Simpson innocent, let me try to explain to you why.

1) My understanding of human character is such that I have never found the motivations attributed to O.J. Simpson for these murders, or the way these murders were committed, compatible with other known facts about O.J. Simpson's personality. I refer you to chapters in my book *Self Control Not Gun Control* (which I gave you) for my points on this.

2) You always make it an either-or between those who say that if O.J. Simpson was framed, it must have been by a racist police conspiracy, or that the physical evidence must have been found, analyzed, and collected in an honest and competent manner. That is a classic false dichotomy. In fact, it is possible to believe that one or two corrupt individuals inside the L.A.P.D.—for motivations which may have had nothing whatsoever to do with race—could have acted to frame O.J.. This is my belief.

3) The bottom line is, all the evidence to date collected proves is that O.J. Simpson's blood was at the crime scene. One could reasonably conclude that O.J. Simpson lied about being at the crime scene without necessarily concluding that he committed the murders. Or one could also conclude that someone other than police—perhaps persons close to O.J. with malice aforethought who committed the murders with the specific intent of framing O.J. Simpson for the murders before they were even committed—planted evidence.

I find it odd that O.J.'s former friend, black L.A.P.D. officer Ron Schipp [*sic*], was seen hugging the Goldman family right after the verdict in the civil trial last night. If I were to think anyone possible of participating in such a conspiracy, a person with both possible motive and opportunity to get into O.J.'s house before the crime and gather personal items of his which could be dropped at the crime scene, he'd be at the top of my list.

I know you think I'm crazy for thinking this way. I regret that; I have all sorts of reasons why I would wish you to think me sane. I bring to this question psychological tools which are more familiar to a novelist than a psychiatrist, in addition to rigorous epistemology. Clear, critical thinking is much too important to me to allow myself to be swept along with popular opinion merely because opposing a popular viewpoint is inconvenient.

Best regards,
Neil

The morning of February 12, 1997, my nagging cognitive dissonance about Ron Shipp suddenly came into stark focus. The thought hit me that Ron Shipp didn't need to be part of any sort of conspiracy in order for him to have framed O.J. Simpson. He might have done it all by himself, because he conceivably could have been so jealous of O.J. Simpson that his jealousy turned into a secret vendetta.

I'd been thinking for a long time that O.J. Simpson likely hadn't murdered his wife because he was a winner—successful in life, lucky in love—and most murders were the acts of pathetic losers.

Ron Shipp had admitted on the stand in O.J. Simpson's criminal trial to having had a problem with alcoholism.

I had been thinking that if O.J. Simpson had been framed, it couldn't have been done by the police— as claimed by some lawyers on O.J.'s criminal defense team —because whoever did the frame would have had to have access to O.J.'s stuff in order to bring it to the Bundy crime scene in the first place.

Never mind whether Mark Fuhrman had found a glove at the Bundy crime scene and planted it on O.J.'s estate at Rockingham. The first question would be: how did those gloves (or that glove, singular) get to the Bundy crime scene in the first place?

This is assuming, of course, that they were O.J.'s gloves and had somehow shrunk between the night of June 12, 1994, and when O.J. Simpson struggled to pull them in front of the jury, many months later.

But Ron Shipp had been hanging around O.J. Simpson's house since Simpson had bought it in 1979. And, Shipp had admitted on the stand to being at O.J.'s house just a week before the Brown-Goldman murders.

Ron Shipp had been a police officer for the Los Angeles Police Department for fifteen years, including seven years in a patrol car, and working undercover, and teaching at the Los Angeles Police Academy, before taking early retirement because of (in his account) job-related stress and incidents related to his alcoholism.

That cross-linking of facts, that there existed an individual who —because of professional experience and personal access to both O.J. and Nicole—could have engineered the murder of Nicole and the frame-up of O.J. perhaps all by his lonesome self, startled me almost out of my wits.

Believe me about this part. In the subsequent week, I visited a hospital emergency room twice suffering from a condition diagnosed as ketosis and dehydration, symptoms of severe dieting combined with a low-grade flu-like infection.

Mystical insights are supposed to happen to you when you fast in the desert, or go up into the mountains where the air is thin. I'd been starving myself for five months, and I was running a low fever. I was congested, so my breathing was shallow.

My body had physically reproduced the conditions historically attributed to mystics and seers. And, I had had a startling vision. I had thought that O.J. Simpson was innocent but had no idea who could have done these murders and framed him for them.

Now I had a notion.

I wrote it up as follows:

Novel or Movie Idea:
The Case of the Perry Mason Case

Logline: A writer with writer's block, to pass the time, watches the murder trial of a celebrity on TV, and playing connect the dots with the evidence, the writer comes up with an outlandish scenario which explains why the accused celebrity was actually framed by an obsessed fan whom the celebrity had allowed to get too close. The strange part is, it turns out to be true.

Plot:

The white ex-wife and ex-wife's white friend of an African-

American celebrity who is famous as a former football star, a sportscaster, a commercial spokesman, and an actor, is brutally knifed to death. Because the celebrity has a reputation of being jealous and sometimes violent, all evidence seems to link him to the murder, including articles of clothing linking the celebrity to the murder site. Just before the murder, the celebrity was in a movie in which he used a knife. Detectives never consider any other scenario than that the celebrity is the obvious murderer, and the celebrity is brought to trial for the murder. Even the celebrity's lawyers think he did it. The celebrity consistently maintains his innocence and is acquitted of the murders by a mostly black jury, but a subsequent civil trial before a mostly white jury finds him liable for the murders. The celebrity maintains he was framed by the detectives for racial motives. On this point the celebrity is wrong.

Throughout the entire process of investigation, two trials, and aftermath, one figure keeps on showing up in minor roles. It is a black police officer who was a fan and hanger-on of the celebrity. He had complete access to the celebrity's house and estate both before the murders and for some times afterwards. The police-officer/fan gets psychological satisfaction from being able to take fellow police officers over to the celebrity's estate to play tennis, and to show his fellow officers how important he is by how he is treated like a friend by the athlete. But at some point, the fan becomes sexually interested in the celebrity's ex-wife. Perhaps he manages to get close to her, perhaps he is obsessed by her at a distance. But in any event, at some point, either rejected by her or never having had a chance with her, he becomes angry with her and jealous of the celebrity, and decides to get his revenge on both of them. He steals items of clothing—a pair of winter gloves the celebrity doesn't use anymore, a pair of expensive shoes from the back of the celebrity's closet—and carefully stalks both the celebrity and the ex-wife. Then, on a June night, after making sure that the celebrity is home alone by phoning him on some pretext, the police officer/fan goes over to the ex-wife's condo to murder her with a knife, wearing the celebrity's gloves and shoes. In the process of murdering her, however, a young waiter returning a pair of eyeglasses stumbles in during the murder, and the fan/officer has to murder him, too. The fan then plants one of the celebrity's gloves at the murder scene, and goes over to the celebrity's house to plant the other glove. The fan is seen by a limo driver waiting to drive the celebrity to the airport as the fan crosses the lawn of the celebrity's estate.

The fan stays close to the celebrity after the celebrity returns from his trip, and even works security for the celebrity at his estate in the period right after the murders. But he is fading from the limelight during the trial, so he comes up with a story about how the celebrity told him he had been dreaming about murdering his ex-wife. He testifies to this during the trial, which is broadcast on TV, and gets his fifteen minutes of fame.

Having done this, he is excluded from the life of the celebrity he used to worship, but he still can't bring himself to fade completely into the background, so he attaches himself to the family of the murdered young white man, and is seen hugging the murdered young man's father after his victory in the civil trial.

Eventually, the writer who is watching all this on TV, connects all the dots, and goes to a detective he knows and presents him with the scenario.

Dénouement:

Yet to be written.

And, when I wrote those words on the morning of February 12, 1997, I had no idea whether I would ever write that dénouement. But I knew I had to see if there might be any truth to it. So that morning I took my little scenario to Owen Smet, a robbery-homicide detective I knew on the Culver City police force, and asked him what he thought.

Owen told me that, first, he was pretty well convinced that Simpson was guilty. That did not surprise me. But he also told me that he thought my explanation was the only alternative explanation of the evidence that even came close to making sense to him, and he was now curious whether Ron Shipp had an alibi for that night.

That evening, I went into an Altavista search on the World Wide Web, and looked up all the hits I could find on Ron Shipp. This led me to transcripts of depositions for the civil trial, and I downloaded a bunch of the transcripts.

The next morning, I did a key word search for Shipp in the transcripts I'd downloaded, and in O.J. Simpson's deposition, found something that made my heart go into my throat.

It was the following sequence:

> Q: The Ron Shipp you knew was a former police officer. Correct?
> A: I know —I knew he couldn't get back on the force, yes.
> Q: Why did you just add that? I didn't ask you that.
> MR. BAKER: Don't answer that question.
> BY MR. PETROCELLI: Q: Well, Mr. Simpson, you appear to have some animosity toward Mr. Shipp. Is that correct?
> MR. BAKER: Don't answer that either. He doesn't appear to have anything. Maybe he does in your eyes but not in mine.
> BY MR. PETROCELLI: Q: Do you have animosity towards Mr. Shipp right now?
> A: I feel sorry for Ron Shipp, yes.
> Q: Explain what you mean.
> A: I feel sorry that he's a troubled person, and I tried to help him before because he had some problems, and I tried to help him, and I feel the same way about him now.
> Q: Tell me what problems he has that you feel sorry for.
> A: Well, the problems I knew he had was drugs and alcohol, and now obviously I don't know. I haven't seen him in a year and a half, two years.
> Q: When did he have the drugs and alcohol problem that caused you to feel sorry for him?
> A: Previous to these incidences.
> Q: When was the last time that you knew or believed that he had a drug or alcohol problem.?

A: Roughly a week or so before Nicole's murders.

Q: How did you find that out?

A: Because he was at my gate.

Q: Uninvited?

A: Yes.

Q: Which gate?

A: The Ashford gate.

Q: How did you see him there?

A: I didn't see him

Q: How do you know he was there?

A: He was on my intercom.

Q: He buzzed?

A: Yes.

Q: What did he say?

A: He asked if he could use my Jacuzzi.

Q: What did you say?

A: Told him, "Ron, I was in bed."

Q: What time was it?

A: I don't know. At night.

Q: Were you alone?

A: Yes.

Q: Was the housekeeper there?

A: Maybe. I'm not sure.

Q: What did he then say?

A: He told me he had a big blond, a "Nicole type." quote, unquote. "You got to see this girl, O.J.. Could he use the Jacuzzi. I told him I didn't think it was on. He told me it was on because he had been there earlier.

Q: When you say you don't think it is on, you can simply turn it on, can't you?

A: Yeah.

Q: So then what happened?

A: He kept saying, "I owe you, Juice. Please, man, I owe you. You got to see this girl."

Q: What does that mean, he owes you?

A: I guess if he owes me a favor. He will owe me a favor.

Q: Oh, he will owe you if you give him this favor?

A: Yeah.

Q: Okay. Then what happened?

A: Well, after he told me it was on, I pushed the gate button for him to come in and told him to watch the dog.

Q: Did he tell you that he knew that the Jacuzzi was on from earlier that day?

A: Yes.

Q: Had he been out to your house?

A: Evidently.

Q: Did you know that?

A: No.

Q: Did he have access to your property?

A: No.

Q: How did he get on the property earlier that day?

A: Well, one of the complaints that I've had previous that I had Cathy discuss with him through, because both Michelle and Gigi had concerns about it, is that he would show up at times, climb the wall and bring whoever group he was playing tennis with without telling anybody. When I was out of town also.

Q: What wall would be climb?

A: The Ashford wall.

Q: Right next to this gate where the—

A: I don't know. I wasn't there to see what part of the wall he climbed.

Q: You had told him he could come on your property and play tennis. Right?

A: Only if he called first. As a matter of fact, I actually had Cathy have a conversation with him about that.

Q: When did that conversation occur?

A: In and around that time, and on previous times she's had to tell him," Ron, you just can't show up at his house."

Q: Mr. Simpson, when you said you wanted him to call first, did you also want someone else to be home when he arrived?

A: I would prefer that, yes.

Q: So someone could let him in?

A: No. So that—I just don't like a lot of people on my property if I'm out of town, and I was gone most of the time, so—and the housekeepers didn't —especially Gigi, because she was brand-new, she didn't know how to handle it, and she had mentioned it—evidently she had mentioned it to Cathy, and then Cathy had mentioned it to me.

Q: Did you tell Mr. Shipp that if no one was home and he wanted to play, he could jump the wall or—

A: No.

Q: or get on the property?

A: No.

Q: So your understanding of your deal with him is that if—that he shouldn't be jumping the wall and getting on the property to play tennis. Is that right?

A: I had no deal with him. I don't think anybody should jump my wall without my permission.

Q: And you told him so. Right?

A: Yes.

Q: Through Randa.

A: Right. And I told him myself. This was something that had happened before.

Q: Now, when he came in and used the Jacuzzi, did you see him that evening?

A: Yes.

Q: You were in bed. Right?

A: Yes.

Q: You came down to see him?

A: No.

Q: Tell me—

A: At one point I did.

Q: What happened?

A: He went to my intercom system out back, buzzed me—

Q: From the Jacuzzi?

A: Well, in the backyard. And buzzed me and said, "Juice, please, man, you got to help me out here. I need a bottle of wine." I think I was speaking with Cathy Randa at that time and—

Q: On the phone?

A: I said, "I'm on the phone, Ron." And he said once again this whole thing, and he described this girl as a "Nicole type." "You got to see her."

And I said, "Ron, I don't even know if I have any wine." He said, "Ah, come on, Juice, please, man." So I got up. I went downstairs. I opened one of my patio doors. He walked in. I told him to look in the bar to see if there was some wine. I found a bottle that came in some—one of the Christmas packages or some package somebody had sent me, and I opened it and —I gave it to him and, as he was opening it, he said, "Man, you should go see her." And I walked out back, and she was I wouldn't say a Nicole type, but she was a big blond, real tall, I would say 5-10, 5-11 blond girl. And she was in the Jacuzzi, and she was talking about what a great property and that she could get used to being here, and asked me to get in the Jacuzzi. And then Ron was coming out at that period of time and said, "Come on, man, why don't you join us? And I said, "No, man, I got to get up early in the morning," and I went back upstairs.

If I'd been looking for evidence of Ron Shipp's obsession with both O.J. Simpson and Nicole, I couldn't have asked for more. Further, Simpson was testifying to Ron Shipp habitually coming onto his property uninvited, jumping his gate, being gently— perhaps at other times not so gently—rebuffed by his idol. The question was whether O.J.'s version of events could be believed. I subsequently downloaded Shipp's own testimony of this event from his cross-examination by Carl Douglas during the criminal trial, and could see by the sorts of questions that Douglas was asking that Simpson had told substantially the same story to his lawyers that he was testifying to in his civil deposition. If this wasn't an indication of absolute truth, it was, at least, an indication of O.J.'s consistency in his version of what happened that night.

We can compare Shipp's own version of the events of that night, during his cross-examination by Carl Douglas.

> Q. When was the last time before June 13th, 1994, Mr. Shipp, that you had occasion to visit the Rockingham location?
> A. Probably about a week before that.

Note that Ron Shipp, not knowing what Douglas is getting at yet, confirms that his last previous visit to O.J.'s house was a week before his visit to Rockingham the day after the murders at Bundy.

> Q. And that was when you visited there with some blond female; wasn't it?
> MR. DARDEN: Objection, your Honor.
> Your Honor, can we approach the sidebar?
> THE COURT: Yes. I take it there's an objection?
> MR. DARDEN: Yes.
> THE COURT: Relevance?
> (Sidebar conference.)
> THE COURT: All right. Mr. Douglas, you may wind it up for the afternoon, please.
> MR. DOUGLAS: All right, your Honor.
> Q. It is true, is it not, that about a week before the death of Nicole Brown Simpson, you visited Mr. Simpson's house unannounced at about 10 o'clock p.m. with a blond female; true?
> A. That was approximately—
> MR. DARDEN: Your Honor, I object to this question. I thought the court sustained it.
> THE COURT: No, overruled.
> Q. You may answer.
> THE COURT: But with some— not very broad here.
> MR. DOUGLAS: Very well.
> A. No, the night that the blond female was over, that was three weeks before. It was a good friend of my wife and we're good friends with her husband. Her name is Lisa Madigan. That was three weeks prior.

Suddenly, after an attorney's sidebar conference, which has given him time to think ahead, Shipp is now claiming that it was *three* weeks before that he had last been at Simpson's house.

Was there more than one visit, possibly with more than one woman?

> Q. Is she about six-foot-one, resembling Nicole Simpson —
> A. No— I'm sorry— she's about— about five-nine, almost five-ten.
> Q. Was this the woman whom you wanted to share the Jacuzzi with?
> MR. DARDEN: Objection.
> THE COURT: The fact that he was over there about three or four weeks ago, that's about it that's relevant, counsel.

And, it appears, the difference between one week and three-to-four weeks was important to Judge Ito in deciding the relevance of this last visit.

> MR. DOUGLAS: Very well.
> Q. When you were there on this occasion, did you ask Mr. Simpson to go and bring you some wine?
> A. That's correct.
> Q. You drink a lot, don't you?
> A. I used to.
> Q. You've had a drinking problem; haven't you?
> A. In the past I have.
> MR. DOUGLAS: We can stop now, your Honor.

The next day, the cross-examination continued. Shipp had had all night to consider what this questioning might bring out, and what he might say about it.

> Q. Now, we talked briefly yesterday about an occasion in June of '94 when you visited Mr. Simpson unannounced, asking to use a Jacuzzi with a friend, do you recall that?
> A. I didn't—that's totally false, totally false.
> Q. Okay, there was an occasion when you came with a friend and asked to use Mr. Simpson's Jacuzzi?
> A. Mr. Douglas, I hope you get your facts straight.
> Q. Would you answer the question?
> A. I went to play tennis, Mr. Douglas. I was playing tennis. After the

tennis game —
THE COURT: Hold on?
THE WITNESS: You're attacking me, let me answer the question.
THE COURT: The jury is to disregard the last comments by Mr. Shipp and Mr. Douglas.
Mr. Douglas, ask your question.
MR. DOUGLAS: Thank you.
Q. Don't you recall an occasion when you called Mr. Simpson at about 10:00 in the evening and asked to use his Jacuzzi, do you recall that, sir, yes or no?
A. No.
Q. Do you recall after he let you use the Jacuzzi that about 20 minutes later you called back and asked him to bring you bottle of wine, do you recall that?
A. You just said 10:00 at night, didn't you say that?
Q. I'm asking do you recall when you called him back to ask him to bring a bottle of wine down to you, in the Jacuzzi?
A. Can I have the times clarified, sir.
Q. 1994, June; if not, May.
A. June; I'm talking about the time, not the day, the time.

Which is a very odd statement for Shipp to make here, since the previous day he *had* been disputing the date of his last visit to O.J.'s house—disputing it by two to three weeks.

Q. It was in the evening, Mr. Shipp. Do you recall that occurring?
A. I do recall that.
Q. Okay. You were with a friend other than your wife, were you not?
A. Yes, I was.
Q. She was blond, was she not?
A. Who was a friend of my wife's, correct.
Q. You say her name is what?
A. Lisa Madigan.

After reading O.J.'s deposition (it was only later that I compared it line by line to Shipp's testimony), I believed that Shipp's visit to Rockingham a week prior to the Brown-Goldman murders indicated such a strong obsession with both O.J. and Nicole that I felt I had to share the pattern I was detecting with the Los Angeles Police Department, which had investigated the murders, and the Los Angeles Country District Attorney's office, which had prosecuted them.

My first attempt was to pay a visit to the West Los Angeles Division of the L.A.P.D.. There I was brought to Detective Ron Phillips, who had initially assigned Detectives Mark Fuhrman and Brad Roberts to investigate the murders in the middle of the night, June 13, 1994.

I introduced myself as a journalist—showing off the back cover author's photo of one of my books as proof that I wasn't just your *run-of-the-mill* nutcase—and somewhat haltingly told Detective Phillips that I believed I had a possible lead indicating another killer than O.J. Simpson for the murders at Bundy. At that point, Detective Phillips told me that he knew beyond any doubt who the murderer was that night, and that the murderer lived at 360 North Rockingham. Phillips wasn't even interested in sitting with me for the five minutes I said I would need to show him the materials I had brought that I thought supported my lead. Instead, he told me that since the case had been investigated by the L.A.P.D.'s Robbery/Homicide Division at Parker Center, *they* would have to listen to anything I had to say. He referred me to the third floor of Parker Center and gave me driving instructions there.

Within an hour, I was met in the lobby of Parker Center by Detective Brian P. McCartin, Robbery/Homicide Division of the Los Angeles Police Department. As he took me up the elevator to the third floor, I told him that this was regarding a double homicide that I thought the L.A.P.D. needed to re-open. He asked me which detectives had investigated it. I told him the detectives who had investigated the case were no longer with L.A.P.D.: Vannatter and Lange.

I give Detective McCartin credit. He didn't give me a dirty look or return the elevator to the lobby at that point. Instead, he took me to an interview booth on the third floor.

Detective McCartin was very professional and very polite. He gave me about forty-five minutes to lay out the reasons why I thought it was possible that the L.A.P.D. could have been misled into identifying O.J. Simpson as their suspect in the Brown-Goldman murders, and why I thought that Ron Shipp should be looked at as a possible suspect. McCartin was naturally skeptical, and told me that he couldn't think of a murder case where an innocent man, particularly one as headstrong as O.J. Simpson, didn't take the stand in his own defense. I suggested that if you had half a dozen lawyers telling you that you shouldn't, perhaps even O.J. Simpson would finally take their advice, regardless of his desire to testify—and his lawyers' reasons for not wanting him to testify might have been that the evidence had also convinced *them* that their client was guilty.

I left Detective McCartin the materials I had put together at that point, and a copy of *Self Control Not Gun Control*, with the chapters relating to the Simpson case indicated.

As Detective McCartin walked me to the elevator, he asked me why I had put this effort in—why was I interested in the first place? I told him that it was simply an unrelenting cognitive dissonance that the physical evidence simply wasn't enough to overcome my doubts of Simpson's innocence, based on my observations of his demeanor during the trial.

Detective McCartin had told me as he escorted me to the lobby of Parker Center that if they decided to re-open the Simpson case, I would be called for a re-interview. But even though he was polite during his interview with me, I knew I shouldn't hang by the phone, waiting for a call.

I was still determined to try to get an investigation going, however, so I decided to take my materials to O.J. Simpson's lawyers.

Both the criminal trial and the civil trial were over at this point, but I knew that if any of O.J. Simpson's lawyers still had any interest in establishing their client not having committed these murders, it would have to be his civil lawyers, because the possibility of an appeal still had not been ruled out. The civil trial depositions I'd downloaded gave the office address in Santa Monica of Simpson's lead civil attorney, Robert C. Baker, Esq., of Baker, Silberberg & Keener.

I printed out another copy of the materials I had presented Detective McCartin, wrote a cover letter to Mr. Baker, and, the following Saturday morning, February 15, 1997, sat on the floor of the hallway outside the law offices, waiting for someone to show up. A handwritten note taped to the door, written to Federal Express, said someone would be in to open the office by noon.

When a woman came to open the office at about 11:00 A.M., I introduced myself, handed her a large envelope attached with rubber bands to a copy of *Self Control Not Gun Control,* and asked her to deliver it to the desk of Robert Baker or one of O.J. Simpson's other attorneys. I then asked if Mr. Baker would be in that day and whether I could wait for him. She told me that he would be in later, but that I could not wait.

I said okay, told her that I felt it important that Mr. Baker look at the materials immediately because they related to the possible innocence of O.J. Simpson, and left.

This was the cover letter I hand-delivered:

February 15, 1997

Robert C. Baker, Esq.
Baker, Silberberg & Keener
2850 Ocean Park Boulevard
Suite 300
Santa Monica, CA 90405-2936
By Hand

Dear Mr. Baker:

I am a novelist, screenwriter, and journalist living in Culver City, who like many others has been following the trials of O.J. Simpson since the murders of Nicole Brown Simpson and Ronald Goldman on June 12, 1994. I am attaching to this letter my recent book *Self Control Not Gun Control* and my biography page from my site on the World Wide Web, as introductory credentials.

Yesterday morning, February 14th, I met for about 45 minutes at Parker Center with Detective Brian P. McCartin, Robbery/Homicide Division of the Los Angeles Police Department, and presented him the attached materials. [I included Detective McCartin's telephone number at Parker Center, taken from the business card he gave me.]

The purpose of my meeting was to present to the Robbery/Homicide division of the L.A.P.D. what I believe is a compelling theory that both exonerates O.J. Simpson for the murders of Nicole Brown Simpson and Ronald Goldman, and identifies the individual who instead both premeditatively committed the double murder and premeditatively framed O.J. Simpson as the murderer.

I only know about these murders what any individual who watched the trial, read the newspaper and magazine accounts, and has done some independent research of publicly available sources is able to know. You, with your far more intimate knowledge of this case, can form a much better conclusion than I can whether the theory I present is plausible or nonsensical. But I believe I have brought to my analysis tools that are far more familiar to a professional writer than they would be either to detectives, attorneys, forensic specialists, or even professional psychotherapists. If I have managed to stumble onto an inobvious truth, these professional tools account for my ability to have done so.

The attached materials include a summary of my theory, written as a "fictional" scenario to create an instant gestalt of the theory, my previous writings on this subject (some of which is included in *Self Control Not Gun Control* and some additional material published on my web site), and excerpts I have pulled from the civil depositions and testimony summaries from the criminal trial of Mr. Simpson, which I believe supports each of the crucial points of my theory.

If Mr. Simpson did not commit these murders, than the individual who did must have an extraordinary set of characteristics. He must have professional training which would enable him to know precisely what circumstantial evidence would be convincing to detectives, forensic specialists, and prosecutors. The likely individual would have a background, therefore, in law enforcement. The likely individual would also probably have to have some background as a professional actor. The likely individual would have had to have had intimate and long-term access both to Mr. Simpson and his family, and his estate at Rockingham, in order to be intimately familiar with Mr. Simpson's personal habits, and to gather the items necessary in order to frame him prior to the murders. The likely individual would have had to have an evident psychological problem such as alcohol and/or drug abuse. The likely individual would have had to have a psychological motivation to wish to punish both Nicole Brown Simpson and O.J. Simpson—a powerful stew of obsession with Nicole, worship of O.J., a life filled with personal frustration and failure. In short, the murderer of Nicole Brown Simpson and Ronald Goldman would have to be an obsessed O.J.

Simpson fan whose self-concept was dependent on O.J., who would seek his "fifteen minutes of fame" through his association with O.J. Simpson, and once removed from O.J. Simpson's circle by Mr. Simpson's incarceration during his murder trial, would find someone else to attach himself to.

I believe the single individual who fits all these criteria is Ronald Shipp. I presented this theory to Detective McCartin in the hope that the L.A.P.D. will re-open the murder investigation of Nicole Brown Simpson and Ronald Goldman on the basis of this theory.

I am presenting this material to you in the hopes that you will understand the gravity of what I am suggesting. If I am right, Shipp is probably let-down and depressed right now, at the conclusion of the civil trial. He may still have items he collected from O.J. Simpson over the years which would be physical evidence of his frame-up of Mr. Simpson. He may be psychologically able to be spooked into providing evidence of his guilt. Both of these reasons requires that absolute secrecy of my theory be maintained so as not to tip him off that he is a suspect. He may have grown complacent and be capable of being trapped if his sense of having gotten away with it is maintained.

Likewise, if my theory is wrong, then I do not wish to see Shipp's life destroyed by premature allegations. We know what the press in this country would do with a theory such as this, and it is not pretty.

If I am correct, however, and Mr. Shipp is proved to be the actual murderer, exonerating Mr. Simpson, I do not believe it is possible for me to overstate the mass psychological trauma this is going to have nationwide. If I am correct, Ronald Shipp not only murdered two innocent individuals and framed a national celebrity for the crime, but he also psychologically raped the entire nation.

I am providing you with the information because I am concerned that Mr. Simpson not despair. Such despair and frustration, knowing that he is both innocent and almost universally reviled, could lead him to damage either himself or others. I will leave it to your best judgment whether, or at what point, you would wish to convey my theory to him, with the understanding that every additional individual who becomes aware of my theory is one more individual who might inadvertently tip off Ronald Shipp that he is a suspect, and frustrate the ability to prove it beyond any doubt.

I would hope, however, that you might find a way to encourage the L.A.P.D. to re-open the investigation so that my theory can either be disproved, or proved.

If I can be of any further assistance, please feel free to call upon me.

Sincerely,

J. Neil Schulman

Attachments

A few days later, after a follow-up call to the office, I received a phone call from Phil Baker, Robert Baker's son, and also one of O.J.'s attorneys in the civil case. He told me that he had looked over the materials, and thought my scenario was "plausible."

Considering that I was presenting a scenario which suggested that elements of the Simpson case were wrong—that gloves and shoes which they had attempted to prove weren't his might have actually been stolen from him in order to be planted—I found Phil Baker's word "plausible" to be extremely interesting, to say the least.

Phil Baker had promised to call me back to discuss this further, but I never got another call and my follow-up calls to his office went unanswered.

After a week, I returned to the offices during regular hours and attempted to make an appointment. I was rebuffed, fairly rudely, by Phil Baker's assistant, Kim, and when I phoned to make one last attempt, Kim told me that the office secretary had informed her how I had tried to force my way into the office the previous Saturday.

Perhaps merely being a large bearded guy in a jean jacket, sitting in an empty hallway with a copy of his book, waiting for a law office to open on a Saturday morning, *is* enough to frighten a woman nowadays. No doubt working for O.J. Simpson's attorneys is also enough to make anyone paranoid.

But asking politely if you can wait in a law office is equivalent to "trying to force your way in"?

I saw how easily someone's paranoia could lead to making up false charges, and wondered how many of the sworn statements in the Simpson case were just as warped by the observer's own prejudices. Faye Resnick's cocaine-induced paranoia, during her observations of encounters between O.J. Simpson and Nicole, came to mind immediately. I saw how to a paranoid mind, simply showing up someplace might be interpreted as "stalking."

CNN had just reported that Simpson attorney and F. Lee Bailey's law partner, Dan Leonard, would be looking into the possibility of an appeal of the civil verdict, so I phoned him next at his law office in Boston.

Leonard took my call. I told him of my conversation with Phil Baker and the materials I had left at the Bakers' law office, and we discussed my views. Dan Leonard said that Ron Shipp had been on the list of possible suspects right from the beginning, but he told me that he didn't know why they hadn't looked into him more closely. I asked Leonard if they had been able to establish an alibi for Shipp for the night of the murders. Leonard told me that if they had, he didn't know what it was.

Again, this conversation ended with promises of further discussion, after Leonard had gotten ahold of the materials I'd left with the Bakers. But my repeated phone calls to Dan Leonard, some of them relating information I'd obtained from other contacts, were never again returned.

I made two more attempts to get an investigation going. The first was through an attorney who passed my materials on to the office of L.A. County District Attorney, Gil Garcetti. Garcetti responded that my materials presented a view of the Brown-Goldman murders that, according to the attorney, "Garcetti said he had never heard before."

But I still don't know if Garcetti had done anything to look into it.

In attempting to find out if there was any investigation happening, I telephoned Detective McCartin at Parker Center the morning of Friday, March 21st. McCartin told me he had passed my book and materials on to Detective Vic Pietrantoni, Tom Lange's former partner. He'd transfer the call.

When Detective Pietrantoni got on the phone with me, he lectured, and I listened.

Pietrantoni told me that he'd looked at my materials and read the chapters on Simpson in my book. While he regarded me as intelligent—perhaps even more intelligent than he was, in his phrasing—he couldn't understand how I could possibly believe Simpson innocent. He asserted to me that Simpson was a life-long bully. He was so certain that Simpson was guilty—he said—that he would bet his son's life on it.

Pietrantoni then told me that he was certain that Simpson was guilty, "Because Simpson confessed to his attorneys. They've been secretly working with us on this case, and sometime soon, you're going to be seeing O.J. Simpson confessing publicly and selling another book about it."

Knowing that this would the sort of thing that could get a lawyer disbarred, if he was doing it without his client's consent, I asked Detective Pietrantoni if he could tell me precisely which of O.J. Simpson's attorneys was working with the L.A.P.D.. He, not surprisingly, refused to tell me.

"You're telling me that O.J. Simpson's criminal attorneys suborned perjury during his trial by putting on witnesses they knew were lying?" I asked.

"Sure," he told me. "Defense lawyers are scum. They do that all the time."

I told him, after he wound down a bit, that in the absence of some proof that Simpson had confessed, I would just have to continue my investigation, and that's when I asked him whether an alibi had ever been established for Ron Shipp.

Detective Vic Pietrantoni, Robbery/Homicide Division of the Los Angeles Police Department, then told me what I most wanted to know. "Ron Shipp was never a suspect," he told me." We never investigated whether Shipp had an alibi [for June 12, 1994]."

A few minutes after my conversation with Pietrantoni, I got a call from Leo Wolinsky, City Editor and Assistant Managing Editor of the *Los Angeles Times*. I had faxed a proposal to him that I work with the *Times* as a free-lancer, to pursue a theory I would bring them that O.J. Simpson was innocent. All I asked (and received verbally from him) was a promise before I told them my theory that they wouldn't proceed on it without me. Wolinsky's call was to set up the meeting for me to present my theory to them for the next Tuesday.

I told Wolinsky what Pietrantoni had just told me about Simpson having confessed to his lawyers, and told him that if this was true, my pending meeting with him regarding my theory might be futile. But he agreed to meet with me anyway, since he was skeptical that what Pietrantoni had told me was true.

The next morning, Saturday, I knew I wanted something more interesting to bring to the meeting with the *Times* than I already had. I didn't know what Ron Shipp's address was, but I had a pretty good idea what neighborhood in Canyon Country he lived in. I drove north for about a half hour until I got to the right neighborhood and saw some boys, maybe around 10 or 12, playing hoops in a driveway. I figured that kids would be less likely to clam up about the address of a neighbor than an adult would be. I pulled alongside and rolled down my car window. "Any of you kids know where Ron Shipp's house is?" I asked.

"Yeah, sure!" one of them went. It turned out that one of these boys went to school with Ron Shipp's son, David. Within seconds, I had a detailed description of what the Shipps' house looked like and how to drive there. It was only a few blocks away.

I followed their directions, which were pretty good for kids. It was better directions than I'd gotten on many occasions from adults. In a few minutes, I was parked in front of a house matching the description and location they'd given me.

It looked like a very nice house.

Then I saw Ron Shipp and his wife Nina—whom I recognized from their picture in *People* Magazine of September 30, 1996, which I'd color-copied from the library—coming out of the house with several other kids, getting ready to go someplace.

I simply sat in my car, about five car lengths away, watching, and trying to figure out in my own mind if this man could be a murderer. I didn't see anything that made me think so. I paid special attention to the size of his feet, which indeed looked pretty big to me.

After a while, I noticed that the Shipps had noticed me. Nina Shipp got into a car that looked to me like a Cadillac and drove away. Then Ron Shipp got into a gray Toyota pick-up and drove past me ... and pulled into his neighbor's driveway right behind me.

He got out and started walking toward me.

I'd already figured out on the drive over what I would say to him if we met.

He came right up to my driver's side window. "Can I help you?" he asked.

I took the opportunity to study him closely. I was sitting down and he was leaning over a little, so I couldn't tell how tall he was, but I could see that he was very athletically built. What I most noticed was the cross on a chain wrapped tightly around his neck. The *People* Magazine article on him quoted Nina Shipp as saying that Ron had been moodier since the Simpson trial and "He spends a lot of time reading the Bible."

"I'm very happy I have this chance to talk to you, Mr. Shipp," I said. "I'm a journalist doing some work on the Simpson story and a detective at the L.A.P.D. told me yesterday that O.J. is about to confess."

"No shit," he said.

"I'd like a chance to talk to you about it, get your thoughts," I said.

Shipp told me that he was on his way with his family to a birthday party in Simi Valley, and he asked me for a phone number so he could call me about an interview later. Call me a coward, but I didn't want to give him my name or my phone number. I said, "Listen, I'll be around this area for the rest of the day. Maybe I could just come back later?"

"That's not the way I do things," he said.

I told him that I'd be in touch again, and he nodded. He got back into his pick-up and drove off.

I am still trying to figure out what that "No shit" might mean.

I got the same "We never heard this before" that had been relayed to me from Gil Garcetti at the end of my meeting of Tuesday, March 25th, when I presented my case to Leo Wolinsky and Joan Goulding, who had overseen the *Times'* coverage of the Simpson trials. In addition to giving these editors the excerpt from O.J.'s deposition I'd printed out, and a copy of my letter to Robert Baker, I also presented them a document I'd whipped up to break down my theory into its main points.

Here's what I presented to them.

10 Reasons to Consider That O.J. Simpson Didn't Do it

1. Time line has always been short for O.J. Simpson to be able to clean up after committing blood-drenched murders and get ready for trip to Chicago.

2. No blood whatsoever on O.J.'s white carpet, which he would have had to walk on with a supposedly bleeding finger up to his bedroom after murders.

3. O.J. able to sign autographs casually at LAX an hour after murders took place.

4. O.J. had just flown into town June 10, 1994 before leaving for Chicago on June 12, 1994 casts doubt on stalking.

5. [We know] O.J. was not using cocaine or alcohol on June 12, 1994 because none was found in his blood on June 13, 1994 when police took it. No previous evidence of O.J. ever engaging in physical violence against Nicole when he was completely sober.

6. If O.J. is obsessing about Nicole just before murders, then why is he repeatedly phoning Paula Barbieri?

7. No evidence of escalating pattern of violence of O.J. against

Nicole; rather a pattern of de-escalating violence between 1989 and 1994. (In 1989 he's physically fighting with her causing injuries; after that, he's just breaking things and shouting). Unlike 1989, when Nicole photo-documents her injuries, Nicole photo-documents no injuries to herself in five years since 1989 because no photos later than that are found in her bank lock box with previous photos.

8. Weak motivation for O.J. to premeditatively murder Nicole. O.J. not romantically very desperate since as a wealthy, attractive, athletic, sports legend and celebrity he can whistle and beautiful women will line up for chance to be with him. List of stunning girlfriends include Paula Barbieri and Tawny Kitaen.

8. Murder method of using knife is odd choice for a man obsessed with cleanliness and neatness. O.J.'s neatness with clothes documented in testimony of Ron Shipp. O.J. won't park his car under a tree because sap might dirty it. O.J. won't allow smoking in his house.

9. O.J.'s documented concern for his children throws doubt on his committing murders a few feet away from his kids then leaving the bodies where his children might discover them.

10. O.J. immediately returns from Chicago when he is informed of Nicole's death and voluntarily makes a statement to police, and gives them permission to draw his blood, against his lawyer's advice.

10 Reasons to Consider That Ron Shipp Did Do it

1. Ron Shipp wears size 12 shoes, same as O.J., and could have been wearing Bruno Magli shoes which left footprint at Bundy crime scene.

2. Ron Shipp has history of career failures, alcoholism, and possibly drug use. He tried out for football team at USC and didn't make he because "I wasn't good enough." L.A.P.D. would not

allow him back on force four months after he quit. His only significant success at acting were small parts playing a policeman that O.J. got for him. By his own sworn testimony he "idolized" Simpson. His main source of ego gratification when he was with L.A.P.D. was bringing fellow officers over to O.J.'s Rockingham house to show off O.J.'s trophies and get O.J. to sign autographs. Long term pattern suggests that his ego was dependent on O.J. Simpson for his major life satisfactions amidst career and personal failures.

3. Ron Shipp is *only close acquaintance* of O.J. Simpson with requisite skills to have framed O.J. As 15-year veteran of L.A.P.D., including undercover work, patrol work, and instructing at L.A.P.D. Police Academy, Ron Shipp has requisite skills to know what physical evidence would be convincing to detectives investigating a murder, and the requisite skills to know how to collect blood evidence in order to frame O.J.. He could have obtained a sample of O.J.'s dried blood at any time previous to murders and liquefied it with saline solution just as criminalists are trained to do so it could be dropped at Bundy crime scene at time of murder and on O.J.'s driveway just after murders. If he's the murderer, he could either deliberately collect liquid sample of Nicole's and Ron Goldman's blood to plant on O.J.'s Bronco, or with saline solution reliquefy mixture of their dried blood splattered on his own clothes while committing the murders.

4. As friend of O.J. Simpson, Ron Shipp was on O.J.'s property frequently, and by his own trial testimony was in O.J.'s bedroom several times before murders. This provides opportunity for Shipp to steal items of clothing from O.J.'s house including Bruno Magli shoes, Isotoner gloves, O.J.'s watch cap, which can be planted at Bundy crime scene, and second glove on Rockingham estate outside Kato Kaelin's room. As a mutual friend of many of O.J.'s and Nicole's acquaintances, Shipp could have had intimate knowledge of O.J.'s and Nicole's schedule for June 12, 1994, and know just when would be an ideal time to commit murders when

O.J. would have no alibi. A simple hang-up phone call to O.J.'s from a payphone just before committing murders could establish O.J. at home without any phone records.

5. Shipp has established pattern of jumping O.J.'s gate to get onto O.J.'s property, even when O.J. is not home. This can be verified with O.J.'s maids, Michele and Gigi, and with O.J.'s assistant, Cathy Randa. He would have had ample opportunity over many years to steal O.J.'s master house key to make a copy. In weeks before murders, O.J. instructed Cathy Randa to tell Shipp that he could not come by house without calling first to make sure it's all right because Shipp is coming onto property when O.J. isn't home and frightening new maid, Gigi. This provides indications both of Shipp's feeling separated from O.J., which is long-term pattern necessary to his ego gratification, and his possible intent in weeks prior to murders to gather items necessary to frame O.J. for murder of Nicole he is possibly fantasizing about.

6. Shipp is athletic man who is physically capable of having committed the double murders, and jumping O.J.'s gate.

7. Shipp is physically similar enough to O.J. to be used in a police line-up. Shipp is a black man who could have been black man Nicole saw looking at her through her window, and could have been black man witnesses reported near Bundy crime scene night of June 12, 1994.

8. One week prior to June 12, 1994 murders (approximately June 3rd to 5th), Shipp is at O.J.'s Rockingham estate with Lisa Madigan, a blond-haired Canyon Country neighbor physically similar to Nicole. In O.J.'s deposition, Shipp is reported as showing up at O.J.'s estate with this "blond Nicole type" late at night to use Jacuzzi with her and show her off to O.J.. By both Shipp's trial testimony and O.J.'s deposition, Shipp asks O.J. for bottle of wine, which O.J. reluctantly provides. In O.J.'s deposition, O.J. says that when Shipp asks O.J. for wine, O.J. is on phone to Cathy Randa, and I postulate it's to complain to Randa about Shipp once again showing up uninvited.

9. According to L.A.P.D. Homicide Detective Vic Pietrantoni, Tom Lange's former partner, "Ron Shipp was never a suspect" and "we never investigated whether Shipp had an alibi" for June 12, 1994.

10. According to deposition of Denise Brown, and Shipp's own trial testimony, Ron Shipp and Nicole were "close." According to Cora Fischman's deposition, in weeks prior to murders Nicole was engaging in sex with many male partners, as well as three-somes with Faye Resnick. This provides possible motivation for Shipp, who already wants to do everything just like O.J. Simpson does, to stalk Nicole, become obsessively sexually jealous of her, and when rejected by her (possibly after one or more sexual encounters with her) to decide to murder her and frame O.J. for the crime.

Conclusions

I postulate that for someone other than O.J. Simpson to have committed these murders, it has to be an individual who

1. Is physically capable of the murders and of jumping O.J.'s gate.

2. Can be physically confused in identification with O.J. Simpson.

3. Can wear O.J.'s shoes.

4. Has law-enforcement skills which can accomplish a professional frame-up of blood and other circumstantial evidence.

5. Has access to O.J.'s estate.

6. Has obsession with both O.J. and Nicole.

7. Has given no alibi to investigators.

8. Has history of psychological problems, personal failures.

9. Has history of substance abuse.

Things to Investigate

1. I postulate that Ron Shipp was romantically obsessed with Nicole. Al Cowlings thought so and reports are that Shipp had

said to A.C. that "he had a shot at Nicole if O.J. wasn't there" and this was A.C.'s reason for thinking that Shipp should be a suspect. Other Simpson friends supposedly have said that Shipp was in love with Nicole. Investigation of Shipp's relationship with Nicole might yield clues.

2. I postulate that on the same day, one week prior to murders, that Shipp brought Lisa Madigan over to O.J.'s Rockingham estate, Shipp also brought Madigan over to Nicole's condo on Bundy. [To the best of my knowledge, now, this did not happen.] This coincides with disappearance of Nicole's keys, which were found in O.J.'s bag in Al Cowling's Bronco when O.J. was arrested after famous Bronco chase. I speculate that Shipp stole Nicole's keys that day, used them a week later on June 12, 1994 during murders, and planted them in O.J.'s bag during time period of June 13, 1994 to June 17, 1994, when Shipp had complete access to O.J.'s house along with many of O.J.'s friends and family. Nicole's keys were found by police in O.J.'s bag when O.J. was arrested June 17, 1994 after Bronco chase. Investigation of Shipp's presence in Brentwood neighborhood of Nicole's condo in period before murders might yield clues (but trail is cold and Shipp might not have been recognized before TV appearance during O.J.'s trial).

3. I postulate that Shipp's wife, Nina, knows, or suspects, that Ron Shipp did it (if Ron Shipp did it). I speculate that (if Shipp did it) Lisa Madigan also suspects it. [This also, apparently, turns out not to be true.] If these postulates are true, this provides leverage to pry information out of one or both of these women.

4. If Shipp brought Lisa to Nicole's condo on Bundy the week before the murders, this would be evidence of Shipp's ability to steal Nicole's keys on date they turned up missing, and the coincidence of the keys disappearing when Shipp was there would be strong evidence of Shipp committing a frame. Identification of Shipp and Lisa Madigan in Brentwood neighborhood near Nicole's weekend prior to murders would be clue.

5. Ron Shipp was not investigated by L.A.P.D. for murders. Following theory of his being murderer might provide evidence to investigators since territory is virgin. But after 2-1/2 years, the trail is cold. Still, much older murders have been successfully investigated.

6. If Shipp did it, Shipp knows that he did, and that O.J. is innocent. This provides main avenue of proving it: by spooking Shipp into making a false move.

7. Shipp wears a cross around his neck and according to Nina, quoted in *People* magazine, Shipp has been reading the Bible a lot since O.J.'s criminal trial. *People* reports Shipp moodier since trial. Shipp might either be using Christianity as a cover for his murders, or might have "found Jesus" out of guilt for murders during an out-of-control period of his life. He might have rationalized not confessing because it would hurt his children. But his guilt, if he is guilty, might make him want to confess, if he feels he is trapped.

8. I did not find upon cursory inspection, nor would I expect to find, anything out of the ordinary in Shipp's lifestyle, two-and-a-half years after the murders. Nazis have led ordinary lives for many years after committing much worse atrocities. The human power to rationalize is almost unlimited. See Woody Allen's *Crimes and Misdemeanors.*

Sitting across from a conference table in Leo Wolinsky's cramped cubbyhole at the labyrinth-like editorial offices of the *Los Angeles Times*, I read this aloud to Wolinsky and Goulding, point by point, and watched their jaws slowly drop. I don't know if their shock was caused by the idea that there might actually be a plausible case for O.J.'s innocence, or merely because of my bizarre imagination at having come up with this.

Our meeting ended with a discussion of the difficulties that would exist in pursuing an investigation of my theory. Wolinsky said he needed to talk to the *Times'* lawyers.

About a week after our meeting, Leo Wolinsky told me had been advised by the *Los Angeles Times'* attorneys that they couldn't participate in a criminal investigation of a private individual who wasn't already under some official investigation. The risks of liability for possible invasion of that individual's privacy precluded trying to establish that he had committed a crime in the first place; the risk of being sued for libel if they published evidence of a crime that they might uncover eliminated any incentive to look in the second place.

Even my suggestion that the *Times* review the official blood toxicology reports from the Simpson case, to look for toxicological or metabolic discrepancies between Simpson's reference sample taken by police the afternoon of June 13, 1994, and the blood drops identified as his which he theoretically left at the crime scene only sixteen hours earlier, was apparently too much of an investigation for O.J. Simpson's home-town paper to undertake.

Apparently, a major daily newspaper engaging in investigative journalism of a crime, independent of those cases already being investigated by the police, is *de facto* against the law today in the United States.

The libertarian part of me was appalled by this discovery, and it encouraged me to continue, in spite of my knowledge that it might be against my best interests.

Besides, the *Los Angeles Times* had deep pockets if they got sued. I was so much in debt already that I was always contemplating filing for bankruptcy anyway.

I was, as they say, judgment proof.

Over the next couple of months I spent pursuing verification of my theory, I developed my speculations into as coherent a picture as I could manage.

I began researching in microscopic detail the physical evidence presented in the O.J. Simpson trials, trying to see if there existed evidence that could destroy my scenario. I re-familiarized myself with the testimony in the criminal trial, and immersed myself in the depositions of the civil trial. I read most of the major books that had been written about the case. I looked for possible motives that could drive Ron Shipp to do those things that my theory had him doing. I tried to find out if he had ever been a police suspect, and whether he had ever established an alibi for the times of the murders.

I tried, without success, to interview Lisa Madigan, the "blonde Nicole type"—the married friend of Ron and Nina Shipp—who had accompanied Ronald Shipp to Simpson's estate a week before the murders. I later found out from one of her neighbors why she wouldn't talk to me. When Shipp had brought her name into Simpson's criminal trial, a TV truck from *Hard Copy* had shown up in front of her house. She wouldn't talk to them, either. I was later able to determine, through these neighbors, that Lisa Madigan was trying to make some extra money for her family by pursuing a career in commercial acting, and had met Shipp in an acting class. In a typical come-on, Shipp had gotten her into O.J. Simpson's Jacuzzi by suggesting that meeting O.J. Simpson might lead to acting parts. I was able to determine that Lisa Madigan didn't believe she had seen anything on her visit with Shipp to O.J.'s estate that would lead her to believe Shipp was planning a murder or frame-up that night. I sure would like to ask her if she saw a cut on O.J. Simpson's left hand that night— a cut that Ron Shipp might have also noticed.

But if Ron Shipp had been trying to set her up with O.J. as a temple offering, apparently she was never a party to the plan.

I tried (and failed) to place Shipp near Nicole's condo at any time closely preceding the murders. I talked to florists near Nicole's condo to see if Shipp might have bought any flowers in the weeks previous to the murders, figuring that if he had, it might be indicative of an attempt to romance her. I came up with nothing. I questioned anyone associated with Simpson who would talk to me, and spent hours discussing my theory with veteran crime writer Joseph Bosco, who had sat in court for the criminal trial and written the fine book about it called *A Problem of Evidence.*

Bosco told me he liked my theory. He just wished there was some way to prove it. He couldn't think of one, either.

In essence, I tried to eliminate Shipp, in my own mind, as a possible suspect.

I wasn't finding any evidence to establish my scenario, but I was also unable to find evidence that could refute my theory about him.

While as a gumshoe I was on a wild goose chase, finding nothing that could encourage me that my theory had any basis in fact, as a writer I was developing a scenario for the murders that I thought could account for all but the blood evidence.

Then, following a lead given to me by one of Simpson's "DNA" attorneys, Robert Blasier, I interviewed a prominent microbiologist (one *not* involved in the Simpson case) who gave me a theory to account for that evidence, too.

The picture I was painting in my mind, a summary of what I had assembled so far, goes something like this.

The Ron Shipp I was postulating as an actor in these events (as opposed to the real-life Ron Shipp, who may bear only a passing resemblance to my model), would have to be a consummate failure, whose main source of ego gratification had to do with his association to his celebrity friend, O.J. Simpson. It was well-known that Shipp used to take fellow L.A.P.D. officers over to Simpson's house to show off his relationship with Simpson, give guided tours of Simpson's memorabilia, and use Simpson's tennis courts.

The Ron Shipp I was inventing had at least this in common with the real Ron Shipp: he hero worshipped O.J. Simpson.

The question in my mind was: did this hero worship turn into a fatal attraction?

My research told me that I was not the first person to suspect Ron Shipp of being involved in the Brown-Goldman murders. Reports said that Al Cowlings had suspected Shipp, as had O.J.'s sister Shirley Baker and her husband, Benny Baker. There were fragments of suspicions published in several of the books about the Simpson case. Supposedly Shipp had been attracted to Nicole, but the feeling wasn't mutual. Shipp's marriage might not have been solid: he was known to make moves on blonde "Nicole types" he met in acting class, and one of them he had even brought over to O.J.'s house a week before the Brown-Goldman murders.

Was this evidence of an obsession that Shipp also had for Nicole?

What if, following the "final break-up" of O.J. Simpson and Nicole, Shipp had made a move on Nicole and was rejected?

What if Shipp had been told to stop coming around to O.J.'s so much, and to call before coming over?

What if Ron Shipp, whose ego seemed so dependent on his association with a celebrity, was being given the bum's rush by that celebrity?

Ron Shipp had, apparently, tried to make an offering of a blonde neighbor of his to O.J. Simpson, a week before the murders, in a possible attempt to get back into his hero's good graces.

O.J. had rejected the sacrificial offering.

Would this hero worshipper react the way Cain did when his offering to the object of his worship was rejected? Would he take out his frustration by murdering the love object of the object of his love?

Did Ron Shipp murder Nicole Brown Simpson to take from O.J. Simpson the two things that mattered most to him: his love goddess and his celebrity?

I started plotting how the planning of the murders would have to go.

Shipp was an ex-cop, and after leaving the L.A.P.D. had tried

starting his own security firm. He could have had electronic surveillance equipment left over he could use on Nicole or O.J.

He could have sneaked into O.J.'s bedroom, grabbed a pair of
shoes from the 40 pairs in O.J.'s closet—a pair from the back so
they wouldn't be missed—and a watch cap and pair of winter
gloves from a drawer—also stuff that O.J. wouldn't immediately
miss.

O.J. habitually hid a master key to his house outside his front
gate, in case he got locked out. Shipp, the ex-cop and O.J. hanger-
on, easily could have known where that key was hidden.

O.J. habitually kept a spare set of keys to the Bronco in his
kitchen. Shipp could have known where those were kept, also,
and grabbed them when he needed them. One of the books talked
about evidence of someone having left O.J.'s kitchen door open,
and the alarm system off, which O.J. discovered when he got
home from a date with Paula Barbieri on June 11th, the night
before the murders.

Then there was the most important question: how could Shipp
have gotten hold of a supply of O.J. Simpson's blood?

It was not an easy challenge.

You don't simply go up to O.J. Simpson at a party and stick a
syringe into his arm. Aside from the social impropriety of it, O.J.
Simpson was reported by his friends to be squeamish about blood.

But what if Shipp managed to get alone with O.J. and got him
to drink some Gatorade spiked with the so-called "date-rape"
drug, Rhohypnol? Or perhaps a tranquilizer such as Xanax mixed
into a glass of Chivas Regal? An unconscious O.J. might not be
all that hard to draw blood from, if you knew what you were
doing. You didn't need to store the blood in a purple-topped tube
with EDTA in it, either. You could either freeze the blood rela-
tively quickly (adding saline solution or even distilled water, if it
coagulated a bit first) or even add some CPDA—citrate, phos-
phate, dextrose, and adenine—which blood banks used as a preservative—good for keeping blood transfusable for up to a month.

Another possibility was to find out if O.J. kept any blood available at a clinic, for autologous blood donation—that is, his own blood that he might need for a knee surgery. In fact, O.J.'s mother had donated blood to herself for precisely that sort of surgical purpose. If you're having chronic knee problems, you might want to store blood long term. If you're going to store blood longer than a month, if you want it to keep for up to ten years, you have to add something like glycerine, and freeze it.

Clip off a few inches of the blood-bag tubing attached to the outside of the blood bag, and you'd have all the blood you need, with no one the wiser.

If Ron Shipp were lucky enough to go through O.J.'s bathroom wastebasket and find some gauze or tissue or toweling with O.J.'s dried blood on it, perhaps it could be reconstituted with saline solution or distilled water into liquid blood again. But how much would the DNA have degraded, and when reconstituted, would it be bright red again? And would there be enough to get the 40 or so drops that you'd need?

But there was one additional possibility I discovered.

If you didn't have enough of O.J.'s blood, Dr. Frankenstein could make more for you.

Dr. Frankenstein, as it turns out, could be anyone with a high-school diploma and a job in a biochemistry lab. Any lab doing criminalistics would do. So would most university labs. It just required a device called a thermal cycler used for PCR testing of DNA, and common lab equipment such as a blood centrifuge. Five thousand bucks worth of lab equipment that could be ordered on an 800 line, paid for by credit card, and delivered by mail, anonymously—and another couple of hundred dollars in chemicals. The techniques had been in use for a decade, and everybody who worked in the field knew it could be done.

Any policeman who'd ever spent any time talking to a lab technician, or had to be briefed on DNA procedures for a criminal case, would know about it, too.

He'd need a drop of O.J.'s blood, as a reference sample. Type the red blood cells for ABO and enzymes. Do PCR on the white blood cells to clone the DNA—as much as you need. Shipp wouldn't even necessarily need a drop of O.J.'s blood as a reference sample. If he had a lab blood report giving O.J.'s ABO type, ESD, and PGM subtype—used in case O.J. needed a blood transfusion—then all he would need is a sample of O.J.'s DNA—and he could get that from a used Kleenex, or a fingernail clipping, or a follicle from O.J.'s hair.

Now you get a test tube of blood of the same ABO type. Centrifuge the blood to separate the red and white blood cells. Heat the red blood cells carefully to destroy the enzymes, while preserving the ABO typing, and pour in enzymes matching your reference sample. Then take the white blood cells and subject them to X-rays or short-length ultraviolet to destroy the DNA. Do PCR testing on the white blood cells to make sure none of the DNA is left. If it is, give them more radiation.

Then take the DNA you've cloned using PCR and mix well with the now DNA-free white blood cells, and mix it back with the red blood cells.

Voila. Instant O.J., suitable for use at the crime scene of your choice.

Of course, Ron Shipp wouldn't have to know how to do this, himself. It would be enough if he knew it could be done. If he could come up with some cover story so a lab technician would do it for him, or simply for cash—and keep his mouth shut when he later suspected he might be an accomplice before the fact to a double homicide—it would be enough. But, in all likelihood, nobody would even believe this sort of blood frame up would ever be done, and would never even look into it.

Detectives just don't have that sort of imagination. You'd have to write science fiction or something even to take this complex a plot seriously.

So, June 12, 1994, Ron Shipp is ready. He has O.J.'s shoes, a watch cap full of O.J.'s hairs, a pair of the Juice's gloves, and a test tube with some of O.J.'s blood—original, reconstituted, or Frankenstein.

He also has a Swiss Army knife that O.J. gave him, along with half O.J.'s other friends.

Shipp doesn't want to use his own car that night, so he drops his car at a dealership for a tune-up, and gets a loaner.

He uses the loaner to drive from his home in Santa Clarita to Sydney Simpson's recital, and there he begins his tailing of Nicole. He follows Nicole to Mezzaluna, and from there to her home. He then drives over to O.J.'s house on Rockingham, and parks somewhere inconspicuous. He's been working for a real-estate company. A computer listing tells him which houses in O.J.'s neighborhood are unoccupied. That's where he parks.

Dressed the way he saw O.J. Simpson costumed in a *Naked Gun* movie—a black commando outfit and a watch cap—Shipp sneaks into O.J.'s Rockingham estate, just as he's done dozens of times before, and positions himself near the tennis courts, which gives him a good view of Simpson's bedroom. There, possibly using a headset to listen to a bug he's planted inside the house, he waits until he sees O.J. lie down on his bed for a few minutes before his flight to Chicago. O.J. has been up since 5:30 that morning. He's been up now for almost seventeen hours. He's exhausted.

Shipp now has his opportunity.

He heads out to the Bronco and opens it, using the spare set of keys from O.J.'s kitchen. The first thing he does is remove the bulb from the ceiling light—a technique he learned years before as an L.A.P.D. patrol officer, to prevent himself from being a target when the door is opened. It's something, perhaps, that only a cop would think of. Even Detective Lange mentions having done this as a patrol officer in his book with Vannatter, *Evidence Dismissed*.

He drives the Bronco over to Nicole's condo, drives around a couple of times just to make sure someone sees the Bronco, then parks in back and enters through the back gate.

He then makes some sort of noise outside Nicole's condo, to draw Nicole outside. She comes out to investigate.

Or if her intercom is working, Ron Shipp buzzes her and says, "Nicole, this is Ron."

And with a bizarre irony, Nicole Brown Simpson, expecting Ron Goldman and not being able to differentiate between male voices on the tinny intercom speaker, comes outside in her bare feet to find the wrong Ron.

Shipp opens the Swiss Army knife and uses it on Nicole, as Mark Fuhrman suggests in his book *Murder In Brentwood*. He kills her. I don't need to tell you how. It's exactly the same way the prosecution's detectives, medical examiners, and criminalists told you it could have happened during the trials of O.J. Simpson. One killer. It's over quickly.

Then Ron Goldman shows up. Perhaps he's there while Nicole's murder is still going on, and tries to save her. Or perhaps Nicole is already dying, and Goldman sees Shipp standing over Nicole's body. "Hey, hey, hey," are, likely, Ron Goldman's last words.

Shipp heads out toward the back gate, carefully dripping blood from the test tube, one drop at a time, as he goes. He walks slowly. The blood drops take on a circular pattern, with no tail indicating movement. He dabs some of O.J.'s blood on the back gate.

Then he remembers that there's more cross-linking and evidence- planting he wanted to do. He circles back to the crime scene and drags the watch cap across Goldman's shirt before dropping it—makes sure he gets blood on the gloves and some of Nicole's hair on it. Collects a small sample of Nicole's blood from the pool surrounding her body. Drops one of the gloves. Rubs O.J.'s shoes that he's wearing against their clothes and makes sure the shoes have the victims' blood on them.

Lucky thing that O.J. and Shipp both wear size 12 shoes.

Shipp is now desperate to get the Bronco back to Rockingham

before O.J. looks outside and might notice it's missing. So he drives like a demon back to Rockingham, with the headlights off.

Jill Shively, the one witness who claimed to have seen Simpson in the immediate vicinity of the murders at the time they probably occurred, was a grand-jury witness whose veracity was compromised because she sold her story before testifying about it, lied about having done so, and was also reported to have committed fraud in the past.

But just maybe Jill Shively is the Girl Who Cried Wolf, and sees O.J.'s Bronco cut her off and almost hit a gray Nissan at the intersection of Bundy and San Vicente. Shipp shouts for the car to move. It's night but light enough for Shively to see a black man costumed like O.J. Simpson in *Naked Gun* driving a white Bronco she recognizes as O.J.'s. Her mind does what witnesses' minds often do, and fits the facts into a firm memory of having seen and heard O.J. in the Bronco.

Shipp glides the car into a parking space next to the Rockingham gate to O.J.'s estate. He can tell that the limousine has already come to pick O.J. up for his trip to LAX for O.J.'s red-eye to Chicago. He makes sure that his bloody shoes leave plenty of Ron Goldman's and Nicole's blood in the Bronco, and uses some drops of O.J.'s blood from the tube as well to smear some blood around.

Then he sneaks back onto the Rockingham estate and behind Kato's room, where he drops the other glove, pre-stained with some O.J. blood.

Then he bangs on the air conditioner outside Kato's room three times, to make sure that someone will look back there and find the glove.

Then he hides.

He waits until O.J. has left for the airport in the limo, and Kato is back inside his guest room.

Shipp uses a bathroom near the garage to clean himself up,

and put all his bloody clothes, shoes, and murder weapon into a trash bag, which he can always dispose of much later. He changes back into his own clothes. He can't leave any of this behind. He realizes that there might be fibers, hairs, prints, his own DNA, etc., that might link him to the crime scene. He's much too obsessive to risk that.

Then Shipp finishes the frame-up, creating a blood trail from the tube of O.J.'s blood from the Bronco to O.J.'s house. He uses O.J.'s key to get into the front alcove, and notes that the security alarm is off. He drips his last few drops of O.J.'s blood inside the alcove, then pads up the stairs into O.J.'s bedroom and grabs a pair of O.J.'s socks from the hamper. He's saved just a few drops of Nicole's blood, taken from her pool of blood at Bundy. He rubs the blood into one of the socks and drops it onto the carpet.

He's brought one more item along for the *piece de resistance* of the frame-up. He's brought along the box from the Swiss army knife that O.J. had given him. He drops it on O.J.'s bathroom sink.

Then he hears something downstairs, maybe Kato, setting the alarm as O.J. called about. He waits until it's quiet then sneaks down the stairs again. As he heads out, he sees that the security alarm is now armed. He turns it off to get out. It's been so many years since O.J. told him the code that O.J. probably doesn't even remember that Shipp knows it. But Shipp, the hanger-on, memorized that code and has used it whenever he needed to get inside O.J.'s house. Now he's using it to get out.

He sneaks out the back of O.J.'s estate and walks calmly over to his car.

He doesn't know how long it will take detectives to make their way over to O.J. Simpson's house, but he knows he's left a trail that any decent detective could follow.

Ron Shipp gets back onto the 405 Freeway and drives back to his home in Santa Clarita.

When he slips into bed next to his wife, Nina wakes up and

asks, "Who was she this time, Ron?"

Ron Shipp confesses a drunken one-night-stand to his wife that never happened.

The next morning, the news of the murders is all over the radio and TV.

Ron Shipp calls O.J.'s house and gets Mark Fuhrman on the phone. This is working even faster than he thought possible. Shipp asks Fuhrman if O.J. hurt Nicole.

The next week gives him an opportunity to enhance his frame-up, as necessary. He still has friends at West L.A. division and at Parker Center, and Shipp starts passing them information about the doings at O.J.'s house, getting information from the ongoing police investigation in return. He's told of O.J.'s interview conducted by robbery-homicide Detectives Vannatter and Lange, and O.J.'s statement to them that he's been having weird thoughts about Nicole. The germ of an idea of how far he can go in further implicating O.J. starts percolating. He will first tell author Sheila Weller, suggesting that the alias "Leo," be used, that O.J. told him he'd been dreaming about killing Nicole. When Weller's book, *Raging Heart*, is published, the prosecutors easily figure out who "Leo" is.

Sheila Weller says, "Leo had a good working knowledge of criminal forensics."

A *very* good working knowledge of it, if my theory is correct.

As an indication that Shipp might never have intended his statements to Weller to be anonymous—but he just wanted it to look that way so he'd have plausible deniability when called to testify: "Leo" is a well-known acronym among police officers.

It's cop slang for "Law Enforcement Officer."

And Shipp admits, under Carl Douglas's cross examination, that he didn't have much expectation of anonymity, anyway.

Later, when Marcia Clark and Philip Vannatter interview him, Vannatter asks Ron Shipp if he thinks O.J. did it. Shipp pauses, then remembers his police training. Never tell an outright lie, since it can be detected by a trained observer. He tells Marcia Clark, "Whoever did this did a heck of a job framing him."

Ron Shipp is the only other person, aside from myself, who has *ever* identified the murderer as the person who did the frame-up. The police and prosecutors denied that there was a frame-up. The defense team asserted that the L.A.P.D. did it.

And, in words reminiscent of MacBeth, Shipp seems to feel he has some kind of guilt of his own to atone for, guilt which may have nothing to do with his having failed to intervene in a domestic violence case, when he declares: "I will not have the blood of Nicole on Ron Shipp."

My letter to Robert Baker of February 15, 1997 shows my state of mind at the time I first identified Ron Shipp as a suspect in my mind. I thought I had a "compelling theory." Now I use the words "theory" and "speculation" almost interchangeably. I had expected, perhaps unrealistically, that I would find some physical evidence to support my theory. That I didn't uncover any has made me doubt my thinking process. Whether this increased doubt is justified or not is a methodological question I have not been able to answer to my own satisfaction.

I think my letter to Robert Baker also establishes that my writing anything about Ron Shipp's possible involvement wasn't something I felt entitled to do in the absence of more compelling evidence. On the one hand, I didn't feel I had the right to invade his privacy if I was wrong. On the other hand, I didn't want to let him know he was being once again looked at with suspicion if I was right.

This is a complex set of both moral and journalistic ethics problems—balancing a pursuit of justice versus the privacy rights of an individual who's never been accused of a crime—that I've had to grapple with throughout my investigation. Even as I decide that I think these questions of mine need to be dealt with openly and in public, I don't think I'll ever be fully comfortable with my decision to write about this, given that my decision to do so has been made in the absence of my finding any physical evidence which would incriminate Ron Shipp for the things I speculate him having done.

It was my original intention not to write about this until and unless an official police or district attorney's investigation had re-opened the Brown-Goldman murders.

I have obviously changed my mind, on grounds that even I consider ethically tenuous.

I ask myself:

Is a far-fetched theory on paper, unsupported by physical evidence, enough reason to possibly subject an innocent private citizen to the ravages of the American tabloid press? Is this just entirely fantasy spun out of an overactive imagination?

Did I, like so many other Americans, just watch too much of the trial of O.J. Simpson?

Have I made this all up in my own mind, simply because there's something magical about O.J. Simpson, and even though I don't even like football, I just don't want to believe him guilty of these horrible crimes?

Or, does this make sense? Is there truth here? Could any of this have actually happened?

Could this case be akin to the murder of *tejano* singer Selena by a close associate obsessed with her, or the fannish obsessions of Robert Bardo, who stalked then murdered actress Rebecca Schaeffer?

Marcia Clark successfully prosecuted Robert Bardo for that murder. I ask myself why she apparently never even considered that this case might be about a fan's obsession with a celebrity—a fan's jealous obsession of a celebrity leading to meticulously detailed pathological acts.

If Ron Shipp did what I speculate, then he was a unique fan with long-term access to his idol and a professional police and security background that enabled him to act out his pathological obsession in a way that a Robert Bardo, or even a Ted Bundy, could never have dreamed.

A fan with the same shoe size as the man he was professionally capable of having framed.

Perhaps Simpson's attorney, Robert Shapiro, at one moment in defense discussion, almost had this figured out. On page 291 of *American Tragedy*, Schiller and Willwerth recount a defense lawyers' meeting of December 22, 1994, in which Shapiro tells his fellow lawyers, "It's possible the killers broke into the Bronco, drove it to Bundy, and committed the murders. They smeared the victims' blood around the inside of the vehicle, drove back, parked it, and dropped the glove off—"

At which point, Schiller and Willwerth report, Johnnie Cochran interrupts and says, "Bob, don't waste our time with this bullshit."

Apparently, discussing their client's possible innocence was irrelevant to the defense strategy.

No wonder, if Simpson was innocent, that no one found "the real killer." Nobody in this supposed search for the truth was really looking very hard.

As I said in 1995, it's enough to make you wish that Perry Mason is real.

Come to think of it, if I'm right, then I made my wish come true.

I tell you one more time. I have no evidence that this theory is true, that the Ron Shipp I've been referring to in this story has even a passing resemblance to the retired L.A.P.D. officer and sometime bit-part actor, Ronald G. Shipp, who, in real life, lives with his wife and two children in a suburb of Los Angeles.

I do not know the true character or psychological makeup of Ronald G. Shipp. I have taken established physical evidence that was used in the case against O.J. Simpson and mixed this evidence with sheer speculation of a possible alternative interpretation. In the absence of physical proof of my speculations, we as a society are morally, ethically, and legally required to regard my speculations as fiction.

Mr. Shipp, if this is merely a fantasy I've made up, you have my sincere apologies. But as an ex-cop, you know that someone should have eliminated you as a suspect three years ago, as soon as they discovered that you wear the same size shoe as O.J. Simpson. Somebody should have asked you if you had an alibi. If you had told them where you were on the night of June 12, 1994, this story might never have been written.

But nobody, apparently, even asked. Detective Vic Pietrantoni of the L.A.P.D. Robbery/Homicide Division says you were never a suspect and nobody ever asked if you had an alibi.

Bill Pavelic, a former L.A.P.D. officer who investigated for O.J. Simpson's defense team, said he was never able to determine if you had an alibi.

And, apparently, the reason you weren't more closely investigated by O.J. Simpson's investigators, in spite of his family's suspicions, was that O.J. Simpson, himself, could never bring himself to believe that you did any of these things.

Could that be because O.J. Simpson knows you didn't commit these murders, because he knows who else did?

Is O.J. Simpson a much better actor than the critics ever thought?

I know this. I think between the two of you, one of you knows which one of you is lying.

And, if by some odd chance, I guessed right, I'd be very careful about that cross you wear around your neck.

Forgiveness comes only after confession and contrition.

If there's anything at all that you need to confess, that is.

Postscript I

Deciding to publish "The Frame of the Century?" has been, perhaps, the most profound decision I've ever had to make in my life.

I have been very careful to state multiple times in the story that I have no physical evidence that what I theorize about the murders of Nicole Brown Simpson and Ronald Goldman is true, that this is a theory—a speculation.

But I also know that once this story is published, it will be reported on by sensationalizers not as meticulous about what they repeat, and it could be assumed by people not paying attention that what I have written is already a proven set of facts.

An unbalanced individual might do something awful to Ronald Shipp or his family. I also lived in Los Angeles during the riots in Spring, 1992, and I understand that anything to do with the Simpson case is a tinderbox if handled indelicately.

Regardless of whether or not my speculation is true, I desperately do not want to trigger anything of this sort. My object in publishing this is to do what I have been trying to do since February 12, 1997: cause someone to confirm or eliminate my theory of the Brown-Goldman murders.

Even if sufficient evidence were found to indict Ronald Shipp, my primary interest in his trial would not be to see his conviction but to see whether there were sufficient evidence to clear O.J. Simpson's name for the Brown-Goldman murders. I would, however, vigorously oppose the prosecution seeking any *greater* penalty for anyone else tried for these murders than were sought against O.J. Simpson when *he* was tried for them. That would be an unconscionable double standard.

My primary reason for publishing "The Frame of the Century?" at this particular time, in the last weeks of May, 1997, is that O.J.

Simpson's Rockingham house, where he still lives with his two young children Sydney and Justin, is in foreclosure, caused by the 34-million-dollar civil judgment against him, and if Simpson is unable to bring his mortgage up to date by next month, he and his children will be forced to move. This would create a dislocation in the Simpson's children's lives once again, and they certainly do not need any more of those.

I would urge the families of Nicole Brown and Ronald Goldman to request the trial judge in their civil suit against Simpson, Hiroshi Fujisaki, not to allow this to happen while the theory I've presented is being investigated as to its truth or falsity.

I hand-delivered an envelope containing a draft manuscript of "The Frame of the Century?" to the home doorstep of Ronald G. Shipp, on Tuesday, May 13, 1997, at approximately 11:15 PM PDT. There were two cars parked at the Shipp house that I recognized as the family's (and I learned that the car I'd seen Nina Shipp driving, which I'd thought was a Cadillac, was in fact an Oldsmobile Cutlass).

My note, handwritten on the outside of the envelope, said, "Mr. Shipp: If you can present me with proof that convinces me that the enclosed is not true, I will stop its pending publication.— JNS"

I also wrote on the outside of the envelope, "Personal and Confidential." I didn't even want Mr. Shipp's wife reading this, if he did not want anyone else to.

The next morning, however, I discovered that my AT&T True Connections number was not working. I phoned AT&T to repair it, but they informed me it would be at least twenty-four hours, even on an emergency basis, to restore it.

I felt it would be terrible if Ron Shipp wanted to get in touch with me and found the number I had given him not working. It would make me seem as if I were trying to defraud him or play a cat-and-mouse game with him.

So, I wrote the following letter, and again drove to his house to deliver it immediately. This time, there were no cars parked at the Shipp house. The envelope with the manuscript I had dropped off only a few hours earlier was gone from the inside of the Shipp's screen door where I'd left it so I could reasonably conclude that Mr. Shipp was in possession of it. I put the letter, also marked "Personal and Confidential" on its envelope, inside the screen door.

My letter follows.

May 14, 1997

Ronald G. Shipp
[Street Address]
Santa Clarita, CA [XXXXX-XXXX]

Dear Mr. Shipp:

Apparently, the above AT&T True Reach [*sic*] number that I use for receiving voice and fax calls has had some problems that I wasn't aware of. AT&T tells me they are working on the problem, and hope to have it working within 24 hours.

Since the manuscript I left with you contains a theory about yourself that you might view as alarming, I wanted to make sure you had a way to reach me in a timely manner.

My cellular phone number is [XXX-XXX-XXXX]. I usually keep it off but I will keep it on until my 500-445-6345 number is working again.

I can also be reached by the above email address, which I check frequently.

Let me repeat what I said in my note to you on the manuscript's envelope. I have no desire to publish a story that might embarrass you if my conclusions are based on premises that can be proved false. If you have any means of proving to me that my theory is simply untrue, I will withdraw the manuscript from its pending publication.

Please be assured, I bear you no malice and my most important agenda is to establish the truth.

Sincerely,
J. Neil Schulman

About three the afternoon of Wednesday, May 14th, AT&T had my True Connections phone number working again.

When I still hadn't heard anything from Mr. Shipp by Friday

afternoon, I telephoned Shipp's attorney, Robert McNeill, to again make sure Mr. Shipp knew how to get in touch with me. After being told by the receptionist that Mr. McNeill was out of the office, I gave my name—and was immediately told to hang on; I would be connected.

After about four minutes on hold, Robert McNeill came onto the line—on speakerphone. I gave him my name, told him that I was an investigative journalist and had dropped off a manuscript with his client, Ronald Shipp, to give Mr. Shipp a chance to give me any information or response he wished. I explained about the problem I'd had with my True Connections number and explained that it had been working for 24 hours and I'd expected to hear from Mr. Shipp by now.

Mr. McNeill asked me if I was trying to get Shipp to "clear" the manuscript.

I said no, but that since I bore Mr. Shipp no malice, and because my manuscript linked him to the Brown-Goldman murders, I felt I had an ethical responsibility to give him a chance to prove me wrong before I published. "I have no desire to harm Mr. Shipp's reputation based on an unprovable theory," I said. That was why I was giving him this chance to respond, I explained to Shipp's attorney.

McNeill thanked me for the information, and we ended the call.

As of this writing, I have not heard or received any communication from Ronald Shipp or his attorney.—JNS

Postscript II

On Sunday evening, May 18, 1997, at approximately 7:15 PM PDT, I drove over to Ronald G. Shipp's house, for the last time, with a friend.

The Shipps' cars were in the driveway and the garage door open so I assume they were home. My friend got out of my car, hand-delivered the final-draft manuscript of "The Frame of the Century?" into the front door of the Shipps' house, then returned to my car and we drove off. The manuscript included everything you are reading, including the first postscript and the bio info about me that follows, and a cover letter.

That cover letter read:

May 18, 1997

Ronald G. Shipp
[Street Address]
Santa Clarita, CA [XXXXX-XXXX]

Dear Mr. Shipp:

This letter is attached to what will be the published version of "The Frame of the Century?" unless you choose to respond to my offer to provide me with proof that my theories are false. As I said in my note to you on the manuscript's envelope, and my hand-delivered letter of May 14, if you provide me with sufficient proof to convince me that I am simply wrong about your having done the things I speculate upon in my story, I will stop its pending publication.

If I do not hear from you or your attorney by Tuesday, May 20, 1997, at noon, expressing a desire to communicate some information to me, I will conclude that you do *not* intend to do so and I will not stop its publication. In the event that I have *not* heard from you or your attorney by Tuesday, May 20, 1997, at noon, you can expect the public release of "The Frame of the Century?" at any time thereafter.

If you do, however, communicate with me a desire to take me up on my offer to respond to what I have written, I am willing to extend to you until noon, Monday May 26, 1997, to present me such proof as you would be interested in providing me.

To put this bluntly, if you have a good alibi for the time of the Brown-Goldman murders, and show it to me, or other proof that you could not have done what I speculate, then I will not publish the story. If you do not present me something that convinces me that I've dreamed all this up, I will feel it ethical to publish it, and will do so with the understanding that what I have written does not constitute anything legally actionable.

I suspect that an element in your decision may be questions about my character. If that question is troubling you, I suggest you or your attorney get in touch with my attorney and friend, [name deleted], at his office at [address deleted], Beverly Hills, CA XXXXX-XXXX. Mr. [deleted]'s telephone number is XXX-XXX-XXXX and his fax number is XXX-XXX-XXXX. Mr. [deleted] was a federal prosecutor for many years and enjoys a sterling reputation. He'll vouch for my honesty and ethics.

Sincerely,
J. Neil Schulman

Attachment: "The Frame of the Century?"

Monday afternoon, May 19, 1997, at approximately 2:00 PM PDT, I dropped off another copy of the final-draft manuscript and my cover letter to Ronald Shipp at the offices of his attorney, Robert McNeill.

On Tuesday, May 20, 1997, at 10:09 AM PDT, I telephoned Mr. McNeill's office and left a message on his voicemail, telling him that I was at home waiting for a call if he or Mr. Shipp wished to inform me that they wanted the chance to tell me anything.

The deadline I'd given Ronald Shipp and his attorney, Robert McNeill to inform me—by phone, fax, mail, or email—that they had any information they wished to present me passed without them having done so.

There was no warning that they considered what I had written grounds for a lawsuit if I published it. There was no denial of anything I'd speculated about.

There was no request, on any grounds, that I not publish this.

We are left on our own to speculate upon Ronald Shipp's silence.   —J. Neil Schulman,
May 20, 1997, 12:15 PM PDT

Part Two

Additional Questions

In Part Two, I answer questions that were raised by Part One of
The Frame of the Century?—*the last version I gave Ron Shipp to
read. Some of these questions were selected from letters to me or
news group posts discussing my book, and I dealt with the ones I
considered interesting and on point. Correspondents requesting
anonymity were not identified.* —*JNS*

From an email letter (anonymity requested) of Thursday, May 22, 1997:

Mr. Schulman,

As a subscriber to alt.fan.oj-simpson, I just came across your posting promoting your book, *The Frame of the Century?*. After downloading your book, I searched it for any mention of the cuts on Simpson's left hand. I found only two references to these cuts in your book. You question why there was no blood from Simpson's bleeding finger on the white carpet of his house, and you ponder whether Lisa Madigan had seen a cut on Simpson's hand on the night of her visit to Rockingham a week before the murders. You fail to account for Simpson's admissions during his 6/13/94 L.A.P.D. interview by Lange and Vannatter that he had cut himself at Rockingham the previous night (6/12/94).

Unless you can work this into your frame-up scenario, it all falls apart. You could, I suppose, attribute the cuts to coincidence, but that would be very weak, in my opinion.

I do not consider the question of O.J. Simpson's left-hand cuts to be dispositive of the case, as much as writers such as Vincent Bugliosi would like us to think so. O.J. said he had possibly "reopened" a cut he'd gotten earlier. He tells Vannatter and Lange during his interview at Parker Center on June 13, 1994, "Mmm, it was cut before, but I think I just opened it again, I'm not sure."

That's why I raised the question whether Lisa Madigan saw a cut the night Shipp was over, an opportunity allowing Shipp to know that he would have to drip blood on the left side of the footprints.

In essence, I wonder whether Shipp, as part of his observations of O.J.—which he would *already* have had to do in order to plan a frame of him—had observed, or otherwise learned of, a cut on O.J.'s left hand at *any* time in the days prior to the murders, which would have allowed him to know which side of the footprints to drop blood. Perhaps he merely overheard O.J. complaining about his left hand having a painful cut on it. I even wonder if he could have set up some sort of trap that would have caused O.J. to cut his hand—something sharp left where O.J. would have to be reaching for something, in a drawer for example.

Or, consider that deciding to obtain blood evidence from O.J. was a last minute decision brought about by a window of opportunity.

Let's postulate that Shipp is observing O.J. at Rockingham the night before the murders, looking for an opportunity to grab the Bronco. Shipp sees O.J. go out to the Bronco, cut himself in there ("Shit!" Shipp might hear O.J. exclaim as he then sucks on the wound to his left hand), and drip blood in the Bronco and all the way back into the house. All Shipp needs to do is sop up some of those blood drops into a paper towel or handkerchief, add a little water when he's ready to use it, and re-drip the blood back onto the walkway at Bundy, on the side of the footprints which corresponded to the hand he saw O.J. tending to after wounding himself. He can then use the residual blood on the paper towel or handkerchief to rub O.J.'s blood on the back gate and inside the Bronco itself.

On page 10 of the Pocket Books paperback edition of Sheila

Weller's book, *Raging Heart*, Weller describes "Leo" (later admitted to as Ron Shipp) driving over to Rockingham on June 13, 1994. Weller's interview with Shipp occurred within weeks of the murders.

Weller writes, "Driving over to Rockingham this evening, Leo said to himself, 'I hope he doesn't have a wound on his hand. And I hope he doesn't want to get me in a corner and ask me questions.' When Leo saw the Band-Aid on the middle finger of his friend's hand, the first tiny alarm bell went off in his mind."

Now this is very interesting. By Ron Shipp's account to Sheila Weller, even before Ron Shipp has supposedly learned of *any* evidence in the case—he's never been at either the Bundy or Rockingham crime scenes, nor does he know what if anything was in the Bronco—he's wondering about O.J. having cut *his hand*. Not his lip, or his arm, or his leg, just his hand.

Now there's a "coincidence" for you.

Shipp's supposed advance worry about O.J. having a "wounded hand" amounts to Shipp telling Weller that he had had a precognition about a wound to Simpson's hand.

Either Shipp is a psychic, or the most specific guesser in human history, or he is lying to Weller about having had to "worry" about a possible wound to O.J.'s hand before he saw it.

If Shipp already knew about the wound to Simpson's hand from having learned about it before the murders, then he had the specific knowledge necessary to frame the blood drops to the left of the footprints at Bundy.

When Shipp called Rockingham the morning of the 13th, he got Mark Fuhrman on the phone, and by Fuhrman's statements in *Murder In Brentwood*, Fuhrman refused to tell Shipp anything more than that Nicole had been murdered. So unless Fuhrman is lying about this point (and to what purpose?), Fuhrman is not the source of any advance knowledge Shipp might have regarding a wound to Simpson's hand.

But even if Shipp had been told about the wound to Simpson's hand by some source who saw O.J. when he returned from Chicago—such as someone at Parker Center or a member of Simpson's family—we need to ask why Shipp would be making up a story two weeks later for Weller, in which Shipp says that he didn't know about the wound already but was worried that there might be one. Even Shipp's statement that he had worried about a wound to O.J.'s hand is far too specific for what was known at that moment in time, before any identification of the blood evidence had been done.

Now, let's consider why Shipp would be telling Weller that, on the way over to Rockingham that evening, he was already thinking about a possible wound to Simpson's hand.

Someone who had seen Simpson's hand since O.J.'s leaving the hotel room in Chicago could have told Shipp about Simpson's wound—but then Shipp is lying to Weller about having hoped Simpson didn't have a wound. If Shipp was told by someone at Parker Center about the examination made of Simpson's wounded hand, then Shipp wouldn't be hoping Simpson didn't have a wound; he would already know Simpson did have a wound and hope about it would be excluded and irrelevant.

But even if we postulate that some other cops had been talking to Shipp about the crime scene evidence, doesn't this still indicate that Shipp already knew that O.J. had a cut hand before any of the blood drops had been analyzed and found to be evidence of a bleeding hand, much less O.J. Simpson's? If someone had told Shipp about what was found at the Bundy crime scene, then why wouldn't Shipp be hoping that Simpson didn't have cuts or bruises on his face or arms from a death struggle with Ron Goldman? Goldman's defense wounds were much grosser crime-scene evidence to detectives and criminalists than five or six as-yet-unidentified blood drops at the crime scene would be—blood drops that on the evening of June 13, 1994, before any blood analysis had been done, could have easily been assumed to belong to one of the victims.

Perhaps Sheila Weller's unpublished notes of her interviews with Shipp would answer these questions—if Weller decides to share them with the public when my questions gain wider interest.

Interestingly, on the night that I delivered a copy of the manuscript of *The Frame of the Century?* to Ron Shipp's house for the first time, I noticed some of my own blood on the white envelope, but did not recall when I'd cut my hand.

You can, indeed, bleed without being able to account for it.

In any event, I do not regard the question of the "coincidence" of O.J.'s having a cut on his hand that makes him look guilty conclusive, since I, for one, think that things do not necessarily happen by random chance and can be calculated as likely or not merely by figuring the odds. Human behavior does not happen randomly. Read what writers such as Robert Anton Wilson say about synchronicity versus coincidence.

The same correspondent asks:

One more thing. On page 38 of your book you say:
"The fan is seen by a limo driver waiting to drive the celebrity to the airport as the fan crosses the lawn of the celebrity's estate."
This is not supportable since Simpson, himself, admitted both in a T.V. interview and in his testimony/deposition at the civil trial that he was the person Park saw entering the house at 10:55 PM on the night of 6/12/94.

Well, I consider that O.J. is simply guessing what Allan Park saw at any given moment. Since Simpson is not considering, as I have, that a second black man dressed in black would have been at Rockingham the night of the murders, O.J. can only conclude that whatever the limo driver saw must have been himself bringing his bags out—so that's the way he would explain it, to himself and others.

But on Page 90 of the hardcover edition of Marc Eliot's *Kato Kaelin: The Whole Truth,* based on 17 hours of Kato's taped conversations with Eliot for a book collaboration that was never published, Eliot writes, "The office [adjoining Kato's guest room] is on the other side of a set of double doors that lead to the main house, which can only be unlocked from O.J.'s side. When Kato turned on the office lights he couldn't help but see how eerie the reflection was through the window. Again he felt uneasy. If anyone were outside, how hard would it be for them to look in?"

This statement refers to a time about a half hour before the three thumps outside Kato's room. Kato recounts to Marc Eliot his already having had a sense of someone around outside.

Human intuition—hunches—do not have to be based on paranormal senses. Hearing a rustling outside on an otherwise silent night, or seeing shadows moving in a pattern the brain subliminally recollects as human movement, could bring about such a feeling. The apprehension that one is being watched, when one does not know whom the watcher is, is not all that unusual, and can properly be regarded as an indication to be taken into account for our investigation.

But there is another indication that someone else may have been at Rockingham that night.

Earlier that evening, Kato had asked Simpson if he could use Simpson's Jacuzzi. O.J. had given permission, told him how to work the jet controls, and Kato had done so. Later, O.J. Simpson had come to Kato's room to tell Kato that he'd left the jets of the Jacuzzi on. Kato is embarrassed. But, in both his trial testimony and his deposition for the civil trial, Kato says that he thought he had turned the Jacuzzi jets off.

Perhaps he had turned them off, and someone else had turned them back on, perhaps to create a white noise so he wouldn't be detected.

I suggest it's possible that whatever sightings there might have been that night—by either Kato or limo driver Allan Park—of a black man in dark clothes walking around O.J's Rockingham property, could have been Ron Shipp, either preparing for, or back from, the murders at Bundy.

Is there any confirmation of O.J. rejecting Shipp's companionship, and of Shipp having access to O.J.'s house and property, other than O.J.'s own deposition?

Yes.

From Marc Eliot's *Kato Kaelin: The Whole Truth*, page 239:

> Ron Shipp was an ex-cop who used to visit the house quite often with friends to play tennis. Sometimes Ron would be on the tennis court with three friends, and O.J. nowhere in sight. "He was always friendly to me," Kato said, "but I know his hanging around bothered O.J. Toward the end, whenever Shipp would show up, O.J. would look at Kato, raise his eyes to the sky, and say, "Oh, no, Ron's here again. I need to talk to him about this."
>
> Shipp got to know the ins and outs of the house. He discovered, for example, that the Ashford gate had a latch that could be opened from the outside. Kato often used it to let himself in when he'd come home late. He preferred using this method because the Rockingham gate worked electronically and it had a slow lumbering motion, which meant having to wait until it opened completely, and then completely shut. On a cold night, with O.J.'s dog barking at his feet, it wasn't the most pleasant way to pass five or ten minutes.

Note that O.J.'s deposition for the civil trial began January 21, 1996, while Marc Elliot's book was published seven months earlier, in June, 1995. This information, documented by Marc Elliot, could not have been derived from O.J.'s deposition, which did not yet exist, and was the first time O.J. had talked about Ron Shipp publicly since June 13, 1994. Nor does Kato, who tells Eliot that he believes Simpson is guilty, have any reason to make anything up about Simpson's relationship with Shipp.

From an exchange of postings in alt.fan.oj-simpson. In a message of May 25, 1997, "Clio" asked:

[W]hy would Shipp murder Nicole, especially considering the allegation that he had a crush on her? Wouldn't he have been more likely to kill O.J.?

My reply:

The question of motivation for the murders of Nicole Brown Simpson and Ronald Goldman asks for speculation, whether one regards the murderer as O.J. Simpson or—as I ask—Ron Shipp. Marcia Clark and Christopher Darden, in their prosecution of Simpson, went to a great deal of effort to establish a pattern of domestic abuse and stalking in their attempt to prove that Simpson had a likely intent to murder Nicole, but even they were never able to come up with more than the barest speculations about what might have been going through O.J.'s mind that would have led him to commit murder.

Nor is motive one of the elements of the crime of murder that a prosecutor has to prove under California criminal law. Only the intent to commit the murder has to be proved.

The question of what could have created an intent in Ron Shipp to murder Nicole is one I speculate on at length. To me, the failures in his life—his being forced to leave the L.A.P.D. for alcoholism and possible other substance abuse, his failure at starting his own security firm, and ending up in a run-of-the-mill job working for a property management company, which might seem a major come-down for a former L.A.P.D. cop—create a fertile field in which the seeds of frustration and jealousy might grow. And, who better than O.J. Simpson, his hero, for Shipp to become jealous of? O.J. must have seemed to Shipp to be the luckiest bastard on the face of the earth: rich, surrounded by beautiful women at his beck and call—and, perhaps, in Shipp's eyes, not worthy of all the blessings that had been bestowed on him.

As for why Shipp might kill Nicole rather than O.J., well, that can get complicated. Clio's question is on point. In common stalking behavior, it is the rival of the love object who is often the target of violence, rather than the love object herself...or himself.

I believe Ron Shipp's primary attachment was to O.J. Simpson, not to Nicole. Ron Shipp had, as stated in his own sworn testimony, idolized O.J. Simpson for years, whether or not that idolization was expressed homoerotically—which, considering O.J.'s homophobia caused by his father being homosexual, would have been particularly confronting to Shipp if any of his feelings toward O.J. were homoerotic. I believe any interest Shipp would have developed in Nicole would likely have been as a consequence of his feelings for O.J.—perhaps to prove that he was up to scoring with his hero's woman. Or, alternatively, it conceivably could have been a psychologically acceptable way to actualize his own inexpressible homoerotic feelings toward Simpson.

One friend of mine, an award-winning novelist, suggested when I showed him the excerpt from Simpson's civil deposition with O.J.'s account of Shipp's visit to Rockingham with what O.J. said Shipp had declared a "blond Nicole type," that perhaps it was in Shipp's mind to create a *menage a trois*—behavior indicating, perhaps, repressed homoerotic desires. I doubt very much that either of the other two persons involved—Simpson or Madigan—would have had anything to do with such a plan, or even necessarily perceived the intent, because who ever really knows what goes on in the hidden recesses of a person's mind?

In any event, if Shipp had, at some point, made a pass at Nicole and been rejected by her—at the same time that O.J. was trying to get him to stop coming around to the Rockingham house so much—then the psychological basis for using Nicole as a means of punishing O.J. for being dissed would be in place.

I emphasize again that this is speculation.

But so is what the prosecution asserted were O.J. Simpson's motives.

In a letter of Friday, 23 May 1997, an attorney I correspond with wrote:

Neil—Read your O.J. piece, it was interesting. Unfortunately you have no evidence to back up your theory, just damn good speculation. Too bad the newspapers are not interested. ... [D]id you consider, while formulating your hypothesis, the revelations of the civil trial? By that I mean instances when O.J. was caught lying—about peripheral matters, to be sure—but nevertheless relevant, like whether or not he ever had those darn shoes (based on the pictures introduced into evidence, I understand that he in fact did, while he denied it). You may know much more about it than I, since I tuned out long time ago.

My reply:

Re. the "ugly ass" shoes. Bruno Magli made more than one style of loafers. O.J. was asked only about the ones he supposedly wore in the photographs introduced at the civil trial, which may turn out to have been faked using computer retouching. But this doesn't mean that O.J. didn't own some other style of Bruno Maglis, which had the sole print found at the Bundy crime scene-shoes that Ron Shipp could have swiped from among the other 40 pairs of shoes found in O.J.'s closet by the L.A.P.D. detectives searching his bedroom.

Even O.J. says, in his deposition for the civil trial, that he doesn't know whether he ever owned a pair of Bruno Magli loafers or not since the only footwear of which he says he ever paid attention to the brand were athletic shoes.

You know, I believe him. If you asked me the brand name of any shoes I've ever bought, I wouldn't know, either. Men are just that way.

So, I don't consider this a lie or a contradiction on O.J.'s part.

Some of the comments in the news group I've noticed have not been designed to promote an exchange of ideas, but merely to insult anyone who stands against the common viewpoint that O.J. Simpson is guilty.
One such comment, posted in alt.fan.oj-simpson on

May 23, 1997 by John Griffin, responded to my offer for a free download of my book as follows:

This is one of the few occasions when you can get exactly your money's worth.

To which I responded:

This is interesting. I write a book in which I use the prosecution's own evidence to come to a different possible murderer, and take the position that those who have been asserting that O.J. Simpson was a victim of a conspiracy, are wrong ... and the *only* people who want to insult me (without first reading my book) are those who believe Simpson guilty.

Griffin responded to my comments in email, but his letter merely engaged in more scattershot *ad hominem*, without responding to anything substantive I'd written, and I assumed he wasn't worth responding to again.

But I was wrong twice. Later on, Griffin did make some substantive comments that I found worth responding to ... and it didn't take more than a few days for me to start getting insults from the other side, too.

Sometimes hostile comments turn into interesting exchanges. In a comment of May 24, 1997 in the news groups alt.fan.oj-simpson, alt.crime, and alt.true-crime, where I'd posted a notice regarding my book, "Jim" wrote from New Zealand:

Ridiculous pap. Obviously he committed the crime. This is just another example of more people without scruples cashing in on a terrible double murder. It's about time someone wrote a book about all these vultures.

I replied, in the news groups:

Now there's an open mind for you.

Excuse me, but you are not God. You do not know what happened. All you can do is what any other human being can do: reconstruct what happened by collecting available facts and creating a pattern of those facts which are then made into a story.

This is what a prosecutor does during a trial.

I have done the same thing, only—using the prosecution's own set of facts—I come to a different possible conclusion.

If you had read my book—which you can do at absolutely no profit to me by downloading it from the web, where I have posted it for free—you would know that I openly acknowledge the desire for profit and recognition as one of the reasons a writer writes anything. But I also ask the reader to understand that a writer's motivations can—and in this case did—also contain the motivations of seeking out truth and justice.

You are free to sneer at my motivations. But I suggest that a little humility, rather than the hubris of unwarranted certainty, is a more appropriate way to approach human affairs.

Interestingly, my comments hit home. I received the following letter in private email:

Hi,

I'm amazed you responded. Thanks for the restraint you showed.

I'm sorry if I offended you. Your book may well be a very good read, but I am concerned about the fact that two murder victims are making a lot of people an awful lot of money. That is not right.

Tell me: do you know for sure who your mother is? Do you think that is open to doubt? All you have to go on is what other people have told you about it. But you do know, don't you? (Unless you are adopted).

I suspect you have absolutely no doubt that O.J. did it. I suspect virtually every other writer who has cashed in on this case knows that too. What will the next angle be? A Martian did it? Manson slipped out of jail for the night and did it?

I am sick of all these books, sick of people making money out of these deaths. Even members of the dead woman's family have cashed in on it.

Thank God I am not an American and don't live in the US. Your society is warped. But someone like you, living there, probably cannot see that.

One final thing: when the murders took place I did not entertain for a second the notion O.J. might be involved. I was an O.J. admirer. In fact I thought he was a lovely chap, a genuinely nice guy despite his fame and wealth. When the police investigation started to focus on him I thought they had it horribly wrong. But, undoubtedly, they were right.

He did it. I know he did it, just as surely as I know who my mother is.

Jim

I replied, in email:

Jim,

I live a ten-minute drive from where the murders at Bundy occurred—and that address is a two-minute drive from my ex-wife's house.

That makes it a story of neighborhood interest to a writer such as myself.

I'm not going to debate my parentage with you, or yours for that matter. But I will suggest that your epistemology needs some work. Whatever you know about the Simpson case is at many removes from what happened. You have had multiple layers of filtering on the information you've received. I suggest that the intelligence community ratings on information might come in useful to you in evaluating whatever you've heard:

RELIABILITY—SOURCE			ACCURACY—INFORMATION
Completely reliable	A	1	Confirmed by other sources
Usually reliable	B	2	Probably true
Fairly reliable	C	3	Possibly true
Not usually reliable	D	4	Doubtfully true
Unreliable	E	5	Improbable
Reliability can't be judged	F	6	Truth can't be judged

I suggest that any information you've gotten through news sources—and a good deal of what was claimed to be news in the Simpson case was nothing more than rumors and conjecture—would have an intelligence rating no better than B3, and more likely D4. This leaves us with the physical evidence in the case, which I've dealt with in my book.

Jim replied in email the same day:

Neil, I am a journalist and had such a crime taken place in my neighbourhood then I admit that I, too, would have been intrigued by it.

But in all honesty I do not find it credible that any reasonable person might still argue for Simpson. He is guilty beyond reasonable doubt.

Your reasoning seems to be that, unless the murderer is seen by 100 witnesses to pump six rounds into a victim then there must always be an atom of doubt. I can't buy that. Not in this case.

A reasonable person would say Simpson is guilty. Sufficient evidence tells us that, in fact screams it out.

Do you honestly believe there is a possibility he is innocent? (And, frankly, I expect you will find a reason not to answer 'yes' or 'no' to this— but perhaps that's the cynical journo in me coming out).

I have seen enough on this case to last me a lifetime but I will try to download your book. However, my PC is several years old and extremely slow so I make be taking on an impossible mission.

Good luck, Jim.

To which I replied:

Jim,

Yes, I think Simpson is innocent. For a long time the physical evidence confounded me, because it contradicted the many other indications of innocence I was perceiving. That contradiction created cognitive dissonance that wouldn't go away until this past February I was finally able to account for the physical evidence. My reasons for thinking him innocent are documented in my book.

I'm not saying Simpson couldn't be guilty. I just think there's more than a reasonable doubt, now, that he is.

I look forward to hearing from you after you've read my book.

Neil

I find, in reading back, that Jim made several comments I want to answer more completely.

Jim said, "[Simpson] is guilty beyond reasonable doubt."

That is the standard of proof in American criminal trials, and in this particular criminal trial, the jury (whatever we think of their cognitive methods) decided that such a reasonable doubt did exist: they acquitted Simpson. Under American jurisprudence, reasonable doubt of guilt, stated in a verdict of "not guilty," has been established in the Simpson case as a matter of law. Since criminal trials in California don't allow a distinction between "not proven" and "innocent," as Scottish courts do, we may even assert that the jury found Simpson legally innocent of the charges against him.

Jim also said, "Your reasoning seems to be that, unless the murderer is seen by 100 witnesses to pump six rounds into a victim then there must always be an atom of doubt. I can't buy that. Not in this case. A reasonable person would say Simpson is guilty. Sufficient evidence tells us that, in fact screams it out."

Of course I disagree, since I have doubts about Simpson's guilt which I think are reasonable. But my main point is that one needs to eliminate possible-in-the-real-world scenarios that suggest evidence could have been manufactured by someone with opportunity and possible motive before deciding "beyond a reasonable doubt" that incriminatory evidence found at a crime scene is enough to convict. I agree that merely suggesting a conspiracy by unknown persons would not be enough to establish reasonable doubt.

But, unlike the defense in the Simpson case, I've been investigating a specific person whom I believe had the opportunity and a possible motive to do it.

I think the prosecution did a pretty good job in defeating the defense's claims that the frame-up of O.J. Simpson could have been engineered after the murders at Bundy were committed. But neither the defense nor the prosecution ever addressed the question I raise about the possibility that an individual exists with the skills, the access, some physical characteristics shared with Simpson, and a possible motive for framing Simpson for the murders at the very time they were committed, before the police even got there.

That, in my view, makes doubt about Simpson's guilt more than reasonable.

Finally, I received letters from several correspondents who believed O.J. Simpson innocent, and Ron Shipp a possible suspect, but they still believed a conspiracy was at work, involving either or both Mark Fuhrman and Kato Kaelin. Representative of that viewpoint was the following letter, sent to me in private email on May 24, 1997. I've inserted my comments.

Dear Mr. Schulman,

I have just finished reading your book and agree with your account of these murders. I must say that I also picked up on Shipp from the very beginning. I believe if you add Mark Fuhrman to this you will find answers where there weren't any before. He was also obsessed with Nicole since his first encounter in 1985. His assistance would have come the next day to ensure the early morning visit to Mr. Simpson's residence. One might also venture he assisted in the murders since he has been shown to have lied about his whereabouts the night of the murders.

My reply:

I'm aware of comments that suggest Mark Fuhrman was interested in Nicole, but I do not use them to propose Fuhrman as involved in the frame-up of O.J. because I don't see it as likely that racist hatred of O.J. Simpson would motivate him to collaborate on a hate crime with a black man such as Shipp as a partner. Further, without Shipp, Fuhrman could not obtain the items necessary to frame O.J. This eliminates Fuhrman, in my view, from any role in my theory.

The letter continues:

I cannot tell you how glad I am that another person has come up with this solution. I am no writer so I simply told people around me. I wouldn't let Kato Kaelin off the hook either. His living on O.J.'s estate was most helpful to the killers.

My reply:

No available evidence indicates to me that Kato was involved in a conspiracy of any sort. And, again, while Kato would have had access to O.J.'s house, he would not have the law-enforcement skills to be able to frame O.J.

It is the nexus of facts that Ron Shipp had access to both O.J. and Nicole, and a body of needed skills, that suggests him to me as a possible suspect. No other individual whose name has been brought into the case, or any other individual I'm aware of from my investigation, fits into both these categories-and Shipp would not have needed anyone else to have done what I suggest and would likely have had to have avoided any additional persons as conspirators because they might eventually turn state's evidence against him in any potential prosecution.

I think, if he did it, he did it alone.

The letter makes its final point:

Shipp would have to have had help committing these murders because of the fight put up by Ron Goldman.

My answer:

I don't agree. I think he would have been athletically fit enough to win a knife fight against an unarmed opponent.

The tool of logic called Occam's Razor cautions us to prefer that explanation which uses fewer, rather than more, elements. I don't want to leave Occam's Razor too many steps behind. I have been motivated by O.J. Simpson's consistent claims of innocence, supported by demeanor evidence, to postulate that one individual with means, opportunity, and possible motive could have committed the murders and framed Simpson for them. That gives us one more element than the theory that Simpson himself committed the murders. I don't want to add any further elements to the theory of a frame-up that aren't warranted by the available evidence.—JNS

A correspondent with an Islamic sounding name wrote me an extensive email letter on May 25, 1997, agreeing with me about Simpson's innocence, but disagreeing with my specific theories of the murders and frame-up. I'll excerpt and answer what I consider the most relevant parts.

Mr. Schulman:

After reading *The Frame of the Century?* I would conclude that it's very much so possible to believe that Ron Shipp committed the murders, especially since no one, as yet, has come forward with any eyewitness testimony. Although your overall theory that Ron Shipp did the murders and frame up is extremely tantalizing to one's intellectual juices, there are a couple of facts in this case that cause me to lay aside Ron Shipp as one who would have committed the crime but was beaten to the punch by stronger, more formidable conspirators.

1.)Simply put, it would have taken more than one person to lure Nicole out of the house and to the point of her attack.

Nicole knew Ron Shipp, and apparently trusted him. He would have had no difficulty getting her to come outside merely by ringing the bell and speaking to her on the intercom.

More than one person had to contain Goldman—regardless of who was killed first. Only the element of surprise, and shock, would preclude the victims from making a sound loud enough to be heard.

I believe it's possible that the killer murdered Nicole first, and Goldman arrived when she was already at least unconscious.

Someone had to open the front gate for Goldman to get in, and at the same time be in complete control of two people, simultaneously.

It's easy for me to postulate that Shipp parked the Bronco in back of the house then came around to the front gate where he rang Nicole's bell. Leaving the gate unlatched might have been an over-sight, or he might have left the gate unlatched for some other rea-son, such as to observe Bundy, and he did not re-latch it.

2.) If you bring out the evidence by Simpson that someone left his door open, and a cryptic message on his answering machine, then you must also mention the evidence by Simpson of his encounter with the Oriental guys on the Santa Monica Freeway, weeks before the murders, where they attempt to intimidate him by refusing to let him pass. This incident upset Simpson enough for him to get himself a gun, and put him in a worried and concerned state of mind.

The encounter with Asians you mention is interesting, but it does not necessarily become part of the Brown-Goldman mur-der case unless a link can be established. There is none I can find so far.

3.) If you mention that Jill Shively saw someone she thought was O.J. Simpson almost run her over, then you must also include that Mary Anne Gerchas would have testified that she saw four men in front of the Bundy residence during the time of the murders. Also, to complete the seeming circle of evidence pointing to more than one person committing the murders, Rosa Lopez would have testified that she heard men in the back of Mr. Simpson's property after he left for the LAX.

I mention Shively only because she would have been a wit-ness for the prosecution. It's my job to account for evidence pre-sented against Simpson, not evidence presented by his defense, which may prove to be irrelevant to the *corpus delicti* of the crime.

4.) You mentioned that Goldman could have yelled out, "hey, hey, hey," when he came upon Shipp murdering Nicole, but I ask you to consider this. As I said before, my understanding is that Nicole's front gate was closed and locked, with some sort of damage to it that required someone to have to open it from the inside. In that case, Nicole came out of her house to let Goldman in? Maybe she never made it to the gate to let him in, while at the same time, somebody more than gladly did let him in?

We can only speculate on the order of events at Bundy, so this is not a part of the *corpus delicti* of the crime I need to deal with. In any case, I suggest that the gate could have been left unlatched from someone coming in earlier.

5.) Robert Heidstra testified that he saw a vehicle turning left (away from Rockingham)! Why, if it was Shipp, would he go that way under the time constraints that he would have been under?

There are streets in both directions that could be turned onto to get back to Sunset Boulevard, the way back to Rockingham. It might simply have been the direction the car he drove was parked—and the same would be true if Simpson were the murderer.

Mr. Schulman, I am a believer in the exposition entitled, *Blood Oath: The Conspiracy To Murder Nicole Brown Simpson*, by Steven Worth. I don't know if you are familiar with his work in this case, but he says that he was contacted by one of the alleged conspirators who decided to come forth (albeit by phone only) and tell what really happened that night.

On my part, after reading the book, considering how the author came about his information, and from what I have been observing throughout the entire case, now including your theory, my personal opinion (which may not mean much—I'm just a common man) —is that the ultimate murders grew from the same tree that produced the Alan Berg murder in 1984 in Denver, and more recently the Oklahoma City Bombing.

That requires a much more elaborate explanation for the murders at Bundy than is warranted by the evidence presented by both the prosecution and defense in the Simpson trial, and by the plaintiffs in the civil action. One does not multiply elements in an investigation without verifying each element independently—and that's my general criticism of the theory that the Brown-Goldman murders required a conspiracy. If Shipp could have done it alone, and I think I've demonstrated that he could have, no conspiracy was necessary, so I don't feel it necessary to look for one.

Finally, I must say I liked the way you teased the readers as to who you felt committed the murders as you gradually revealed Ron Shipp as the culprit. But what I was most surprised about was who you didn't consider in your scenario. You make mention of the similarities of Shipp and Simpson, but what about Marcus Allen? He was sexually intimate (allegedly) with Nicole. He had what one could assume, a burning motivation to kill Nicole, namely, to protect his marriage and wife from finding out his exploits. And you mention similarities, well what about these:

O.J. Simpson	Marcus Allen
Black and 6' 2" tall	Black and 6' 2" tall
approx. 205 lbs.	approx. 205 lbs.
interracial marriage	interracial marriage
intimate with Nicole	intimate with Nicole
wears size 12 shoe	wears size 12 shoe
uniform no. 32	uniform no. 32
famous and wealthy	famous and wealthy
Flight Out Of Lax That Night	Flight Out Of Lax That Night (supposed vacation?)

Who appears to be more of an O.J. clone and admirer than Marcus Allen?

If Marcus Allen had the abilities Ron Shipp had to do a professional frame-up of forensic evidence, then I would have looked at Marcus Allen as a suspect. It is the fact that Shipp fulfills the requirements of access to both Simpson and Nicole, *and* has the technical background to frame-up forensic evidence, that makes him worthy of investigation. Marcus Allen doesn't fulfill those requirements to be considered since he wouldn't know what to do in order to make a frame-up of evidence convincing to detectives and prosecutors.

My correspondent then gave me a long list of questions which to his mind indicated a conspiracy.

I answered him, "I believe all your questions fall into areas I have examined in my book: either establishing the reasons why Simpson should be considered possibly innocent, or then looking for alternative explanations of the crime. But, any alternative explanation has to deal with the evidence as presented against Simpson, with as few additional elements as possible.

"Conspiracy theories make the mistake of multiplying elements. I've tried not to do that, and I believe, by eliminating a conspiracy as a likely answer to the Brown-Goldman murders, I have been able to identify the one person who all by himself could have accomplished both the frame-up and the murders themselves."

My correspondent followed up my response with additional comments and questions.

You say that Allan Park testifies that he sees a dark figure walking across Simpson's driveway. This is probably an oversight on your part, but Park never says that in his testimony. Clark asks him where does he first see the defendant, and he responds by saying (and pointing to the arrow on the map of Simpson's property) that the figure was at the point where the driveway starts and where Simpson's walkway leading to the front door ends, when he first saw him. It was Marcia Clark who then suggested, slyly, and added that the figure was walking across the driveway and into the house.

This question was raised by a previous correspondent. Remember that my object is to account for the most *damaging* possible interpretation of prosecution evidence against Simpson. If Marcia Clark is claiming that Allan Park might have seen Simpson from a point nearer to the lawn than he thought, then I have accounted for that possibility by pointing out that Park might have combined two different sightings (one of Simpson walking back into his house, one of a similarly dressed black man, Shipp, on the lawn) into one memory. If Park did not see anyone on the lawn, then there is no fault, because it does nothing to damage Simpson's innocence, nor does it damage my theory of Shipp as a possible framer/murderer.

Relying strictly on the evidence as presented at trial, Kato Kaelin heard the thumps on the back wall, and he realized someone was out there. But do you think it more likely to be Ron Shipp bumping and knocking around back there, possibly bringing attention to himself, or someone who didn't know the makeup of the area? Or who intentionally produced the bumps? I just can't shake or throw aside, or take lightly, in good faith (and I don't think anybody else looking for the truth should either) what Rosa Lopez, a mere next door neighbor (ordinarily, neighbors make good witnesses) said she heard. *men talking.* Sounds like conspiracy to me.

I think Shipp could have been back there to plant the glove and make noises so that Kato would later tell someone that someone was back there, so they could find the glove.

As far as Rosa Lopez's earwitness account of talking back there, she would have heard that for certain around 6:30 AM, when Fuhrman took others back there to show them the glove. If she heard this while she was asleep, she might have thought she heard this earlier as well, and projected her memory back in time by several hours. With an untrained observer, this sort of mis-witnessing is so common as to be an ordinary element considered in any police investigation.

I never believed Fuhrman planted the glove. I never believed Fuhrman planted anything—except the blood on the socks—but he [aggressively] not only threw Vannatter and Lange off course, but emphatically placed them on the wrong course towards Simpson.

Here's the thing. The question of whether blood was planted on the socks became an issue in court because Vannatter carried a tube of Simpson's reference sample blood back to Rockingham. But it was *Nicole's* blood, not Simpson's, that was identified on the socks, so Vannatter's actions, though quirky, become irrelevant to this question.

For Fuhrman to have planted Nicole's blood on the socks in Simpson's bedroom, Fuhrman would have had to have collected some of Nicole's blood from the Bundy crime scene before proceeding to Rockingham. But, when would Fuhrman have had the opportunity to do so, with a dozen other officers protecting the crime scene from tampering before Fuhrman even got there? None of the cross-examination by the defense ever established such an opportunity, so I eliminate Fuhrman as a single actor capable of having done that.

Now, once the blood samples are collected by the criminalists and returned to L.A.P.D.'s Scientific Investigations Division, Fuhrman is completely out of the loop, since he works at West L.A. Division, and wouldn't have access codes at S.I.D. So, we are left with Vannatter and Lange, as detectives, and L.A.P.D. technical staff, dealing with the blood at that point—and while they may have made mistakes, I can't find any likely motive why they would have participated in a conspiracy to frame Simpson at an early point. Later, when their incentives for finding incriminatory evidence against Simpson are higher, because their reputations are on the line, the samples are already at the California Department of Justice and Cellmark Diagnostics labs being analyzed—and the window of opportunity for them to tamper is long gone.

Mr. Schulman, I really don't think we disagree too much, except to say you believe Shipp pulled it off alone, and you want to stay away from conspiracies without linking proof of one, which is fair. But Ron Shipp was a loser. He failed eventually in everything he tried to do with success. To say, after that track record, that he pulled off the "Frame of the Century" may be giving him more credit than he deserves. I don't know. But I wish you well in your continued investigation of this matter and if it turns out that you're right, then you deserve all the good that comes to you.

Shipp served for fifteen years on the L.A.P.D. before leaving because of personal problems. He had a problem with alcoholism, but judging from his appearance on the witness stand, and in interviews, and in my one encounter with him, he appears capable of well-reasoned action and decisive action while sober. Just because a person has chronic failures does not mean that he is incapable of success in all instances. It is the very fact that the high standards in law enforcement require consistent alertness which might have been Shipp's downfall. It does not mean that he had to be usually incompetent; he probably was competent 99% or more of the time regardless of any problems. It's that 1% or less of the time that he might have engaged in actions while impaired that would have caused life failures— but that is a different question than testing his competence to take action when he was determined and sober.—JNS

What is *J. Neil Schulman's* alibi for the night of June 12, 1994?

A few days ago, a writer friend of mine who believes that O.J. Simpson is guilty, thought I was being unreasonable in asking Ron Shipp to provide an alibi for the night of June 12, 1994, three years later. "Do you remember where *you* were at the time of the murders?" he asked me.

"I know it was right in the middle of promoting my book, *Stopping Power*, which had just come out," I said. "But where I was precisely the night of June 12, 1994? I don't remember."

"My point exactly," my friend said.

Was I being unfair? I hadn't had one of my close friends murdered that night, in an incident that tended to freeze a moment in time as graphically as the JFK assassination, so perhaps I have no specific reason to remember that night or wonder where I was at the time. I certainly had no idea that I would ever be writing about those murders.

But I wanted to find out anyway. So, on May 26, 1997, Memorial Day, when I had a spare moment, I dug out my tax records from 1994, which included credit-card bills, cancelled checks, and phone bills, as well as merchant batch deposits for my bookselling business. I also checked my computer for any files or messages that were stored in my hard drive, with file dates in June, 1994.

I found no checks I'd written on Sunday, June 12, 1994. I found no credit-card records that I'd purchased anything on June 12, 1994. I batch-deposited no credit-card merchant sales on June 12, 1994. I found no computer messages from June 12, 1994.

According to my L.A. Cellular phone bill of June 23, 1994, I made one call from my cellular phone on June 12, 1994, at 1:06 PM. It was to my ex-wife's number and I was charged for one minute. It was not a roam call, so I knew I was in my home area, rather than out of town that weekend, promoting my new book.

Then I checked my home phone bill.

Bingo.

My Pacific Bell telephone bill dated July 4, 1994 (I guess Pacific Bell doesn't allow its computers time off to celebrate American Independence Day) includes calls for June 12, 1994. Five calls I made that day were outside my free calling area, and generated billing records, either AT&T long distance, or Pacific Bell local long distance.

At 9:45 AM, I called my parents in Texas, an AT&T call. The call lasted 17 minutes and I was charged $2.38 at direct-dial weekend (night) rates.

At 5:13 PM, I called friends in Massachusetts, another AT&T call. The call lasted 14 minutes, and I was charged another $2.38, this time at direct-dial *evening* rates.

At 5:27 PM, I called Gary Kleck, Ph.D., a criminologist who had advised me on technical matters for *Stopping Power*, at his home in Tallahassee, Florida. The call lasted two minutes and I was charged $0.34 at direct-dial evening rates.

At 10:26 PM, I made a call to Canoga Park, local long distance. The number is no longer in my files, so I called it today and the message phone that answered was not a name I recognized. But I was connected to this number for seven minutes and Pacific Bell charged me $.40 at direct-dial night rates. I also called this same number at 6:07 PM two days earlier, and was connected for three minutes and charged $.033 at direct-dial evening rates.

My final call for June 12, 1994 is a Pacific Bell call at 10:39 PM. The number I called is 818-403-0399. I was connected for two minutes and charged $0.14 at direct-dial night rates. I don't mind giving out that number because it's the public dial-up computer bulletin-board line for The Bullet Box, a Second Amendment rights BBS operated by my friend, Dan Feely. I have a bunch of other calls to that phone number on the same bill, all lasting between two and three minutes. That's how long it took my computer back then to dial into the board and exchange pre-compressed Tomcat message packets.

The software on my computer was a shareware version of Procomm Plus. It didn't allow for automatic timed call-ins to BBS's to pick-up messages. I had to be home to do it manually.

So, at the approximate time of the Brown-Goldman murders across town, I was at home, at my desk, downloading, and possibly uploading, computer messages.

I was able to find out where I was that night within about a half hour's looking.

Oh, and one more thing.

My shoe size is 10-1/2 Wide and I couldn't win a knife fight if you tied my opponent's hands behind his back.

Addendum, May 30, 1997

I can now tell you precisely what I was doing the Sunday of the Brown-Goldman murders, and whom I was on the phone with for seven minutes beginning at 10:26 PM that night, during the precise period of the murders.

As I said, if you read up a few paragraphs, I no longer had this number in my personal phone book and did not remember making either of the two phone calls to that number that weekend, almost three years ago.

But I'm a persistent son of a bitch, and don't like to leave mysteries unsolved. Also, when I told my friend about my "alibi" computer call to Dan Feely's computer bulletin-board, my friend said, "Someone else could have been using your computer. It's a weak alibi."

So I called Pacific Bell today and asked if the number on my bill was owned by the same party who'd owned it on June 12, 1994 when I got my bill. Pacific Bell said yes. That person, whose name I did not recognize, was, according both to the outgoing phone message I'd gotten when I first called and Pacific Bell, is Loni Specter.

So I called Loni Specter at 9:30 or so this morning.

I may not have remembered Loni Specter. But Loni Specter remembered me.

Loni Specter was the entrepreneur who had organized the Home/Auto/Personal Security (HAPS) Expo held at the Century Plaza Hotel in Los Angeles the weekend of June 10-12, 1994. A week earlier, Loni had called me to participate in a debate on gun-control to be held during the Expo, and the two of us had tried to find someone representing a pro-gun-control position to debate me. Loni reminded me that we had tried to get Gloria Allred to debate me, but she wanted too much money. Ironically, not long after that, Allred ended up as a counselor to the Brown family, and spent a good deal of her KABC radio program attacking O.J. Simpson's claims of innocence.

Since Loni and I couldn't get anyone to debate me, I ended up doing two seminars, Saturday June 11, 1994, and Sunday June 12, 1994, at the HAPS Expo at the Century Plaza Hotel. There weren't very many attendees at the HAPS Expo despite heavy advertising on KABC; but lots of police officers, security personnel, and safety equipment salespeople in attendance at the Expo would remember seeing me there on both days, including writer, self-defense-instructor, and now KMPC talk-show host, Paxton Quigley, whose Saturday seminar I attended at the HAPS Expo.

I can now pretty well reconstruct what I was doing Sunday, June 12, 1994.

I was home in the morning, phoning my parents. I went over to the HAPS Expo sometime in the late morning or early afternoon and gave my final seminar to a largely empty room, spent some time behind a table trying to sell copies of Stopping Power, spent some time chatting with Paxton Quigley, who'd cancelled her second seminar due to lack of attendance, and was home by late afternoon, when I telephoned friends in Massachusetts. I don't remember whether I went out again that evening, but I was home by 10:26 PM, when billing records show I called Loni, possibly returning a call from him on my machine, and likely to commiserate with Loni, for the duration of the seven-minute call, about the small attendance, which had caused him to lose a bundle on the event.

After I was done talking with Loni, I logged onto the Bullet Box BBS at 10:39 PM and downloaded the day's Tomcat message packet, which took about two minutes.

I wouldn't have been free until 10:41 PM to jump into my car, drive across town to 875 South Bundy, arriving about 10:55 PM, the time O.J. Simpson was seen by limo driver Allan Park, and also about the time that Nicole's neighbor Steven Schwab testified he found Nicole's Akita wandering on Bundy with bloody paws. That pretty well eliminates me as a suspect in drawing a woman I didn't know outside, at night, and then knifing to death this unknown woman and another man I'd never even heard of.

Now, can Ron Shipp—who was long-time friends with both the accused murderer and one of the victims, who wears the size shoe that made footprints in the victims' blood, who is more athletically capable of the crime than the man who was tried for them, who was coming uninvited onto the accused's property for weeks before the crime, who had a police background including undercover work and who had "a good working knowledge of forensics"—account for his Sunday night, June 12, 1994, as I have done?

Another participant, also using the handle "Jim" in the news group alt.fan.oj-simpson, writing on May 25, 1997, posted the following message:

This guy admits that he formed an opinion of whether Simpson could have committed the murders based on a 10-second encounter with him in 1980 at a screening of *The Empire Strikes Back*. He claims that because Simpson told his son Jason to follow the advice of Yoda, he was raising his son with "strong values." From this he concludes that Simpson would not murder his wife 14 years later. Talk about being *star struck*!—Jim

I replied in the news group:

Jim,

It's not being star struck. It's called a first impression. O.J. Simpson made a good one on me, on an occasion when he wasn't trying to put on a show for anyone.

But, I agree, that would be a rather thin basis to form an opinion, if that was all I had to go on.

Why don't you deal with the other 2,900 words I wrote on that topic?

Apparently, Jim was more than upset with me. On May 25, 1997, he posted the following message in three news groups—alt.fan.oj-simpson, alt.crime, and alt.true-crime:

You base this *theory* on Ron Shipp not having an alibi. Yet you have no idea if he had an alibi or not. Because he was never asked if he had one by the principles in this case that is *good enough* for you to postulate that this man is guilty of a brutal double murder? If you were any kind of reputable journalist you would have made it *your first priority* to find out if he had an alibi or not. Since you did not even have the decency to do this before accusing a man of the most heinous of crimes you will get *no* respect from me (and I would hope other reasonable people) in this news group.—Jim

I replied in the news groups:
Jim,

I spent three months trying to determine whether Ron Shipp had an alibi. Eliminating Ron Shipp as a potential suspect was the main question that propelled my investigation. I asked detectives at the Robbery/Homicide Division of the L.A.P.D.. I asked Simpson's lawyers and investigators. And, most importantly, I gave Ron Shipp the opportunity to prevent publication of *The Frame of the Century?* entirely by giving me any proof whatsoever that my theories were wrong. I provided Shipp with the penultimate draft of the manuscript, and both Shipp and his attorney, Robert McNeill, with the final draft of the manuscript.

I've recounted my offers to Shipp in the postscripts to *The Frame of the Century?*

I quoted my second letter to Ron Shipp.

This only seemed to upset Jim more. He replied in the news groups on May 27, 1997:

Ron Shipp has stated in a number of interviews that he has been the target of numerous crackpots who did not agree with his position in this case. He stated that he had even received death threats. Who do you think you are that *any* individual, much less one who has been harassed for the past several years, should have to explain their whereabouts for *any* time period to you? Frankly it is none of your business where he was. If you have *evidence* that he had no alibi, that is one thing, but to demand that someone provide you with their whereabouts, or you will label them a double murderer, is repulsive, and I would imagine actionable. I just hope I get to serve on the jury!—Jim

I replied:

Jim,

Sure, I'm willing to answer your question-in front of a jury, if necessary.

In a polygraph examination, if necessary.

I have no way of making you believe my answer, but I'll give it to you anyway.

I agonized over the decision of whether or not to publish the fruits of my investigation. I consulted with other journalists with experience in these matters. I thought long and hard about the possible consequences, not only to Ron Shipp and his family, but also to my own family.

That goes with the territory of being human. You make choices.

I gave Shipp the chance to silence me from continuing to question his involvement in the Brown-Goldman murders, simply by proving to me that the pattern of his involvement that I was detecting was false. He chose to remain silent, as is his right. But the consequence of his standing on that right was made known to him in advance: that I would publish. I did.

Who am I to have investigated, theorized, and created scenarios about a homicide? I'm a guy who thinks a lot and feels a lot, that's who. I'm a guy who's willing to get involved. And, I have a gift of being able to express myself, which God has bestowed on me.

I could talk about the role of a free press in ferreting out truths which make people uncomfortable.

I could talk about the consequences of nobody ever daring to speak their minds unless their thoughts are officially sanctioned. Our current legal climate comes close to that, by intimidating major media organs from engaging in independent investigations of crimes that are not already being investigated by government agencies. That de facto policy is bad for a free society.

Before I published, I went to the police, to the D.A., and to the

Los Angeles Times to let them do their job: find out if there was anything to my theories. They have the resources to verify or falsify my theories which no free-lance writer can have. They didn't do their job, so I published, in the hope that the attention to my theory will cause them to reconsider.

Now you, of course, are free to continue thinking I am wrong headed. I have no expectation that I will convince you that I did what I perceive to be necessary and good, a pursuit of truth and justice.

But those are my main reasons. I'm not saying personal interests didn't play a function also. I'm only human, subject to the usual temptations. But, you know, it will be God's job to judge me on those charges. And I'll accept the verdict from that court without protest.

Sincerely,

J. Neil Schulman

Also, on May 27, Jim posted the following in alt.fan.oj-simpson:

If anyone knows how to contact Mr. Shipp or his attorney Robert McNeill (apparently) I would appreciate the info. He should be informed that this "book" is being publicly distributed via the net.

If anyone in L.A. could get this information to Mr. Shipp or his attorney, I'm sure they would be interested.—Jim

I replied, posting Robert McNeill's law office address and phone, then added:

"Of course, if you read my final postscript, then you already know that I delivered to McNeill's office a final draft of the manuscript before publication, to allow him to advise Ron Shipp on whether to respond to my offer not to publish if he proved to me that my theories were wrong."

On May 29, 1997, Jim replied in the news group:

Thank you for the information. While I don't agree with your methods and approach to this publication, I do respect your honesty and forthrightness in dealing with me. ...

While I understand that you gave him a copy of the final draft, my concern is that he may not know that it is now publicly available. My intentions are to let him know it is, so he may take any action he deems necessary.—Jim

As is only proper.

In the news groups alt.fan.oj-simpson, alt.crime, alt.true-crime, "Bill" posted on May 26, 1997:

Perhaps in the next edition you could include at least one fact to support your theory that this fellow framed O.J... Re-read it carefully and you will see that there isn't a single one here. Also missing are motive, means, and opportunity.

I must point out that, based on what is in the book, we can't rule out that the individual in question (I don't think it is fair to mention his name) was staying in the Lincoln Bedroom on the night in question, or even sleeping over at Judge Ito's.

Bill

I responded in the news groups:

Bill,

I have indeed established a possible motive, means, and opportunity. That statement makes me doubt that you actually read my book.

By a process of elimination, I am able to rule out, by logic alone, all but one man for having framed Simpson because no one else I'm aware of has *all* the following characteristics:

1) Wears the same size shoe as Simpson.
2) Would be physically similar enough to Simpson to be confused for him in a police line-up.
3) Had intimate knowledge of both Simpson and Nicole's lives and belongings.
4) Had proven repeated access to O.J.'s estate.

5) Had a set of skills from 15 years on the L.A.P.D. necessary to be able to perpetrate a frame-up of forensic evidence.

6) Had a set of emotional characteristics consistent with a possible intent to commit the frame and the murders.

7) Declines to provide an alibi for the night of June 12, 1997.

That gets us a long way forward.

I have been able to find a few clues, mentioned in *The Frame of the Century?*, but I admit, they are not many, and they are not proof.

You ask for facts. Good. I want facts, too. But uncovering new facts usually requires the power of subpoena and search warrants.

I have been trying to get the police, or the D.A.'s office, to do such investigation necessary to prove or eliminate my theory since February 13, 1997—and publishing my book is a means to that end.

Bill wrote back in email on May 26, 1997:

First, let me point out that I am not now, nor have I ever been, more than mildly interested in the O.J. extravaganza. I downloaded and read your book because of its revisionist theme only and had never even heard of Ron Shipp. So, I have no vested interest in either side of the O.J. debate. I am certain, though, that your premise is unsupported by any facts.[The list] is meaningless. If Shipp's shoe size were 10, one could merely suggest he wore size 12 shoes as part of the frame-up. If it were 13, he could have carried a shoe to the scene and planted the shoe print. If he wasn't at the scene, he could have made sure his hired killer wore size 12 shoes. If the only killer he could find wore size 8 shoes, he could have paid him to take a size 12 shoe to the scene, or hire a partner who wore size 12 shoes. Do you see what I'm getting at? As long as I am unencumbered by facts, I can suggest a dozen ways your suspect could have been responsible for the shoe print. The same goes for the rest of the list. Without evidence, it is all meaningless.

I wrote back:

Bill,

Sorry, your logic doesn't work. If Shipp wearing size 12 shoes is irrelevant, then O.J. Simpson's wearing size 12 shoes is equally irrelevant.

As for proof, we start with clues and indications, and try for proof. My object is to show that there is an uninvestigated person who passes the threshold requiring investigation.

In the news groups alt.fan.oj-simpson, alt.crime, and alt.true-crime, Joyce Roberts wrote on May 26, 1997:

Mr. Schulman:
I really don't know why you wrote this book, or why you are offering it to us for a free download, but I suspect you dreamed up this angle on the case to attempt to jump on the O.J. gravy train.

I responded:

No, I dreamed it up for the same reason that Clyde Tombaugh discovered the planet Pluto. Gravitational irregularities in the orbit of Neptune suggested an additional, as yet unseen, body exerting an influence in Neptune's orbital path. Tombaugh pointed a telescope at where mathematics indicated such a body would have to be in order to affect Neptune's orbit—and discovered a planet there, which was subsequently called Pluto.

I did the same thing. I'd previously defined certain facts that would have to be true if O.J. Simpson had not committed the murders at Bundy. The prosecution's evidence would have to be explained, without merely arguing that the police had planted it all, or were completely incompetent. Logic said that someone who *could* have accounted for the presence of such evidence would have to have certain characteristics.

I surprised even myself when an individual whose name was already associated with the Simpson criminal trial fulfilled all those characteristics—and then some.

My continued investigation, attempting to eliminate this person as a potential suspect, instead kept finding clues and indications which made my suspicions grow even stronger.

My report on the procedures I went through in attempting to prove or disprove my theories, and what those procedures came up with, comprise the bulk of *The Frame of the Century?*

The posting continued:

You are, as they say, a day late and a dollar short with the Ron Shipp theory.

I responded:

I have to say I am at a loss to understand why people who post in news groups think no one who doesn't read their writings can possibly reach any conclusions without their help. I suppose reading criminal trial transcripts, depositions, doing personal interviews, digging through court records, and reading the books written by and about a case's participants doesn't count for anything.

This is around the fifth or sixth comment I've noticed suggesting that I am not the first to propose the Ron Shipp theory. That is not news to me. In my book, I point out that one of Simpson's civil attorneys, Dan Leonard, told me early in my investigation that Shipp had been a suspect from the beginning, and other books I read mentioned that Al Cowlings, Shirley and Benny Baker, and others thought Shipp was involved right from the beginning.

Bringing up Shipp's name as a possible suspect is not my unique contribution to this discussion. My unique contribution is putting some meat on the bones of the theory by showing why Ron Shipp is the only other person than Simpson who has all of the prerequisites to have been able to account for the physical evidence presented against Simpson in his two trials.

I've done something which, to the best of my knowledge, no

one else has done previously. I simply haven't been idly speculating about one person or another having committed the murders and the frame-up. I defined what the framer/murderer
would logically *have* to have accomplished, then found someone who fit those characteristics.

It doesn't mean that Shipp did it. It does, however, mean that
there's reasonable cause to investigate whether he did it—and,
having previously failed to get the authorities to re-open the investigation—my publishing the book is my only remaining means
to create public awareness of the necessity of re-opening the
investigation, of whom, and why.

The posting continued:

I think O.J. is probably innocent, and I would love to have a way to
identify the real killer, but your premise is too far-fetched for me. We've
been over all this before.

I replied:

What is more far-fetched? That a celebrity who's in town for a
couple of days in between business trips, who's been up for 17
hours, decides in a fit of pique to drive over to his ex-wife's house
and decapitate her for no good reason ... or that an obsessed fan
goes off the deep end and decides to punish his hero for dissing
him—using a means that only he had the professional skills to
use?

**John Griffin responded to my analogy regarding
the discovery of Pluto, in the news groups
alt.fan.oj-simpson, alt.crime, and alt.true-crime, in
a posting of May 29, 1997:**

You should use the "Nemesis" story rather than the Pluto story. The
observations of planetary orbit perturbations ("gravitational irregularities,"
indeed!) *were* the discovery of Pluto. The visual sighting was just
entertainment, as there was no doubt that it was there. If the discoverer

had ignored the evidence, his story would have been strikingly similar-at least in that regard-to yours.

I answered:

First of all, I'll accept your re-phrasing as more "astronomically correct" than mine. I meant "gravitationally-*caused* irregularities in the orbit of Neptune. I didn't mean to imply by ambiguity that there was anything irregular about Neptune's own gravitational force. (Although, if you recall, this was how Neptune was previously discovered, also, by its gravitational effect on the orbit of Uranus.)

"Perturbations" is the correct astronomical term, of course, but my phrasing was an attempt to create an analogy. A perturbation is a disturbance in the regular elliptical orbit of a celestial body such as a planet or moon—that is, an orbital irregularity. I was analogizing a similar irregularity in the case against O.J. Simpson.

Now we get to the crux of your question. Suppose the orbital perturbation of Neptune had failed to lead to Clyde Tombaugh's sighting of a planet. Let's assume that astronomers had looked for years without seeing anything that could account for the orbital perturbations. That would have required a new paradigm, such as "dark" matter—and might have prompted this hypothesis years earlier.

The Nemesis or "Dark Star" hypothesis is much more similar to your attempted defamation of Ron Shipp, in that it was contrived as a remotely possible explanation of a certain phenomenon, and it hasn't been taken seriously.

In case anyone doesn't know (and cares), someone hypothesized that a "Brown Dwarf" star orbits the sun at a distance of 1-2 light years, completing one orbit every 26,000,000 years. At its closest approach to the sun, its gravity kicks a gaggle of comets out of something called the "Oort Cloud," causing them to enter the solar system. The resulting collisions with Earth could explain the periodic mass extinctions in the fossil record.

Some similarities with Neil's story are: 1. No one has shown that the mass extinctions are related to any astronomical phenomena; 2. No one has observed the Oort Cloud; and 3. There is no evidence of involvement of any Brown Dwarf, Nemesis or otherwise.

In this exercise, Simpson is Pluto (totally defined by evidence) and Shipp is Nemesis (pure speculation)—and I'm not *even* suggesting that he's a Brown Dwarf.

Now, this is why my analogy to the discovery of Pluto is on point and your bringing up the Nemesis hypothesis isn't.

If the orbital perturbations of Neptune had predicted a celestial body that was never visible, then a dark star hypothesis would have been in order. In fact, to extend your analogy, that's precisely what all the conspiracy theories regarding the forensic evidence of the Brown-Goldman murders have been.

But, I had already detected irregularities in the case against Simpson, and was looking for something that would account for these irregularities, and found it in the person of Ron Shipp.

It would have been a "dark star" hypothesis only if my postulated conditions had never led to the sighting of something that could account for the detected irregularities.

But I think this paradigm is closer to the truth:

Suppose the only debate was whether or not there were, indeed, orbital perturbations of Neptune. One side of the debate is that the mathematics which shows orbital perturbations must be wrong because nobody has been able to find a celestial body that accounts for these supposed perturbations; the other side of the debate is arguing that the perturbations are real but that we must postulate dark matter in order to account for the perturbations.

Then I come along and say: you're both wrong. There is a planet there which we've all seen through our telescopes, all along, which accounts for the perturbations, and one does not need to postulate any dark matter to account for those perturbations.

Then I get attacked from both sides. "The mathematics don't

require your planet!" one side says. "Your planet doesn't account for the perturbations and we still need to look for a dark star!" the other side says.

You don't have to tell me that my analogy isn't perfect. I understand that the mathematics of astrophysics are precise enough that this isn't something that would actually be debated. In astronomical terms, it would be more like arguing whether Pluto's moon, Charon, could account for certain perturbations in the orbit of Neptune.

My old friend, Robert Heinlein, once said that there's nothing that people, especially scientists, are more loath to give up than their pet theories.

And that is no less true when one is trying to establish a new paradigm in a case which everyone has been heatedly, endlessly debating on different terms since its inception.

People with new paradigms are always called whacko, as I have been in these news groups.

If Simpson is "Pluto," then Shipp is "Charon."

A friend of mine who has extensive and sometimes esoteric knowledge in matters military, forensic, and legal, brought up several interesting questions to me, in conversation, about the blood evidence in the Brown-Goldman murders.

He wondered if blood spatter patterns could show whether blood had been reconstituted to a different consistency than would naturally be present in blood drippings, and whether that might indicate which, if any, of the methods I postulated in *The Frame of the Century* could have been used.

He asked about the black sweat shirt that L.A.P.D. criminalist Dennis Fung found in O.J. Simpson's hamper in the search of June 13, 1994, that Fung did not collect. My friend was interested in whether experiments might have been done on black sweat shirts of different types to see if drips of blood would be detectable by visual inspection alone.

Marcia Clark writes on page 376 of her book *Without A Doubt*:

> I was studying a picture of Dennis crouched near the laundry hamper in Simpson's master bathroom. He was holding something dark in his hand. I looked closer. Could it be? It had to be. Jesus! It was the dark sweatshirt Kato had described Simpson wearing when they drove to McDonald's! Why hadn't anyone told me about this? Those sweats had to be tested for blood immediately. Unless, of course, they had never been collected.

Clark calls Fung into her office.

> "Do you remember going through Simpson's hamper when you were at Rockingham on June thirteenth?"
> "I think so," Dennis replied in his usual fog of distraction.
> I handed him the eight-by-ten.
> "Tell me if you collected the item of clothing you're holding in that picture."
> "I know I didn't book any clothing out of the bathroom," he replied. "Why?" I could see awareness dawning.
> "You must have known that clothing in the hamper was likely to have been worn recently by the defendant. In a knife killing there's bound to be some trace evidence, if not the blood of the victims. So why didn't you take the sweats?"

Fung replies,

> "Well, I looked to see if there was blood on them. I figured if they'd been used in the murder the blood would be big and obvious. I didn't see any, so I put them back."

Clark replies to Fung,

> "But if the killer stood behind his victims, he might get only a fine spray on him, if that. You can't see a fine spray on black clothing. Not in normal light."

Clark writes: "You shouldn't have to tell a criminalist this."

Well, perhaps you shouldn't have to because Clark's theory about an invisible-to-the-eye "fine spray" of blood being the only result from this double knife killing is just about impossible, just as criminalist Fung had at first thought.

On pages 402-403 of her book, Clark describes the testimony of L.A. County Coroner, Dr. Lakshmanan Sathyavagiswaran, as to how the knife killing of Nicole Brown Simpson was accomplished.

> At the outset of the attack, Nicole had confronted her killer face-to-face and struggled very briefly. Then she'd turned and had been struck in the back of the head, which knocked her against a wall. That accounted for the concussion that rendered her unconscious. After her attacker delivered one vicious slash to the throat, Nicole fell or was dropped onto the second step. She remained there unconscious, moving little or not at all, bleeding profusely.
>
> Judging by the condition of her brain at autopsy, Dr. [Lakshmanan Sathyavagiswaran] concluded that Nicole had lain there for at least a minute before her assailant resumed his attack, this time pulling her head back by the hair and administering the coup de grace.
>
> "How did that fatal wound occur?" [prosecutor] Brian [Kelberg] asked the coroner.
>
> "My opinion," replied Dr. [Lakshmanan Sathyavagiswaran], "is that the head was extended backwards and the knife was used to cause this incised stab wound from left to right."

As far as how Ron Goldman was knifed to death, Clark is much briefer, writing on page 35,

> He'd fallen or been pushed backward and was slumped against the stump of a palm tree. He was wearing light blue jeans and a light cotton sweater. Lying near his right foot was a white envelope containing a pair of eyeglasses. Goldman had injuries to the neck, back, head, hands, thighs. He'd apparently put up a fierce struggle.

My friend pointed out to me that the description of how Nicole was killed was similar to how a sentry would be killed with a knife in a military raid.

We looked up the book *Silencing Sentries* by Oscar Diaz-Cabo

(Loompanics Unlimited, 1988), a training manual written for U.S. military Special Forces personnel.

Diaz-Cabo writes, "Sentry removal with a knife requires that the operator be a rugged, highly disciplined and trained individual. Killing with a knife is a very gory job and can upset an undisciplined operator."

He also describes two techniques for silencing a sentry with a knife that are consistent with the murder of Nicole in that it can be done by a single attacker, from behind.

In one, Diaz-Cabo writes:

> Wrap your free hand around the sentry's mouth and pull his head sharply backward while simultaneously positioning the knife deep in his throat. Follow immediately by circular-cutting the sentry's throat and neck as you pull back and twist, forcing the sentry and yourself to the ground.

In Diaz-Cabo's other relevant technique:

> With the knife in a blade-out hammer grip, thrust the blade through the sentry's neck approximately two inches below the ear. Drive the blade through the neck and cut outward through his throat. Immediately wrap your knife hand's arm around the sentry's throat and pull back, throwing him and yourself to the floor.

Neither technique, which both require falling to the ground holding the victim, is likely to leave the attacker's clothing free of large amounts of blood.

The book also includes a true account of just such an incident, occurring in 1968 at Khe Sahn, Vietnam, written first person by U.S. Marine PFC L.J. Seavy-Cioffi. Seavy-Cioffi is going through enemy lines to retrieve Marine casualties, and his account tells us something of what an attacker might be thinking and feeling in such an encounter.

Seavy-Cioffi writes:

> I was crouched with [an] entrenching tool inside the darkness of the

bunker. I could see his form now squatted just outside my door. I had room laterally for a considerable stroke against the side of his head, like the swinging of a baseball bat, but I wanted to be absolutely sure he wasn't a Marine. His form was small. ... There was a glimmer of light from a grenade explosion and I caught sight of his uniform and rifle silhouette. He was one of the North Vietnamese, all right. I swung furiously and with all my might; I was about 2 feet away from his bare head. He jerked back and my sweaty grip slipped from the handle. He went falling back against the opposite trench wall with the entrenching tool's spike embedded into his head. I looked up and down the trench and saw no one else. He rolled over and laid on the floor of the trench with the spike buried just over his ear. I didn't like looking but he was making the most bizarre hissing sound that I ever heard another human being make. It sounded absolutely like an air hose. That is the only way to describe it, and it was nearly as loud. I hoped he was at least unconscious. I pulled the spike out and drove it in again, higher into the side of his head. He quieted; but then in a few seconds, he was gasping. Not moving, just gasping for air. I didn't want to kill him necessarily, really only wanting to quiet him. But I wondered why he wasn't dead with two blows like that into his head ....

He was still gasping though not as much as before; but somehow I had to quiet him. There was a Marine bayonet a few feet away and I picked it up quickly trying to decide where to stab him. I was worried about stabbing him in the heart because I didn't know if he could still cry out. After deliberation, I decided on cutting his throat. I asked God to forgive me for what I was about to do to another human being; but then figured what-the-hell and tried telling myself that he was probably going to die anyway and this was an act of mercy. ... I tried cutting his throat. It was impossible. The damn bayonet was as dull as a butter knife. Next, I tried stabbing and slashing at his throat to open it up like hoeing a roe, it was that dull. Blood was everywhere. I felt numb. At this point I was a wild man. I was somebody else and yet me. I clicked bone with the blade tip and realized I had torn down into his spinal column. Now he was no longer gasping but gurgling. "When is this man going to die?" I thought. "When?" His chest was making wild, frantic heaves and a haunting gurgling rattle was desperately respirating out of the gap I had torn open in his throat. ... Then, as an afterthought, I went back to the unconscious and dying N.V.A. and covered his head with three sand bags, muffling his death rattle. "Why didn't I think of that sooner?" I remember thinking at the time.

This account contains eerie similarities to the murder of Nicole Brown Simpson.

Both killings take place in small areas—a bunker or a small

enclosed walkway.

In both cases, the victims are hit on the head before having their throats slit.

In both cases, the throat is cut all the way back to the spinal cord.

In both cases, the victim is smaller than the attacker.

(And, of course, we know that Seavy-Cioffi and O.J. Simpson have both been trained to commit ruthless combat kills. *Not.*)

In Marine PFC L.J. Seavy-Cioffi's description, "Blood was everywhere."

And massive amounts of blood would have been on the black sweat shirt that Dennis Fung found in O.J.'s hamper, if Simpson had worn it while knifing Nicole and Ron to death, regardless of Marcia Clark's speculations about there possibly being only an invisible spray of blood which a trained criminalist could miss.

Aside from the improbability that Simpson could have avoided getting massive amounts of blood on his clothes from such an encounter, is there anyone aside from me who sees how unlikely it is that a man who basically spent his life playing golf, doing TV, chasing beautiful women, and raising young children could do something so brutal to his ex-wife, no matter how pissed off he was with her? And how on earth, having done so, he could casually sign autographs and joke around an hour later, as if nothing were wrong?

Where is it in O.J. Simpson's background to act like a hardened Marine in combat?

That O.J. played football, a sport where every player is heavily padded to *avoid* injury, and Simpson's particular talent was running?

That Simpson was shown how to simulate hand-to-hand combat techniques on the set of the TV pilot *Frogman*? Learning how to do a stunt on a shooting set, where each move is carefully choreographed to avoid any possible injury, isn't going to prepare someone emotionally and physically for the gore of an actual knife assault and brutal murder ... when the opponent is not an enemy soldier but an intimate ... when your children are asleep and might wake up to see Daddy murdering Mommy ... and especially not a man like Simpson, whose friends have said he wouldn't even bait a fish hook because of his squeamishness about blood.

You say I'm obstinate in requiring that there be no other way the forensic evidence could have come about before getting past these doubts based on human psychology? You're damned right I'm obstinate. As Oscar Diaz-Cabo wrote, "Killing with a knife is a very gory job and can upset an undisciplined operator."

Within an hour of these murders, O.J. Simpson was signing autographs at the airport, his old self. I seriously doubt whether even Marine PFC L.J. Seavy-Cioffi could have been that cool an hour after he bashed the head and cut the throat of an enemy North Vietnamese soldier—an incident which Seavy-Cioffi says elsewhere in his account gave him recurring nightmares for years afterwards.

As to the question of whether a police officer such as Ron Shipp would have the background to engage in combat this cold-blooded, well, that depends entirely on the particular police officer's background. Some policemen have to engage in hand-to-hand combat with criminals regularly; others don't. Anybody who has seen the Rodney King video knows how brutal the combat a policeman engages in, as part of the job, can get.

I have not had a look at Ron Shipp's L.A.P.D. personnel files, which are considered private, nor have I interviewed anyone who knew Ron Shipp during his years on the L.A.P.D., to get any answers. The answer to this question, however, could be answered by the other L.A.P.D. police officers who worked with and supervised Ronald Shipp.

In two places in her book, *Without A Doubt*, Marcia Clark wonders about the lengthy amount of

time the killer stayed at the Bundy crime scene. On page 280 she writes,

The contusion [to Nicole Brown's head] was critical because it lent support to other findings that Nicole had been attacked, but left alive and unconscious for at least a minute or two before the coup de grace to her throat. This indicated that Simpson had stuck around after the first attack on Nicole. Now, why would a man who had just committed murder hang around to risk getting caught, not to mention missing his alibi flight to Chicago? The crucial minutes of Nicole's unconsciousness were clearly Simpson's window of opportunity to kill Ron.

And, Clark wonders on page 403 of her book:

"So what was the killer doing during the minute or so between the first and second cuts to Nicole's neck? Lakshmanan left open the possibility that he had used this interval to murder Ron Goldman."

An alternative interpretation, Ms. Clark—and one that supports my theory—is that the killer was someone other than Simpson who was hanging around to plant the evidence that would frame O.J.

In another message published in alt.fan.oj.simpson, John Griffin replied to one of my previous postings:

J. Neil Schulman wrote:
"I have indeed established a possible motive, means, and opportunity. That statement makes me doubt that you actually read my book."
That should say "I have indeed attempted to establish..." or maybe "I have indeed promulgated for my own purposes..."

My response:
This is an observation without critical effect. Yes, I have attempted to establish, and I have published it purposively. But I also have established the points that no one else whose name has ever been brought into the case against O.J. Simpson had

been to his house hundreds of times and "idolized Simpson" (Shipp's trial testimony), was close to Nicole (Denise Brown civil-trial deposition), was coming onto Simpson's property uninvited and was being pressured by Simpson to stay away from Simpson's house (Simpson's civil trial deposition, Kato Kaelin's statements to Marc Eliot), had an extensive law-enforcement background including "a good working knowledge of forensics" (Sheila Weller's book, *Raging Heart*), and has established no alibi (L.A.P.D. Robbery/Homicide Detective Vic Pietrantoni, Simpson investigator Bill Pavelic, Shipp's declining my offer not to publish my book if he gave me an alibi).

These facts encompass motive, means, and opportunity.

First, you settle on Shipp for your silly little story, and then you contrived: "1) Wears the same size shoe as Simpson."
What does the same size as Simpson have to do with anything if you deny he had anything to do with the murders? Were you trying to say "..same size as the bloody Bruno Magli/Silga Real Killer spoor?"

Your challenge fails on two counts. My book is accounting for prosecution evidence that argues size-twelve shoe-prints in the victims' blood at the Bundy crime scene are incriminatory against Simpson; showing that another individual known to the police and prosecutors, with the skills, access, and possible motive to have framed Simpson, also could have left those bloody shoe prints is significant. Also, I'm arguing that Simpson was one of the intended victims of the murders, vicariously, which means that he did indeed have something to do with the murders.

"2) Would be physically similar enough to Simpson to be confused for him in a police line-up."
I could tell them apart easily, and I've only seen Shipp in pictures. You aren't saying "they" all look alike, are you?

Shipp and Simpson are black men of the approximately same age, size, and body type, who share the same shoe size. The crime

took place at night, which makes facial features hard to distinguish. Yes, that's close enough for a police line-up under these
circumstances, for what little eyewitness testimony this case has
had.

"3) Had intimate knowledge of both Simpson and Nicole's lives and
belongings."
Belongings?! Where in hell did you get this intimate knowledge of "both
Simpson (sic) and Nicole's" personal relationships?

This is both arch and disingenuous. I'm not claiming intimate
knowledge for myself. I'm accounting that Shipp had it.

"4) Had proven repeated access to O.J.'s estate."
Oh…that's your launch point for that giant leap…I see.

Yes. It's a necessity. Without that access, the frame-up is impossible. Necessary but not sufficient, however.

"5) Had a set of skills from 15 years on the L.A.P.D. necessary to be able
to perpetrate a frame-up of forensic evidence."
  Could you describe these skills and what experience Shipp had in
applying them? Just kidding…I know you can, since they're fundamental
to your goofy little story.

Is there an actual point here? Knowledge of forensics is an
important part of the training and experience of an L.A.P.D. officer, especially for an officer who at any time in his fifteen years
on the force wished to advance in his pay grade.
    And now we have reached the threshold of necessary *and* suf-
ficient.

"6) Had a set of emotional characteristics consistent with a possible intent
to commit the frame and the murders."
  I think that's one of the most "pussy" statements I've ever heard.
"Consistent with a possible intent"?? That sounds a lot like your cool

"possible likelihood" nonsense.

You criticize me, on the one hand, for making categorical statements of fact, then criticize me when I am careful not to make my statements more categorical than are warranted by the facts.

I'd call my precise phrasing "epistemological rigor," if you'd care to look up the big word.

Are there any psychologists around here? Somehow, making this wishy-washy declaration based on seeing the guy on TV or whatever just doesn't add up.

I don't see why observing a person's demeanor on a TV screen, makes the observation less worthwhile. The TV camera was observing live and unedited. And, that is not my only source of observations, or grounds for my statements, anyway.

"7) Declines to provide an alibi for the night of June 12, 1997."
I don't think Shipp has done any such thing. If someone appeared to be stalking me as you've apparently been stalking Shipp, I wouldn't give the asshole the time of day either.

Ronald G. Shipp saw me waiting for him on one occasion, approached me, and I immediately identified myself as a journalist, which he subsequently learned is true. That's hardly stalking. I also provided Shipp and his lawyer extensive information on my professional background, including publishing credits and TV/film sales with major newspapers, magazines, book publishers, and production companies, as well as my business telephone and fax numbers, my business mail address, and own attorney's name and address. I provided Shipp two drafts of my book manuscript.

That is hardly the behavior of a stalker or a mentally deranged person. It is the behavior of someone whose assertion that he will publish a manuscript that raises serious questions about oneself in relation to culpability in a capital felony needs to be taken seriously. Because of my previous publication, and the interest in the Brown-Goldman murder case, Shipp and his attorney had good reason to conclude that my manuscript would find a publisher and cause further inconvenience to Shipp, including possibly official investigation with powers of subpoena and search warrants. They also had to consider that any lawsuit against me for libel would give me the power to issue subpoenas and search warrants against Shipp, and force his deposition under oath, as part of an affirmative defense that my theory could be true.

If Shipp is, in fact, innocent, and he could head all this off merely by providing me with an alibi, I'd say he had plenty of incentive to do it. Any lawsuit against me would only bring more attention to my theories. Furthermore, my never asserting his guilt in the crime, combined with my obvious attempts to be fair by providing him the chance to prevent publication by providing me evidence that my theory is wrong, would be evidence in a court that there is no malice on my part and a libel suit, especially against a publisher with deep pockets to defend against such a suit, would fail.

There is very little up side for Shipp to remain silent if he was uninvolved in the Brown-Goldman murders and could, as I did experimentally myself with under an hour's effort, establish an alibi for the night of June 12, 1994.

"That gets us a long way forward."
Speak for yourself! You're all alone, and that is your only claim to any uniqueness.

I am hardly alone in thinking Ron Shipp worthy of suspicion in the Brown-Goldman murders. And I have been receiving quite favorable responses to my book, from people who are less dogmatic in their beliefs than you are.

"I have been able to find a few clues, mentioned in *The Frame of the*

Century?, but I admit, they are not many, and they are not proof."

Especially when you contrast them to the plethora of clues that lead any and every logical analysis to O.J. Simpson's doorstep.

Those few clues are part of a theory that also accounts for *all* the evidence that links O.J. Simpson to the Brown-Goldman murder. No contrast is required.

"You ask for facts. Good. I want facts, too. But uncovering new facts requires the power of subpoena and search warrants."

You've been declaiming your own success at doing just that, much to the amusement of all. On this contradictory point, I agree with you.

What contradictory point? I found some facts, enough to warrant further investigation, but not enough to indict, which requires the powers of subpoena and search warrants to determine if there's enough to go to trial.

"I have been trying to get the police, or the D.A.'s office, to do such investigation necessary to prove or eliminate my theory since February 13, 1997—and publishing my book is a means to that end."

In your dreams. Any detective who thought there was any justification for investigating Shipp or anyone else would be on it like a hen on a June Bug. He would have visions of everlasting fame and fortune, book deals, the talk show circuit, busty babes and All-American Hero stature dancing in his head.

Before my book pointed out that there is only one person associated with the Simpson case who fulfills the necessary and sufficient conditions to have framed O.J. Simpson, that threshold had not been reached . Now we will see if it has been. That is something that neither you nor I, nor our dreams, will determine.

If this is really the best deconstruction that is possible of my work, then I am more confident than ever of the probative value of my research.

"Ojokay" in alt.fan.oj-simpson, wrote a message titled "A plea to all pro-J's…" on May 28, 1997. Finally, I was getting attacked from the other side.

I replied:

Dear ojokay:

First, I want to thank you for posting your message, even though it's an *ad hominem* attack without specific content. Your posting serves to prove that my theory attacks the sacred cows both of those who are married to the idea of Simpson's guilt—no matter what the evidence might show—and those who are married to the idea that only an arcane conspiracy could account for O.J. Simpson having been tried for these murders.

Both positions, when they abandon reliance on facts and logic, become an *idée fixe*—an obsession.

Let me deal with your post.

Usually, I try to post humorous crap in here (even if some of you don't get the humor), but this is a serious plea to all pro-J's. I am proud to call myself a pro-J [pro-O.J. Simpson—*JNS*], as I feel any honest and close examination of the evidence against Mr. Simpson leads any reasonable person to conclude the man is innocent. I have and would again also gladly debate any no-J [anti-O.J. Simpson—*JNS*] about the case with confidence in my position. The facts already known point strongly to O.J.'s innocence.

One of the clearest impressions I have gotten from the majority of no-J's is that they rarely talk facts or evidence, instead always trying to divert the various arguments with nonsense, personal attacks, and irrelevancies. This is the main reason I rarely post anything serious in here anymore.

But, when you posted this, did you notice that you have done the same thing you accuse your opponents of: relying on personal attack rather than dealing with facts or evidence?

Physician, heal thyself!

You can't argue with the majority of no-J's on any serious level. They have their anti-O.J. "religion" and as anyone knows, you can't argue against someone's "faith" and "beliefs."

However, as a die-hard pro-J, one of the things I've always had to try to guard against, is freely *giving* the no-J's ammunition. If I come off as some pro-J nut, throwing out wild speculations and hypotheses based upon very little fact, I validate a typical no-J's opinion of us pro-J's as wacky fools. There is no need to do this. One can argue O.J.'s innocence very effectively based upon the facts and evidence already known. There is no need to speculate, especially if it is all out of left field.

Though Freed's book *Killing Time* has much speculation, a lot of it is very reasonable, based upon the facts. But this J. Neil Schulman issue, to me, is the worst kind of *crap* for any pro-J to defend.

Your opening shot of *ad hominem*. Now, I look for your conclusion to be supported by some facts. (And, by the way, I read Killing Time as part of my research.)

I read the whole thing carefully, twice as a matter of fact, and as a strong supporter of O.J., I must appeal to all pro-J's to completely disregard this nonsense.

Second *ad hominem*.

Mr. Schulman's *The Frame of the Century?* is ridiculous.

Third *ad hominem*.

His theory of Shipp's role is ridiculous.

Fourth *ad hominem*.

His reasoning is ridiculous.

Fifth *ad hominem*.

His conclusions are ridiculous.

Sixth *ad hominem.*

And in fact, anyone who takes this crap seriously, does Mr. Simpson and his cause a great disservice.

Seventh *ad hominem.*

Please note that I am a pro-J saying this. Sure, I would love "new information" to come along that would prove conclusively what I believe the facts and evidence already point to, Mr. Simpson's innocence. But we don't *need* this kind of drivel, fellow pro-J's.

Eighth *ad hominem.*

This kind of crap makes us all look really bad, and I would implore all my fellow pro-J's to *not* in any way defend Mr. Schulman and his foolishness.

This compound sentence gives us the ninth and tenth *ad hominems.*

It makes us all look like a bunch of Heaven's Gate loonies.

Eleventh *ad hominem.*

[I've eliminated his twelfth *ad hominem* here, as it brings up a subject I'll be discussing in the next reply.]

Schulman needs serious medicine. I'd suggest lithium…

Ad hominem number thirteen—and I see. Anyone who puts forward a view that you disagree with (still without offering any substantive arguments) needs a psychiatrist.

Does it upset you to know that deciding persons who disagree with you need a psychiatrist was a hallmark of the Soviet Union?

Schulman writes well, but this is pure fiction, folks. At the very beginning as a matter of fact, and throughout he keeps wondering out loud whether he is writing fiction or non-fiction. This is fiction, folks. His wild speculations have very little basis in fact or evidence.

I'll tell you what my speculations do have a basis in: logic.

Sir Arthur Conan Doyle wrote that once you have eliminated the impossible then whatever remains, however improbable, must be the truth. That is the dictum I followed in *The Frame of the Century?*

I show the reasons why we must consider O.J. Simpson innocent. Presumably you agree with that supposition. Fine. Once we postulate O.J. Simpson innocent, we are required to account for the forensic evidence against him.

One has to eliminate any theory which cannot account for someone having O.J. Simpson's blood before the murders.

One has to eliminate any theory which cannot account for someone having the skills to plant the evidence so it will be convincing to detectives, and, after withstanding laboratory analysis, to prosecutors.

Other things being equal, one has to prefer any theory with fewer elements to explain than a greater number of elements. This means that if one individual can be shown to be able to fulfill all the conditions, we are supposed not to postulate a second. Simpson did not fulfill the conditions of background or demeanor consistent with the corpus delicti of the Brown-Goldman murders, so I found sufficient reason to allow in one more element: a second individual who could commit a frame-up. I have found no sufficient reason to add in any individuals beyond that.

One has to prefer any theory where there are indications of a formation of an intent to frame-up O.J. Simpson for the crime.

Now, if you can name for me any other individual who fits into these categories, other than Shipp: name him.

If you can give me a reason to prefer a conspiracy theory which has more elements to a theory of one individual with the required capabilities—which Occam's Razor tells us we must prefer—then give me those reasons.

Otherwise, your attachment to conspiracy theories to explain the Simpson frame-up breaks with logic.

Besides this, throughout his piece, he discounts and eliminates other speculation and theories, such as police/D.A.'s office tricks and planting and conspiracies, all of which can be directly *supported* by the true facts and the known evidence.

No, I'm sorry, that is not what I did and, by the way, it's not even what I would have *had* to do.

I am required to explain the evidence that exists which links Simpson to the crime scene. This my theory does. I am not required to explain any other evidence which does not link to another individual or group of individuals. It may be considered not part of the *corpus delicti* of the crime unless such a linkage can be demonstrated.

All of this is done to throw the whole case into one man's lap, Mr. Shipp. But there is not one shred of credible evidence that Shipp was involved.

Incorrect. Shipp's statements to Sheila Weller indicates his foreknowledge of Simpson's wounded hand.

The removal of the light-bulb from the Bronco's ceiling is a standard procedure for an L.A.P.D. patrol officer, which Shipp was for eight years.

Shipp's answer to Vannatter's question about O.J.'s guilt, that "Whoever did this did a heck of a job framing him," has him stating not that Simpson did it, or that Simpson was framed by the police, but that the frame was done *by the murderer*, which Shipp would know if he had, indeed, done precisely that, himself. This comes damn close to being a confession if the rest of my theory holds up.

Shipp's visit to Rockingham with a "blond Nicole type" indicates obsessive behavior patterns.

Shipp's not getting back onto the L.A.P.D. after resigning indicates a pattern of life failures which can premise obsessional behavior.

Shipp's continually coming by Rockingham secretly in the weeks before the murders indicates a pattern consistent with obtaining items from O.J. that could be used in a frame-up of evidence.

In fact, placing all of this in Mr. Shipp's lap is as ridiculous as placing all the blame on O.J.

There were only one set of size-12 footprints at the Bundy crime scene, proving one killer. Both O.J. and Shipp wear size-12 shoes. That narrows the field of suspects dramatically.

I hope pro-J's can see this point clearly. Regardless of what no-J's say, this case is very complicated with many unanswered questions and anomalies.

Which my theory answers and resolves more than any previous theory.

We can't just reduce it all to placing all the blame on one of O.J.'s friends, especially if all the reasoning behind such an assertion has little basis in fact.

The Frame of the Century? shows the basis in fact.

This is exactly what the no-Js are trying to do with O.J., throw all guilt and suspicion _his_ way, regardless of the problems with that theory. Schulman's Shipp theory is _all_ speculation,

Provably untrue.

and it is _all_ bullshit.

Ad hominem number fourteen.

I would sooner believe O.J. is indeed guilty.

So, when push comes to shove, you prefer complex conspiracy theories to believing in O.J.'s innocence. I suspect your belief in O.J.'s innocence is merely a consequence of your distrust of authority, which is too contrarian to be useful in any discussion.

So please, please, please, all pro-J's, do not give Schulman and his wacky delusions *any* credence whatsoever.

Ad hominem number fifteen.

To me, his mission seems to be one of disinformation, if anything.

Ad hominem number sixteen.

If one studies the UFO/alien abduction phenomenon, one can clearly see wacky cases which are thrown into the serious, fact-based discussion, which just make the whole subject a farce.

Ad hominem number seventeen.

Witness the recent "alien autopsy." Anyone who takes Schulman seriously, especially those of us that still support O.J., is taking Schulman's "bait" and giving no-J's more ammunition.

Presumptive *ad hominem* against anyone who agrees with me. A well-known writer once called this "the argument from intimidation."

Schulman's work belongs in the *Weekly World News*, not in any pro-J's serious understanding of this case, nor in their efforts to defend and argue O.J.'s innocence.

Ad hominem eighteen.

I would not be surprised if Schulman were trolling this news group even now, laughing his ass off that anyone would take him seriously.

Ad hominem nineteen.

Again, to all pro-J's, we don't need this kind of thing to "infect" our purpose here, to see justice done with regards to Mr. Simpson. If Schulman's kind of crap is allowed to take hold of our minds and hearts in our attempt to justify our opinion that O.J. was/is indeed falsely accused, there is no end in sight, except for the total and inevitable rejection of all pro-J's as wacky idiots.

Ad hominem number twenty against me, and number two against anyone who agrees with me.

I know most no-J's already feel we all *are* that, but they are the ones with the problem, as any pro-J who has ever tried to have a reasonable argument with one of them knows. We can continue to try to show them the error of their ways with facts and reasonable, evidence-based theories (or humor?), or we can accept and defend Schulman's type of wild, baseless dementia, and let the no-J's off easy.

Ad hominem number twenty-one.

Lets not.

And, you have engaged in twenty-one *ad hominem* attacks on me, and two on anyone who might agree with me, without offering a single substantive refutation of any point I make in *The Frame of the Century?*

You do this anonymously, from an email account which does not require any identification.

My true email and mail addresses, and my phone number, are

attached to my messages.

I'm willing to stand by my opinions, publicly. Are you?

Why should anyone, on either side of this discussion, take *you* seriously?

Sincerely,

J. Neil Schulman

It is not only strangers who suggest that someone who takes a minority position among the intelligentsia needs psychiatric help. One of my friends, a bestselling crimewriter, said that to me in a phone conversation when I asked help in my investigation. My friend was not joking.

I have to say, I think that anyone who suggests psychiatric treatment for someone who disagrees with them is engaging in some of the most offensive tactics possible—an hysterical appeal to the authority of the mundane.

People like this need a serious wake-up call.—JNS

In my Web-published edition of *The Frame of the Century?* I gave an additional motivation for my continuing investigation, which I have deleted from the first section of the book for this edition. It was the subject of the twelfth *ad hominem* attack made by "Ojokay" above.

I wrote,

But as I sit here today, I must now witness to an additional reason I still believe O.J. Simpson is innocent.

It's a reason that, as a lifelong rationalist, has made me profoundly uncomfortable. I did not take willingly to an acknowledgement of the existence of God, but personal experiences both prior to and after my undertaking this investigation forced it on me.

So, in February, 1997, I asked God if the theory I will present in this story is correct.

Asking God a question, especially in the view of those who believe in God, is not considered a sign of madness. There is a well-known technical term for asking God a question. It's called a "prayer."

But, perhaps less commonly, the Voice I had come to recognize as God's answered me, and said, "Yes, my son."

Having a voice you identify as God answer you in your head is, sometimes, considered a sign of madness.

Fortunately, this Voice has never asked me to do anything crazier than pursue the investigation of an unlikely theory. When I told God after a while that I thought I was on a wild-goose chase, He answered me, "Chase the wild goose, my son."

I have, regardless of our views of my sanity, done that.

Hearing voices—even if you think it's God's voice—is not good enough evidence to be entered into a court of law. Furthermore, if my call to God reached a wrong number, and it *wasn't* God on the line, then either I latched onto a supernatural God impersonator, or my imagination alone has led me on that wild-goose chase.

Only God knows.

And that's the point.

I deleted those paragraphs from the first section of this edition because the context for its inclusion was being missed. I never intended those few words to indicate that I expected anyone to take it seriously as evidence for the truth of my theory; only that it explained my persistence in pursuing it.

Nonetheless, my expression of a purely subjective, non-rational motive for pursuing this investigation has undoubtedly gotten me written off as a nut case by people who otherwise might have cooperated with me ... and might even have saved me from a lawsuit by Ronald Shipp, who could use those paragraphs to dismiss me as a fringe writer not worth even cursory consideration.

I included the statement only for the sake of intellectual honesty. Nonetheless, one (of many) of those who thought I made a strategic blunder by including these words was a fellow science-fiction writer.

In the first year after O.J. Simpson was charged with the murders of Nicole Brown Simpson and Ronald Goldman, I must have had several dozen lunches and phone conversations with my friend, science-fiction author Dafydd ab Hugh, in which we discussed the case.

Dafydd is an admirer of Vincent Bugliosi's approach to the case, and I found, in retrospect after reading Bugliosi's book *Outrage*, that much of the argumentation that Dafydd had been making to me matched up with Bugliosi in both content and style. Our arguments got heated at times, but I felt Dafydd had crossed the line when I emailed him a copy of an excerpt from earlier in this book, in which I answered a challenge about Ron Shipp's not having provided me with an alibi, which I felt gave me the ethical right to publish.

Dafydd emailed me on May 31, 1997:

The question isn't whether Mr. Shipp can present an alibi, but why he should have to present one to *you*.

I replied:

If he could have presented an alibi to me, he should have done so because my track record indicates that I can get published in major media outlets, and people with more clout than I have will repeat my questions, *louder*—and I obviously wasn't being deterred by questions of legal exposure.

Neil

Dafydd wrote back:

I will be shocked as hell if you get this published in any "major outlet." The word of God may be perfectly convincing to you, but I think even you will agree that it won't be very convincing to a newspaper editor.

And in the unlikely-in-the-extreme chance that some reporter does take it seriously enough to question Shipp, he can worry about his alibi then. But all he knows about you is that you staked out his lawyer's office, staked out his house, and have a Web page.

And I replied, in part:

All I wrote in my piece was that I'd had experiences which, in spite of my rationalism, gave me reasons to believe in God, and that I prayed for and got confirmation of what I had figured out by mundane methods.

But, my mentioning that I prayed to God for guidance in the piece isn't an important element in the methodology I used, first of all, since I had my theory in full six days before [my prayer was answered]. All [this] did was give me courage to keep on pursuing my theory.

This makes me a whacko only to readers of *The Skeptic* Magazine, who consider that anyone who doesn't worship bell curves as explanations for everything in the universe is a mystical barbarian unfit to live in The Age of Science. Which, if you'll excuse me, is arrogant and presumptuous nonsense.

Now, the market will determine whether I sell my book, but ... *you* get some endorsements from Milton Friedman and Anthony Burgess, and have had Heinlein rave about one of your books in front of a crowd at an L-5 Society meeting, and sell to the *L.A. Times* six times, and get the cover of *National Review* before you tell me my writings can be dismissed as equivalent to any nut case who can write any damned thing just because he has a web page.

I know I'm venting here, but cut this out. It's threatening my high regard for you.

And Dafydd both phoned me to explain what he meant, and emailed the following:

Neil, it's precisely *because* I have such a high regard for you and your writing, and *because* I'm your friend, that I'm telling you that you're wasting your time with this crusade. It's driven everything else out of your head, it seems to me. ...

You rightly received high praise from Friedman and Burgess and Heinlein for your two novels; and the praise you got from Prager and Heston you rightly earned for your first gun-control book. But what you're doing now is not going to enhance your reputation, it's going to destroy it... because like it or not, and even whether true or not, the way you present it in the manifesto you published on your Web page comes across as whacko.

You're pissed because I said that all Shipp knows about you is your stakeouts and Web page-but that's the simple truth. Everything else about you is being buried by this. I'm telling you because I *am* your friend. Even if you were right about Shipp, *until you can prove it,* you shouldn't publish anything (not even on a Web page). If you're right, all you've done is given Shipp time to come up with a good alibi; if you're wrong, you've just created tons of aggravation for an innocent man.

Look, I'm not telling you to drop your investigation; I think at the bottom you're going to find nothing, but that's because I'm 99.9% convinced that Simpson did it. But I would never tell you to stop investigating. But even Jack Anderson waits until he has *some* evidence before he goes public.
...

My advice, *as your friend,* and as someone who greatly respects and admires your earlier writing, is to withdraw this entire manifesto *until and unless* you come up with actual evidence... something that will convince someone in the world besides yourself. Otherwise, you do yourself, your reputation, and even this cause a grave injustice. ...

I value our friendship and I respect your earlier writing; but unless you go about it more subtly than you have so far, this crusade isn't going to result in exonerating O.J.... it's going to destroy *you.*

To which I reply, in full: only time will tell which of us is right.
—J. Neil Schulman,
June 1, 1997

Ron Shipp's "Alibi"

An analysis of Ron Shipp discussion with Larry King
on the third anniversary of the murders
of Nicole Brown Simpson and Ron Goldman

Excerpts from *Larry King Live*
Aired June 12, 1997—9:00 p.m. ET

Larry King Live Excerpt 1:

> KING: This is the third anniversary of those tragic murders in Brentwood. We are devoting tonight and tomorrow night's program to them. .... Joining us now in Los Angeles are Ron Shipp, former friend of O.J. Simpson, former police officer, and a major prosecution witness. ... Ron, what do you think-where were you three week-three years ago tonight?
>
> RON SHIPP, SIMPSON PROSECUTION WITNESS: Three years ago tonight, actually, I was at home. I didn't hear about it until the next day.
>
> KING: And how did you hear about it?
>
> SHIPP: I was in the bank doing some business. And my mom paged me. She had heard about it. And she paged me. And I called her right away.
>
> KING: First reaction?
>
> SHIPP: Totally—I was totally shocked. And I called the house right away. That was my first reaction at which time Mark Fuhrman answered the phone. And he confirmed that it was actually true.
>
> KING: So when you called the house, it was Fuhrman who answered the phone?
>
> SHIPP: Right.

The first thing that strikes me is Shipp's use of the word "actually" in response to Larry King's question of where he was that night. It's subtle, but Shipp instantly reacts defensively, as if his assertion that he was at home might not be believed.

Mark Fuhrman, in his book *Murder in Brentwood*, describes Shipp's call to Simpson's house, where Fuhrman answered.

> "I'm a good friend of O.J.; my name is Ron Shipp."
> "Ron, this is Fuhrman."
> His tone warmed to that of a friend. I had known Ron for nine years.
> "Mark, what happened? Is everyone okay? O.J. didn't hurt Nicole, did he?"
> I couldn't tell him anything.
> "Ron, it's not my case."
> "Mark, you can trust me, you know that."
> "If it were my case, things would be different. But I can't, it's not my case. Sorry, buddy."

Shipp asks Fuhrman, "Is everyone okay? O.J. didn't hurt Nicole, did he?" Yet, if he is telling Larry King the truth, he has already heard from his mother of Nicole's death, which she relayed to him likely from early news reports. Shipp's question to Fuhrman is either again "precognitive"—such as his relating to Sheila Weller that he wondered about possible injuries to O.J.'s hand before he knew one existed—or Shipp is planting the idea in Fuhrman's mind that O.J. should be a suspect—which is hardly the behavior of the friend that Shipp claimed he was, and grounds for continued suspicion regarding his true agenda from his first recorded moment of involvement.

Larry King Live Excerpt 2:

> KING: Ron, did you ever think early on that it might have been your friend?
> SHIPP: Only because of what she had mentioned to me that she said one day he might kill her. It popped in my head briefly, but then I said no way. He couldn't have done this. I wanted to believe he didn't do it.
> KING: When did your opinion change, Ron?
> SHIPP: That night when I got over to his house and had the conversation with him in his bedroom. That's when I—in my mind, I was just totally convinced he had killed both Ron and Nicole.
> KING: Because he said something significant to you, right?
> SHIPP: He had said the three things that he said to me.
> KING: Which were?
> SHIPP: The lie detector test, he didn't want to take it. He asked me

about the DNA, about the blood, and the thing about the dreams killing her, and just his demeanor and everything, it just—in my mind, I just knew he had done it.

Here we have Shipp repeating hearsay from Nicole, which we earlier heard from Faye Resnick and Denise Brown, that Nicole told people that O.J. would "kill" her if he ever caught her with another man. Yet, the one time that O.J. did encounter Nicole having sex with another man—with Mezzaluna restaurants manager Keith Zlomsowitch—O.J. just rang Nicole's doorbell to let them know they could be observed, then returned the next day to chide Nicole about having sex where she could be seen by their kids—then shook Zlomsowitch's hand and said, "No hard feelings." We are left with O.J.'s statements about killing Nicole having perhaps the same weight as a teenage girl's statement that "My father told me he'd kill me if he catches me with a boy in my room." If Shipp was as close to Nicole as he relates to Larry King in the fourth excerpt (following), where he says he was an "extremely" close friend of Nicole's, then he would have known about the Zlomsowitch incident from Nicole, and would not have had a good basis to interpret these statements as serious threats during his conversation with Fuhrman. I think it at least possible that Shipp is reinventing what his initial state of mind was, based on information he later got from Faye Resnick's and Denise Brown's statements.

Shipp does give an explanation of his initial question to Fuhrman by saying that, "It popped in my head briefly, but then I said no way. He couldn't have done this. I wanted to believe he didn't do it." But then he asserts that his opinion didn't change until his testified-to encounter with O.J. in the bedroom, the night of June 13, 1994, when O.J. supposedly asked about D.N.A. and polygraphs, and told Shipp, with a little laugh, that he'd been dreaming about killing Nicole. But if this encounter never really happened—as Shirley Baker's and Arnelle Simpson's testimony that O.J. was never alone and that Shipp never went upstairs suggests—then Shipp's continued assertions become a significant reason to doubt his testimony and grow concerned about his actual motives.

Larry King Live Excerpt 3:

> KING: We're back. Ron Shipp, how has your life changed in the last three years?
> SHIPP: I'll tell you, in the beginning, it was really kind of bad for me, because I work for a property management company, and a lot of the area that I work in is South Central. So it was kind of—it was rough on me doing my job. You know, I work with a lot of HUD properties, and I'd be walking down the street, and I'd—they'd call me names—you know, people would call me names. It was like horrible.
> KING: Like a black turning against a black?
> SHIPP: Yeah, it was pretty bad in the beginning.
> KING: Has that diminished?
> SHIPP: Yeah, quite a bit. It's been a lot—especially since the civil trial has been over, but it was pretty rough. It was pretty messed up, Larry.

A career change from being a Los Angeles Police officer working in West Los Angeles to being a property manager working in South Central Los Angeles might have seemed a come-down for Shipp, and the idea that he could no longer be spending his time hanging out at O.J.'s estate might have been a source of frustration and envy in the period just before the June 12, 1994 murders—and a source for possible motives.

During Shipp's cross-examination by Carl Douglas during the criminal trial, the following exchange is highly significant:

> Carl Douglas: You're not really this man's friend, are you, sir?
> Ron Shipp: Well, I— okay, I— all right. If you want me to really explain it, I guess you can say I was like everybody else, one of his servants. I did police stuff for him all the time. I ran license plates.
> That's what I was. I—like I said, I love the guy.

Obviously, Ron Shipp's relationship with O.J. Simpson was not what he wanted it to be. It was more one-sided than he wanted: fan to celebrity rather than a mutual friendship between equals. And, at the point when Ron Shipp was no longer on the L.A.P.D.

and could no longer effectively be one of O.J.'s "servants," it may well be that O.J.'s tolerance for Shipp frequently bringing guests onto O.J.'s estate to be given guided tours and use O.J.'s tennis courts was lowered—and Shipp felt himself "dissed" when asked by O.J. and Cathy Randa not to come over without calling for permission first.

The hurt and resentment that Shipp displays for O.J. could not be more obvious.

Larry King Live Excerpt 4:

> KING: Let's get a call. Jacksonville, North Carolina, hello.
> CALLER: Mr. Shipp, have any of your and O.J.'s old friends shown you support, despite testifying against him?
> SHIPP: I tell you in the beginning also—no, they didn't, but afterwards, I think after things—as time went on, I got calls again. I lost a lot of good friends in the beginning, and it was very hurtful. But a lot of them have come back—you know, after—especially after the civil trial.
> KING: You were a good friend of Nicole's, were you not, Ron?
> SHIPP: Oh, yeah, extremely.
> KING: So it would be safe to say you miss her.
> SHIPP: I miss her. I think about Nicole every day, and like with Kris—you know, was talking about and Faye—you know, if there's a positive thing that came out of this, it's the attention to the domestic violence. I think that's the best thing that's come out of this whole thing.

Here we have a stronger statement than we've ever before had of Shipp's emotional bond with Nicole: "extremely" good friend. And, three years after her murder, he still thinks about her every day? This is a statement of significant grief, equivalent to losing a wife or a child. It suggests a level of emotional involvement which, when mixed in with other suspicions, suggests the need for further investigation.

Larry King Live Excerpt 5:

> CALLER: Hello. My question is for Mr. Ron Shipp.
> KING: Yeah.
> CALLER: I'm wondering, exactly what was it about the friendship with him and O.J.? What was it that changed in your friendship that made you take the view that you have right now?

SHIPP: Nothing changed until I was in his room that night—you know, I mean, as far as I was concerned, I was there to support him. That's why I went to the house the night of the—next day. But after I talked to him, and I realized—you know in my mind, that he had done it, I was like, this is it.

CALLER: What changed your mind about—what was it in your friend-ship that changed your mind that made you believe that he actually did this? (CROSSTALK)

SHIPP: I was a police officer for 15 years, okay? And I've done I don't know how many investigations and interviews with people, and just certain ways when people talk to you and certain things they say, and knowing O.J. for 26 years, his demeanor, and just certain things he said. I mean, why would you ask about DNA if you didn't care about your blood?

KING: Yeah. What would happen do you think if you ran into him, Ron?

SHIPP: It's ironic. I went golfing with a buddy of mine last week, and as I was coming off the golf course, the waitress came in and said, hey, do you know that O.J. just came on? But I didn't run into him. If I did run into him, I don't know—I couldn't say.

Shipp's assertions of his skills as a police officer is a double-edged sword. Shipp uses it to assert his grounds for being suspi-cious of O.J. Simpson—but these same claims of skills can ex-plain how Shipp would have had the capabilities to have framed O.J. Simpson and deflected suspicion from himself for three years.

Now that Ron Shipp has gone on the record as to his where-abouts at the time of the Brown-Goldman murders, can he sub-stantiate his alibi?

1) Was Mr. Shipp home alone, or was he with his wife Nina, or either of his children, or anyone else, who has a clear recollec-tion of seeing him at home between the hours of 8:00 PM and midnight? Is there any substantiating proof of Mr. Shipp being at home that night? Is Mr. Shipp or any witness willing to state this under oath, or in a polygraph exam?

2) Do the Shipps' phone records reflect any outgoing telephone calls indicating that Mr. Shipp was at home; or, is there anyone who called him that night whose billing records indicate that they spoke to him at home between approximately 8:00 PM and

midnight?

3) Is there any neighbor who can testify to having a recollection of seeing the Shipps' automobiles at home that night?

Conversely, is there anyone who can testify to seeing Ron Shipp anywhere away from home between the hours of 8:00 P.M. and midnight, the night of June 12, 1994?

These questions become particularly important when you see something that I, myself, almost missed completely.

It's in the last excerpt from Larry King's interview with Ron Shipp, right at the end of the show.

> SHIPP: Nothing changed until I was in his room that night—you know, I mean, as far as I was concerned, I was there to support him. That's why I went to the house the night of the—next day. But after I talked to him, and I realized—you know in my mind, that he had done it, I was like, this is it.

Did you see it? "That's why I went to the house the night of the —" and there's a *pause* before he corrects himself, and says: "next day."

These excerpts are copied directly from the transcript as posted by CNN on its web site, with no punctuation alterations.

Did Ron Shipp almost tell Larry King's caller that he went to O.J. Simpson's house the night of the *murders*?

—J. Neil Schulman, June 21, 1997

Part Three

New Allegations

"Headcase!"

On January 16, 1998, KABC AM Los Angeles talk-show host Larry Elder, an attorney who withstood a campaign by fellow blacks to remove him from the air, partly because of his hostility to the notion of O.J. Simpson's innocence, was once again calling the acquitted O.J. Simpson a murderer on his show, and criticizing any of his listeners who agreed with the criminal-trial jury that there was reasonable doubt of Simpson's guilt. Up to that time I had not made any attempt to present *The Frame of the Century?*'s theory on radio or TV. But as a regular listener to Larry Elder's show, and as a libertarian who agreed with much of Larry's political commentary, I felt Larry was being offensive to his listeners. I was in my car listening so I called in to the show from my cell phone, but after getting through and being placed on hold over 45 costly minutes without being put on the air, I hung up and waited until I got home to call in again.

Several times before I called in to his show this past January 16th, I had met Larry Elder in the studios at KABC while visiting Dennis Prager, with whom I'd become friends after appearing on his KABC talk show. When Larry arrived at the studio at the end of Dennis's show, and just before Larry's show, Dennis had introduced the two of us. On one of those occasions I'd given Larry an inscribed copy of my book *Stopping Power*, and on another occasion an autographed copy of *Self Control Not Gun Control.* On still another occasion, when Larry had been weathering some particularly vile accusations of being a "self-hating black" from his callers, I'd told him it was painful for me as a listener to have to hear him being verbally abused, and advised him that in my opinion he didn't have any obligation to keep such attack-callers on the air.

I had emailed Larry Elder for the first time on November 3, 1997, telling him about *The Frame of the Century?* and inviting him to download it. My letter had read, "I don't expect you to agree with me. I don't even much expect you to regard me as being in my right mind. But I thought you might like to be aware of at least one intelligent white guy who thinks even to this very day that O.J. Simpson might have been the victim of a frame-up for the Brown/Goldman murders—and it had nothing to do with race, did not involve a conspiracy, had nothing to do with Mark Fuhrman, drugs, or the Mafia, and of which the L.A.P.D. and the prosecutors were as much victims as everyone else." I'd attached the "dust jacket" web page, with a description of the book and links to download it, to that letter. I'd never received a response to that email, and had no way of knowing whether Larry had downloaded or read the book.

But, on December 30, 1997, I had also emailed Larry a copy of a short article I'd written titled "Tyll There Isn't You," about KABC talk host, Ed Tyll, who at the time had been given the last two hours of Larry's show. Tyll had done an ignorant anti-gun rant on his show, then cut off any caller who sounded intelligent and informed, who called in to disagree. I'd called in and had been cut off the moment I started mentioning my credentials.

I'd written:

My fellow Americans, the purpose of these words is to try to get a major company to divest itself of one of its holdings. Then I'd like the new owners to fire one of their employees. The company is Disney, the holding is Los Angeles's KABC 790 AM Radio, and the employee is talk show host Ed Tyll, who recently took over the second two hours of Larry Elder's afternoon talk show.

Now, I wasn't exactly pleased with KABC cutting back Larry Elder's time, even though Larry is fully capable of annoying the stuff out of me. Larry's a libertarian whom I agree with on issues ranging from economics to crime; but I also find his repeated attacks on the criminally exonerated O.J. Simpson to be disgusting. But at least Larry is honest.

I can take an honest disagreement.

Larry had written back to me the next day, December 31, 1997, as follows: "Dear J. Neil: You are, of course, quite right. About almost everything you've said— and I don't just mean the gun issue."

So, nine weeks after I'd emailed him about *The Frame of the Century?*, and two weeks after he'd sent me a friendly letter in response to email in which I'd again mentioned my disagreement with him regarding O.J. Simpson, I called in to Larry Elder on KABC, presuming that he would know who I was. I knew Larry was hostile to what I was going to say on the air, but I presumed, because of our prior acquaintance and correspondence, that Larry would give me a reasonable opportunity to present my theory in brief.

My presumption that he knew who I was may have been wrong, but my presumption that he would be fair to a reasonable call was correct. Larry did give me that opportunity, and he listened politely to my ten-minute or so presentation, as I outlined for his listeners the main elements of the theory. All his questions were reasonable and polite. After giving the reasons why I thought we needed to accept the possibility that O.J. Simpson could have been framed for the murder by Ron Shipp, I stated clearly that I was *not* accusing Ron Shipp of anything; the most I was doing was saying Ron Shipp had never been investigated by the police;

and given the circumstances I had uncovered, we couldn't rule out my book's theory until Shipp was eliminated as a suspect in the still-open Brown-Goldman murder case. I was calling to establish that it was possible for a reasonable person to believe that there was reasonable doubt of Simpson's guilt. As I said, Larry listened politely to my presentation ... until the moment he ended my call by playing a recording that shouted, "Headcase!"

The next call after mine was Ron Shipp, whom Larry said had been listening to the show and had called in. But when Shipp got on the air and Elder and Shipp started discussing when they would go play tennis together again, I understood who had likely telephoned whom.

Whether Ron Shipp called in to Larry Elder or Larry Elder had phoned Shipp, my call-in had achieved a result far better than I had hoped for. Before I published *The Frame of the Century?* I had given both Ron Shipp and his attorney, Robert McNeill, copies of the manuscript to review and an opportunity either to prevent its publication entirely by presenting me evidence that my theory was impossible, or by giving me a response I could include in the book. Neither before nor after the book's website publication, and its subsequent thousands of readings, did Ron Shipp or his attorney respond to my offer, get in touch with me, or publicly utter a single word in response to its theories about where Ron Shipp had been, and what he might have been doing, the night of June 12, 1994.

Shipp's on-air phone conversation with Larry Elder following my call-in broke this policy of silence. As he had six months earlier on *Larry King Live*, Shipp claimed that he was at home the night of the murders. But more interesting to me than Shipp's repeated claim was Larry Elder's reaction. Larry Elder phrased it as a joke, but his discomfort was obvious and the serious point was made: Ron Shipp had admitted that he had a weak alibi for the night of June 12, 1994.

After the show, I once again emailed Larry Elder, replying for the first time to his December 31st email. I quoted his compliment about my Ed Tyll article, then wrote:

Dear Larry,

Thanks for your good words on my Ed Tyll piece. Perhaps you haven't put together who I am. You've met me in studio several times when I was visiting Dennis Prager. I gave you copies of my books *Stopping Power: Why 70 Million Americans Own Guns* and *Self Control Not Gun Control.*

And, I'm also the Neil from Culver City about whom, at the end of my call-in to your show today regarding my book on the O.J. case, you played that charming little audio clip yelling "Head Case!" Yes. I'm the same guy who presented to you the theory of Ron Shipp's involvement.

Now, it's apparent that you're friends with Ron Shipp, and think he's a nice guy who possibly couldn't have anything to do with the Brown-Goldman murders. Of course, that's precisely the opinion just about everybody would have had about O.J. Simpson himself, if you'd been asked about him on June 11, 1994. He's even more charming than Ron Shipp.

I understand the forensic evidence in this case and how overwhelming it seems. The problem is, Ron Shipp was fully capable of having brought every bit of evidence to the Bundy and Rockingham crime scenes before Officer Robert Riske showed up at Bundy at 11:45 PM June 12, 1994.

Shipp's call in to your show today, declaring that he was home with his wife at the time of the murders, was only the second time that he has said where he was the night of the murders. The first time he was asked was on *Larry King Live*, June 12, 1997—the third "anniversary" of the murders.

Shipp also dissembled about his knowledge of me when he called into your show today. I gave him the final two drafts of my manuscript, and the final draft to his attorney Robert McNeill, before I published it. I gave him full opportunity to give me an alibi, promising that I would not publish if he gave me one. They declined to do so and I published only then.

The problem for me in eliminating Shipp as a suspect is that Shipp has done nothing to prove his assertion of where he was, and he has never been asked about it officially, which would allow for statements from Nina Shipp and their kids, polygraphs, checking of phone records, etc. I also told you that I have evidence that implicates Shipp. Some of this evidence isn't in my book, and I can't talk about publicly without compromising sources. But I assure you that Ron Shipp has a dark side which I have witnesses to and that he is for certain lying on when he first knew about the murders, and perjured himself on the stand on major points. He has also lied about what his relationship was with both O.J and Nicole at the time of the murders.

This doesn't make him the murderer of Nicole Brown Simpson and Ronald Goldman. But it does mean he needs to be investigated, which he has not been.

You can download my book, *The Frame of the Century?*, in full at http://www.pulpless.com/ojframe/, where I've made it available for free download since May 31, 1997. Over 7,500 readers have already done so, and I've gotten positive reviews and comments on it.

I don't know what your definition of a head case is, but if I'm one, then so is any journalist who decided that facts require more investigation than their face value.

Best regards,
Neil

Larry wrote back the next day, January 17, 1998:

Dear Neil,
Glad you liked "headcase".

I wrote back, the next day (January 18, 1998): "Oh, yes, Larry.

I'm always thrilled to be insulted in a public forum by someone whom I respect. I live for it."

Larry continued:

As for Shipp, the motive would be....

And I answered:

Dear Larry,

To answer your question, you know that motive isn't one of the elements of a murder that needs to be proved. The reason for that is that actual motives are events that occur in the mind and are unknowable. All we can do is observe what people have done before and then, once we are convinced that they have committed a crime, look backwards and try to speculate on what their motives were for doing it.

The rest of this letter has to be off the record. I have sources to protect.

I have plenty of evidence for Ron Shipp being jealous and resentful of O.J. Simpson. Homicidally resentful? Maybe.

I also have a credible witness to Ron Shipp claiming to have had a sexual relationship with Nicole. Enough of a relationship for jealousy to be a motive for murder? Maybe.

I have a credible witness to Ron Shipp having committed serious felonies while still in the L.A.P.D. (in fact, while wearing the L.A.P.D. uniform) and after he'd left the department, and to Ron Shipp bragging that when he was in the L.A.P.D. he had "snuffed" people.

You ask Ron Shipp's motive? I don't yet know. But I know he lied on the stand to make O.J. look guilty. That's evidence of malice. I know he's lied about when he first found out about the murders. That's indicative that he has something to hide. I know that he had access to every piece of evidence that links O.J. Simpson to the crime scene—including O.J.'s blood—prior to the murders. And I know that he had the forensic skill to be able to plant that evidence against O.J. Simpson.

Could there be another motive which I haven't yet found? Could money be involved? I don't yet know. But maybe.

That's not enough of a case to bring to trial. But what I have found at this point requires a police investigation of Ron Shipp that has yet to be made. I'd like his fingerprints compared to the unidentified prints found at the Bundy crime scene. Since he was not an L.A.P.D. officer on June 13, 1994, this has never been done. I'd like his phone and credit-card records checked. I'd like his alibi for the time of the murders checked out, polygraphing both him and Nina if there are no other witnesses. Shipp said to you that he was in home in bed with his wife the night of June 12, 1994. All evening? From what time? At 10:00 PM, or only after midnight?

I suggest you download and read my book. Then, I suggest you and I get together for dinner.

I also seriously suggest that you do not discuss this letter with Mr. Shipp. If I'm right about him, you'd be placing my life, and the lives of my family, in danger.

Best regards,
Neil

Larry did not respond to this email.

On February 10, 1998, I wrote Larry again. He was a featured speaker at the upcoming Libertarian Party state convention and I was getting press credentials to cover it. By this time, Ed Tyll's KABC show was history and Larry had his entire show back. (I credit the TV commercials run by an anti-censorship campaign more than I credit my article, but I wasn't about to let Larry forget that I'd been one of his supporters.)

I wrote:

Larry,

I'm going to be at the Libertarian Party State convention this coming weekend. Do you have some time while you're there when the two of us can talk in private? If you can promise me that it will be absolutely off the record, there's something we need to talk about.

Congratulations on getting 5-7 back. Maybe my piece on Ed Tyll was one of the things that helped bring it about.

Best regards,

Neil

Elder wrote me back February 11, 1998, "Would love to, but I'm pressed for time. Perhaps we can talk at the convention."

On February 15, 1998, after his Libertarian Party convention address (where I asked Larry a question about drug legalization which was aired when Larry's speech was later broadcast on C-SPAN), Larry Elder and I met privately for about a half hour in a private conference room adjacent to the banquet hall at the Los Angeles Hyatt Regency Hotel where the Libertarian Party was meeting.

Larry and I chatted amiably for a few minutes, and I made sure he remembered me both from our previous meetings, our email correspondence, and my call in, before I gave Larry reasons why I thought it would now be in Ron Shipp's interest to meet with me to discuss these allegations privately before I published them. I asked that he approach Shipp about setting up such a meeting. I invited Larry to participate in such a meeting. Larry agreed to approach Shipp with my request.

I gave Larry a print-out of *The Frame of the Century?*, along with a another set of hardbacks of *Stopping Power* and *Self Control Not Gun Control*, and paperbacks of my two novels. We ended our meeting with a mutual understanding that Larry would approach his friend Ron Shipp about meeting with me. Either Larry or Ron Shipp would get back to me by phone or email within a day or so.

On March 1, 1998, when I still hadn't heard anything back, I emailed Larry,

Larry,

I haven't heard from you since our meeting at the Libertarian Party convention in which we discussed you bringing to Ron Shipp a proposal that we meet. I assume this means that he rejected the idea.

If my assumption is correct, did he give you a reason for declining which you found satisfying?

Best regards,
Neil

There was still no response. A week later, on March 7, 1998, I tried one last time:

Larry,

Still haven't heard from you regarding our meeting. (My last email to you reproduced below.)

My unlisted home phone number is [XXX-XXX-XXXX], and my unlisted home fax number is [XXX-XXX-XXXX].

Best regards,
Neil

Again there was no response. Another offer to meet with Ron Shipp, which I made through Robert McNeill, also went unanswered by Shipp.

On May 26, just prior to publication of the new additions to this book, I emailed a copy of the above to Larry Elder. My cover letter read:

Dear Larry,

I'm currently assembling material for a third section of my book The Frame of the Century? I gave you the earlier parts when we met this past February 15th at the Hyatt Regency Hotel, after your address to the Libertarian Party state convention.

The first new material in the book is about my call-in to your show, our correspondence, and our meeting.

I'm attaching a text version of the new material I've assembled so far to this email.

If you have any comments, please email me immediately, as I intend to publish this on my web site immediately after finishing the work, which I expect to have done within the next day or so.

Best regards,

Neil

Larry wrote me back on the 25th,

Dear Neil,

Even if I played tennis with O.J. Simpson, I would still conclude that he murdered two innocent people.

As for your ridiculous assertion that Ron Shipp did it or was involved, not even Simpson says such a thing. You might recall, Simpson has said on several occasions, "the key to this crime lies in the world of Faye Resnick."

Why don't you ask for the June 12 whereabouts of Oprah Winfrey or Stone Cold Steve Austin? Why not demand an investigation as to whether their prints are at the crime scene?

I'm sorry you feel that just because you've spent considerable time formulating a theory, I'm obligated to give it an airing, no matter how preposterous I believe it is.

Larry

I immediately replied, responding point by point:

Larry Elder:

Even if I played tennis with O.J. Simpson, I would still conclude that he murdered two innocent people.

JNS:

Fine. I also know several old golfing buddies of O.J. that are convinced he did it. Irrelevant and immaterial, counselor.

Larry Elder:
As for your ridiculous assertion that Ron Shipp did it or was involved, not even Simpson says such a thing. You might recall, Simpson has said on several occasions, "the key to this crime lies in the world of Faye Resnick".

JNS:
True. This gives us three obvious possibilities. (1) O.J. did it and is trying to throw people off as part of a cover up. (2) O.J. didn't do it but knows who other than himself did do it, and is trying to throw people off for some unknown reason—such as, perhaps, fear of some grave consequence if he fingers the real killer. (3) O.J. didn't do it, doesn't know who did it, and has a theory which, like everyone else's, can be right or wrong.

Larry Elder:
Why don't you ask for the June l2 whereabouts of Oprah Winfrey or Stone Cold Steve Austin? Why not demand an investigation as to whether their prints are at the crime scene?

JNS:
Okay, Larry, tell me what part of the following is irrelevant or incorrect:

Shipp is known to have had an alcohol and cocaine problem, and is reported to have supplied cocaine to Simpson in the 1980's. He had a habit of hanging around O.J.'s house uninvited so often, and in O.J.'s absence, that Simpson's maids complained to him about it, and Simpson had to have his assistant, Cathy Randa, tell him to stop coming around so often. Simpson had also complained about Shipp's uninvited visits to Kato Kaelin, too.

Kaelin reports that, prior to the murder of Nicole, Shipp had familiarized himself with the access and security features of O.J.'s estate. A week before the murders Shipp showed up at Simpson's house, uninvited, late at night with a blond female. Shipp awakened O.J. and repeatedly told O.J. that the woman was a "Nicole type," and demanded that O.J. come down and meet her—and to bring a bottle of wine. Simpson reluctantly complied while complaining about the incident on the phone to his assistant, Cathy. In the weeks before her murder, Nicole had complained to O.J. several times that Shipp was coming around her house unwanted, also, and telephoning her repeatedly as well. I have this from two sources.

Shipp had a background as an L.A.P.D. officer for 15 years, then had gone into the field of private security and investigation for a year, before going into commercial property management. Shipp had bragged to one of his security clients that when he was a cop he had "snuffed people." Shipp also had run a scam on this same client to frighten his client into believing that a woman who had been stalking him before was stalking him again. It was a lie; the woman was 6,000 miles away at the time Shipp made this claim. The client paid off Shipp and fired him, telling him he never wanted anything to do with him again.

On the morning of Nicole's murder, Shipp long-distance telephoned this same client, whom he hadn't talked to since he'd fired him for his deception three years earlier, at 5:30 AM Los Angeles time, June 13, 1994, to tell him that Nicole had been murdered. Shipp later testified in the Simpson criminal trial to having first learned about Nicole's murder between 10:00 AM and 10:30 AM, while standing in line at the First Interstate Bank, and receiving a page from his mother. Shipp has repeated that claim publicly ever since. Shipp also testified that Simpson had confessed to him in a meeting in the evening on June 13, 1994 that Simpson claimed he'd been dreaming of murdering Nicole. However, another friend of both Simpson's and Shipp's at the time has told me that it was *he* who'd had a dream before Nicole was murdered—a dream that Nicole had murdered O.J.—and he'd told Shipp of his dream. This friend says Shipp just took the dream he'd told him about, flipped it around, and said O.J. had said it.

Shipp has told different people different stories of where he was the night of June 12, 1994. He told one reporter that he'd had a fight with his wife that night and was out with another woman. He's also said on a TV interview that he was at home that night. Shipp's wife isn't on the record at all about this, and considering that they have two kids together, she isn't likely to turn Shipp in for lying about this, even though Shipp has cheated on her before. In other words, Shipp does not have even a consistent alibi for the night of the murders.

So tell me. Should the L.A.P.D. have looked into whether Shipp was a possible murderer of Nicole? Were there warning signs, the sort of danger signals Gavin de Becker wrote about in *The Gift of Fear*?

Since Shipp had both intimate access to the homes of both O.J. Simpson and Nicole, since he has expert background in surveillance and forensics, since he might own electronic surveillance equipment, since he wears size-12 shoes like the shoe prints found on the Bundy walkway, since he could have known about Simpson's planned trip to Chicago, since he knew where O.J. kept his spare keys, since he could have known what code name O.J. Simpson had his knee surgery under at Cedars Sinai hospitalæwhere O.J. kept an autologous supply of his blood for autologous transfusion ... don't you think the possibility that he committed the murders and framed Simpson for them should at least be eliminated as a possibility?

Larry Elder:
I'm sorry you feel that just because you've spent considerable time formulating a theory, I'm obligated to give it an airing, no matter how preposterous I believe it is.

JNS:
And I'm sorry that just because you've committed yourself to a belief in O.J. Simpson's guilt on your radio show, and have been

attacked unmercifully and unfairly for your position, that this leaves you unable to consider new facts unemotionally.

You're entitled not to believe anything you like and not to air anything you don't want to. It's your microphone. You can call me a headcase all you like; that's your privilege.

But, Larry, how many things have our reasoning processes caused us to agree on? We agree on legalization of drugs, the usefulness of guns in self-defense, on the necessity for allowing the free-market to work, on the benefits of choice in education, on the importance of individual character and initiative over race. Both of us could be called headcases for any one of these positions.

You know that my previous books have received endorsements from people you respect like Milton Friedman, Charlton Heston, and Walter Williams.

Doesn't that indicate to you that you need to deal with my challenges rather than dismissing them because you find my conclusion improbable?

Let me state it outright. In all probability, O.J. Simpson murdered Nicole Brown and Ronald Goldman, because that's where the weight of forensic evidence lies.

But if there could have been a frame-up of this evidence, as I have demonstrated, then its weight is meaningless and probability analysis goes out the window.

I'd like to think that you're capable of analysis based on fact rather than emotion. What am I to conclude?

I've repeatedly tried to get Ron Shipp to prove me wrong, prove me a headcase. When we met you agreed to bring my offer to meet with Ron Shipp to him, and to get back to me with his answer. You didn't do that. What does that tell me about your commitment to respect and truth?

Shall I also take it from your lack of comments on the materials I emailed you that you have no revisions you wish to make regarding my account of our correspondence and meeting?

Larry Elder responded in email:

Dear Neil,
Okay, I'm tempted. Headcase!
Larry

Early morning, Wednesday, May 27, 1998, I finished my draft on this section of the book. I emailed it to Larry with the following cover:

Larry,
I have completed work on "Part 3: New Allegations" of The Frame of the Century?. This new section is about 25,000 words long, and extends the length of the book by about half again.
I added your reply to my letter and my response to the material. This is your last chance before web publication to say to me anything you'd like included in the book, or anything you want corrected.
Best regards,
Neil

Larry wrote me back that morning:

Dear Neil,
Yes, there are two more things. Please add them to your book since you seem intent on including me.
First, I think your theory that Ron Shipp might have committed these murders is one of the most irresponsible and idiotic things I've ever heard. Move over "Colombian necktie."
Second, as for my "promise" to raise the issue with Ron, and to get him to respond to the charges, I have a different recollection. I recall saying that I would consider doing so. I considered it, and elected not to insult him or waste his and my time to respond to charges that neither Simpson, Cochran, other members of the defense, nor any other of the principal players who have written books about the case have made.
To repeat, headcase. Put this in your book.

Larry

My final comment to Larry Elder until he chooses to bring up the subject, himself: "Done."

Wasz There a Conspiracy?
A possible contract on
Nicole Brown Simpson

One of these days, somebody is going to make a movie about my friend Joe Bosco. If it's made sometime in the next decade or so, he'll probably be played by Matthew McConaughey, who only needs to grow a mustache to look quite a bit like Joe—and he already talks like him. And, depending how the storyline goes, it's either going to be directed by Oliver Stone or Martin Scorcese.

Aside from being a top-notch true-crime writer—one regarded highly enough by Judge Lance Ito that he gave Joe one of only four permanent author's seats in the gallery of the O.J. Simpson criminal trial—Joe has a secret life as a poet, and I suspect his first love is writing novels. But it's as author of a nonfiction book about the O.J. Simpson case that Joe came to my attention, and therein begins a tale that's as much about Joe as it's about the story he's been pursuing.

What makes Joe Bosco into an almost mythic figure, even at close range, is that he's a 1940's character living at the morning twilight of the new millennium. He's the perfect combination of worldly cynicism and strident idealism, the sort of guy who's way too liberal for the Old South and way too conservative for New York. That probably explains why he spends most of his time in Los Angeles, which will take almost any eccentric.

Joe Bosco is almost impossible not to like, even when he's yelling into the phone telling you what an asshole you are for doing something he regards as below his lofty standards. What cuts across time, and makes Joe destined soon to be a major motion picture, is that he's the sort of journalist that you don't see in real life anymore: the reporter who cares only for the truth and who'll get his story no matter what and no matter where it leads. You can threaten to put him in jail for not revealing a source.

He'll take jail without a thought. You can take pot shots at him, beat him up and leave him bleeding in an alley, leave threatening messages for him, run his car off the road, or have an editor tell him to drop it or else, and he'll patch himself up, take a swig of Glenlivet, and be back on the story the next day, with a new editor, if necessary. You also get the feeling that even killing him wouldn't stop his story, since he has his own Baker Street Irregulars working silently in the background—some of them quite prominent in their own right.

I first telephoned Joe Bosco almost a year ago to the day that I'm writing this—April 23, 1997. I got his phone number from Directory Assistance; he believes a journalist needs to be reachable by the public, any one of whom might just have that key clue he's been searching for. I was calling Joe to discuss with him my own investigation of the Simpson case. Our first conversation lasted about four hours.

Joe's approach to the story differed from mine. I had a working hypothesis on who other than O.J. Simpson might have committed the murder of Nicole Brown Simpson and Ronald Goldman that I was trying to test true or false. I was in the business of psychological profiling and looking to connect lines at an imaginary axis with speculation based on logic. I had pattern lock and I was Fox Two seeing if my missiles would hit their target. Joe didn't care much for either profiling or speculation. He just wanted to see where the facts were leading. My approach was that of the science fiction writer. His was that of the street reporter back when reporters actually hit the bricks and editors didn't fill the paper with official pronouncements.

Where all this was leading is that I was trying to find out if the fourth prosecution witness against O.J. Simpson in the criminal trial, ex-L.A.P.D. cop and Simpson hanger-on Ron Shipp, could have been the actual murderer and framed O.J. for it. I ended up writing a book on my pursuit of that question called *The Frame of the Century?*

Meanwhile, Joe had already written and seen published his book on the Simpson case, *A Problem of Evidence*, and as far as the world knew, Joe had moved on to other stories, such as the Ennis Cosby murder.

I knew better. Slowly, as Joe got to know me better, he was willing to trust me with what exactly was still keeping him involved in the Simpson case, with the same understanding that I was letting him know about leads and sources I was developing: neither of us would try to beat the other into print on the other's investigation. This has kept me out of print on the Simpson case for most of the last nine months, because if what Joe was investigating panned out, it threw my own investigation onto a different path. I was pursuing a "lone nut" theory. Joe was pursuing a "second gunman" theory.

It is only the release of a document leaked onto the Internet that has smoked Joe out, and allows me for the first time to talk about what Joe Bosco has been investigating, and how his investigation impacts upon my own.

To the best of my knowledge, Joe has been interviewed only twice on the subject of his continued investigation of the Brown-Goldman murders. The first time he mentioned it was to the *Los Angeles Times'* Bill Boyarsky at a casual meeting at the Van Nuys courthouse on January 5, 1998, where both Boyarsky and Bosco were covering a case involving defense lawyer (and former L.A. County deputy prosecutor) Larry Longo. Boyarsky, now the *Times'* City editor, wrote about their meeting in his "The Spin" column of January 12. In that meeting, Joe told Boyarsky that he "was working with the DAs office on 'a reinvestigation of certain aspects of the O.J. Simpson case.'"

Boyarsky wrote,

> Bosco, after looking around to see if anyone in the cafeteria was eavesdropping, told me that during one of his many journalistic investigations, he interviewed a state prison convict who alleged that in January, 1994, he had been hired by a "very close associate of O.J.'s" to fol-

low Nicole Brown Simpson and then to shoot her to death. Bosco told
me that the convict insisted that the Simpson associate made a $7,500
down payment on the hit, with a promise of $7,500 more after the mur-
der was committed. But the hit man supposedly reneged on the deal,
robbing the Simpson associate of the second payment. The hit man
allegedly took off in a sport utility vehicle stolen from Simpson's post-
Nicole girlfriend, Paula Barbieri. He later wrecked the vehicle after
committing several robberies. Police arrested him and recovered a di-
ary purporting to detail Nicole Simpson's movements, a fact that came
up briefly during the Simpson trial.

Boyarsky expressed his opinion to Bosco that the imprisoned
felon didn't sound like a very credible witness. Bosco agreed with
the point, but said he had corroborating evidence.

Some of that corroborating evidence came into my hands
through one of my own sources. An on-line reader of *The Frame
of the Century?* emailed me to offer me assistance in my investigation. Unlike the dozens of other offers of this type I've received,
this particular reader was connected to principals in the case,
and was actually able to offer concrete help. Among the documents this reader was able to provide me were photocopies of
several police reports involving the prisoner Joe Bosco had told
Boyarsky about. There was the February 1, 1994 evidence booking report from the felon's arrest the previous day, which confirmed the existence of items taken from Paula Barbieri's sports
utility vehicle, including the notebook, a camera, and several
handguns. And there were several pages from an interview with
the felon done by L.A.P.D. detectives on August 23, 1994, several
months before the start of Simpson's criminal trial.

When I saw these documents, I already knew about the significant parts of their content from my discussions with Joe Bosco.
I already knew the name of the felon. And Joe hadn't even had to
tell me whom the felon named as having ordered him to follow
Nicole Brown Simpson and later steal Paula Barbieri's vehicle—
the person the felon claimed had hired him to murder Nicole. I
figured that name out on my own. But I wouldn't even have been
interested in this aspect of the investigation were it not for my

conversations with Joe Bosco. It was Joe's story and I was ethically bound not to write about it until either Joe had written about it—or until it otherwise showed up in the news.

70-3.11.20 (4/92) Tape No.	**STATEMENT FORM** *CL*001364

STATEMENT FORM — *CL*001364

Page 1 of ___

Wt. No.	DR No. 94-08 17431/2
Name WASZ, William	Date/Time of Interview 8-23-94 1230	Location of Interview
Resid. Add.	City	Zip Code	Phone
Bus. Add.	City	Zip Code	Phone

Sex	Desc.	Hair	Eyes	Hgt.	Wgt.	DOB	Age	Drivers Lic. No./Other ID	State

Interviewing Officer(s) C. LeFall/A. Luper	Serial No(s). 20154/17516	Division RHD

Other Person(s) Present

Statements: Use third person. Include who, what, where, when, why and how.

SEE ATTACHED FOR NARRATIVE

LAPD detectives statement on interview with William Benson Wasz.

Wasz, William
Page 2

CL001365

On August 23, 1994, 1230 hours, Detective Luper ▆▆▆ and I,
Detective LeFall ▆▆▆ conducted an interview with William Wasz
at ▆▆▆▆▆▆▆▆▆▆▆▆. The interview began
when Detective Luper explained to Mr. Wasz the reason for the
interview. The interview was focused around obtaining a
handwriting exemplar and obtaining a statement regarding the
notebook.

Mr. Wasz informed the detectives there was no reason for him to
provide them with handwriting exemplars. He stated that the
small notebook belonged to him and all entries were written by
him. To make sure the detectives were talking about the same
small notebook, Mr. Wasz stated, "We are talking about the
notebook that I wrote something about guns in it right?" The
detectives replied "Yes."

Mr. Wasz informed the detectives that the small notebook fit in
the pocket of his larger leather binder. HE took it out because
it was easy for him to carry. He said there were several pages
missing because he would write his phone number on them and give
it to the girls.

When asked about the January 6th and 7th entries, Mr. Wasz
informed the detectives that during the month of January, he was
using cocaine heavily. He stated he stayed high most of that
month. January 6th and 7th, 1994, he did follow Nicole Simpson
and recorded her activities for those two days. Mr. Wasz implied
there was an outstanding debt and the debt was taken care of
before any further action was taken. He stated he was a runner
and he would travel from the Valley area to Brentwood and all of
the area surrounding Belair.

The detectives asked Mr. Wasz if he ever made a delivery of
cocaine to Nicole or O.J. Simpson. Mr. Wasz refused to answer
but said the group surrounding O.J. Simpson were heavy users.
Mr. Wasz refused to go any further with that topic. The
detectives then asked about Mr. Kardashian's involvement with
drugs. Mr. Wasz replied with the question asking the detectives
how well did they know Kardashian. The detectives reply was not
very much. Mr. Wasz asked the detectives, did they know about
Kardashian's involvement in the movie industry. Mr. Wasz advised
the detectives to look into the background of Mr. Kardashian
because he is not all that clean.

Mr. Wasz was asked about the stolen vehicle he was apprehended
in. He replied the people whom he was working for called him by
telephone and informed him he had only 30 minutes to get that
particular vehicle. They told him where the vehicle was and told
him that the keys would be in the vehicle. He got a ride to the

---

CL001366

Wasz, William
Page 3

location, saw the vehicle parked, the keys were in the ignition.
He got in the vehicle and drove off. He kept the vehicle until
he was apprehended.

Mr. Wasz was asked about robbing the people he had worked for.
Mr. Wasz's reply was, when he felt he was going to jail, he would
burn all of the bridges before he got apprehended.

The last issue the detectives talked about with Mr. Wasz was some
letters written to his girlfriend. The detectives showed Mr.
Wasz several handwritten letters. Mr. Wasz looked at the letters
and replied, "Those are some of the letters I've written to my
girlfriend, where did you get them?" The detectives responded to
his question. Mr. Wasz informed the detectives that he had to
talk to his lady about that.

Newport Beach Police property report, arrest of William Benson Wasz

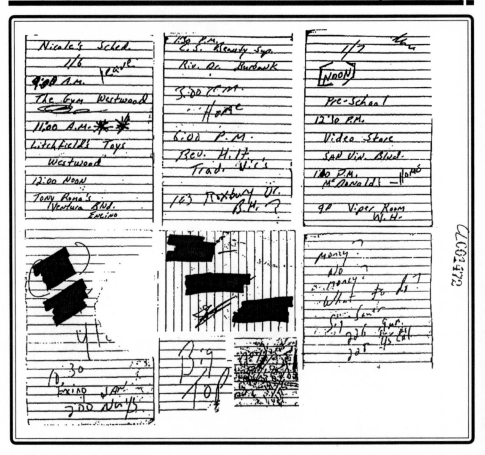

William Benson Wasz s handwritten notes made while tailing Nicole Brown Simpson.

The story still hasn't been in the *Los Angeles Times*, or *Time* Magazine, or on CNN. Joseph Bosco's byline has yet to tell us the whole story of his investigation. But major parts of the story have now appeared on a World Wide Web news service, and a key document has been leaked to what the leaker has referred to in an anonymous Usenet posting as "major media and selected journalists." I was one of those journalists. So I now feel free to write about those aspects of the story that have either previously appeared in print, or which were given to me by a source that is not Joe Bosco, and which impact upon my own investigation. This is not one journalist trying to steal another's thunder. This is still Joe's story and, ultimately—as the person with the access to the key witness and that "corroborating evidence" he told Bill Boyarsky about—Joe will have to tell it.

So consider this an appetizer, and Joe Bosco will eventually give you the main course in some journal of record.

On early morning Wednesday, April 22, 1998, an email letter was sent by a person with the email account "whistle_blower@altavista.net," and signing her/himself "Whistle Blower." The copy I received was addressed not only to me at "J. Neil Schulman" <jneil@loop.com>, but also to "Matt Drudge, Drudge Report" <drudge@drudgereport.com>, "Robert Sterling, The Konformist" <Robalini@aol.com>, "Ian Goddard" <igoddard@erols.com>, "Larry Elder" <the_sage@larryelder.com>, "David Bresnahan" <david@talkusa.com>, and "Wired" <editor@wired.com>. An April 23, 1998 posting in multiple Usenet news groups, also from "whistle_blower@altavista.net," contains the same text, minus a graphic file titled "proffer.gif" attached to the email I received.

It reads as follows:

Dear Editor:

Enclosed in this email is a document that claims proof that there was a conspiracy to kill Nicole Brown. I'm sending you a text version of the document followed by a scanned graphics file of the actual document. My identity has to be secret because I don't want to get anyone in trouble. But I don't trust the Los Angeles County District Attorney's office to properly investigate this information. They've known about this for too long without doing anything. It's time for the truth, whatever it is, to come out.

I don't know whether this information will end up proving that O.J. Simpson was innocent of killing Nicole Brown and Ronald Goldman or whether it will prove that he was part of a conspiracy to kill Nicole. Either way, this information proves that the criminal prosecution of Simpson was botched.

The document contains the name and address of the writer and the recipient. It's up to you to see that the claims made in this document are investigated, and either proved false or verified.

Because of security worries, I will not be responding to any messages sent to the email account I'm sending this to you from.

Yours truly,
Whistle Blower

LAW OFFICES OF LAWRENCE M. LONGO
7871 W. Manchester Ave.
Suite E
Playa del Rey, CA 90293
(310) 457-3911
Fax: (310) 457-0146

March 16, 1998

Mr. Curtis A. Hazell
District Attorney Office
210 West Temple Street
Los Angeles, CA 90012

Re: Attorney Proffer of William Benson Wasz

Dear Curtis:

Pursuant to your request I would like to make an attorney proffer for your consideration. It is my understanding based upon my conversation with you that you might be interested in information my client could provide in regards to a solicitation to commit murder of Nicole Simpson Brown by Robert Kardashian.

I have spoken to my client and I believe that he would cooperate with the District Attorneys Office in connection with this investigation.

In the fall of 1993, Bill Wasz came into contact with Paula Barbierti, Robert Kardashian and O.J. Simpson. The contact with these individuals was made at the Roxbury in West Hollywood.

Just before the New Year, Robert Kardashian met with Wasz in his home in Encino and offered him an assignment. The purpose was to follow Nicole and take pictures of her with any man whom she might meet with romantically. The surveillance of Nicole took place on January 6th and 7th, 1994. This information was documented in a Notebook- the notebook is currently in the custody of the LAPD. The three phone numbers in the book belong to O.J., Kardashian and Barbieri.

On about January 14 Bill Wasz met Robert Kardashian again in his Encino home. At this meeting Kardashian offered Wasz $15,000 if he would kill Nicole with a 25 caliber bullet to the head.

Robert Kardashian also told Wasz he was to steel Paula Barberi's car and use it during the murder. The murder was to take place at the Rockingham estate and not at Nicole Simpson's home on Gretna Green.

On January 24 at approximately 10am, Kardashian called Wasz at his room at the Saharan Motel on Sunset Blvd. In Hollywood, Kardashian told Wasz to steal Barbieri's car from a parking garage in Beverly Hills between 3 and 4 O'clock while she was having her hair done.

After Wasz stole Barbieri's car he drove to a Mall in West Valley where he met Kardashian. While at the mall Wasz took an envelope containing $7,500, which was to be partial payment for the killing.

—————————————————————————————— LAW OFFICES OF LML   PAGE 02

If you desire to interview my client in regards to the above information please contact me as soon as possible.

If you have any further questions, please do not hesitate to call me.

Very truly yours,

LAW OFFICES OF LAWRENCE M. LONGO

LAWRENCE M. LONGO

Lawrence Longo is the same Larry Longo that Joe Bosco and Bill Boyarsky were observing at the Van Nuys courthouse on January 5, 1998, when Joe first mentioned the substance of this document—minus the names.

David Bresnahan, who received the same email from "whistle_blower@altavista.net" that I did, was not constrained as I was from breaking this story. So, on Thursday, April 23, *WorldNetDaily*, on its website at http://www.worldnetdaily.com/exclusiv/980423.ex.hired.tokill.nicole.html, ran a bylined story by David Bresnahan headlined, "New evidence of plot to kill Nicole Brown" and subheadlined "L.A. County D.A.'s Office sitting on witness charge?" Knowing that Bresnahan had received the same email that I had, I was probably one of the first to seek out his website at http://www.talkusa.com, looking to see if he'd written about it. Bresnahan had not let any moss grow under his feet … and I hit pay dirt in that I was now free to write about this, myself.

Bresnahan's story relied heavily on the "Whistle Blower" document, but Bresnahan did what any respectable journalist would do and verified the authenticity of the leaked document before publishing. He phoned Larry Longo's number on the document and got confirmation from Longo's office that the document was genuine. Then Longo's office put Bresnahan in touch with Joe Bosco, who had brought William Wasz to Longo in the first place.

As Bresnahan's article tells it, "'Very early after the murder, Mr. Wasz appeared across the radar screen, and very early both sides put out that he was just bogus,' said Bosco in a phone interview. 'So we all forgot about it. A couple years later I find out the information both sides put out wasn't true. So I started visiting Mr. Wasz in prison, and I've been doing so for about a year. And I've been talking to some people at the District Attorney' Office who are friends of mine.'"

Now, let me make clear at this point that my own investigation into the Brown–Goldman murders was premised on two assumptions. The first was that the prosecution's main evidence against O.J. Simpson had not been either tampered with or otherwise "compromised and contaminated" after it was collected by L.A.P.D. criminalists. If evidence had been tampered with, in my view, it had been done by the murderer (my theory only required one) in order to frame O.J. Simpson for the crime before the first police officer arrived at the crime scene.

My second assumption was that of Occam's Razor: if a logical explanation could be made with fewer complications, that explanation was to be preferred to a more complex one until proven otherwise. I didn't need William Wasz's claims of a contract put out on Nicole Brown Simpson in order for my theory to work. I had my own theory which I was investigating, and Occam's Razor said it could have been done by a single individual who was *not* Robert Kardashian.

Joe Bosco does not share my assumptions. Joe Bosco tries not to have assumptions at all.

But *if* William Benson Wasz told Joe Bosco the truth, then my theory was entirely compatible with it. My theory did not require Ron Shipp to have murdered Nicole Brown Simpson, and frame O.J. Simpson for it, for personal motives, although my book speculated about possible personal motives. If William Wasz had been originally hired to murder Nicole, and not only failed to do so but was subsequently in prison, then it was logical that if another attempt was to be made on Nicole Brown Simpson, another person would have to be found to do it. If Ron Shipp had yet to be eliminated as the June 12, 1994 murderer of Nicole Brown Simpson, he had also yet to be eliminated as a contract killer.

And here's where my own investigation came into play again. I had developed a reliable source close to principals in the Simpson case who'd had both personal and business contacts with Ron Shipp prior to the Brown-Goldman murders. During these contacts, my source informed me, Ron Shipp had "bragged

about snuffing people while on the L.A.P.D.." My source had observed Ron Shipp, while acting as a private investigator and bodyguard, wearing a black commando outfit which my source said
Shipp had referred to as "my SWAT outfit." My source told me
additional facts about Ron Shipp's activities which led me to believe that it would not have been inconsistent with past activities for Ron Shipp to be capable of committing serious crimes.

Additionally, Dominick Dunne, on page 151 (hardcover) of his
book *Another City Not My Own*, told of a meeting his pseudony-
mous avatar had with a close friend of O.J. Simpson's, also pseud-
onymous, during Simpson's criminal trial. The facts of this meeting and the discussion had also been fictionalized to a certain
extent, but Dunne related that the man he'd met with told of
receiving a telephone call from another Simpson friend telling
him of Nicole's murder. The problem was the timing of the phone
call, which in the book is referred to as "the night of the murders" and in fact, I have learned from my source, was between
5:30 AM and 6:00 AM Los Angeles time, June 13, 1994. That is
about the time that Detectives Phillips, Fuhrman, Lange, and
Vannatter are first climbing O.J. Simpson's gate at Rockingham
to get into the estate—before they've spoken to Kato Kaelin or
Arnelle Simpson, before O.J.'s personal assistant Cathy Randa
has been called, and before O.J. Simpson has been located or
called at his hotel room in Chicago.

At the time he wrote his book, Dominick Dunne did not know
which Simpson friend had made that telephone call, but he
learned after his book was published that it was Ron Shipp. The
problem with that is that Ron Shipp, in his sworn testimony during the criminal trial of O.J. Simpson, and later on *Larry King
Live*, has consistently maintained that the first he learned of
Nicole's murder was at 10:30 AM, Los Angeles Time, June 13,
1994, when his mother paged him while he was standing in line
inside the First Interstate Bank.

In other words, Ron Shipp perjured himself during O.J.'s criminal trial about when he first learned about Nicole's murder—and did so to cover up knowledge that he shouldn't possibly have had for at least four-and-a-half more hours.

That makes much of Ron Shipp's testimony likewise incredible.

Questions about William Benson Wasz's credibility are central to his claims. The fact is, the words of a convicted armed robber and cokehead have no veracity on their own.

But we do know these facts. Paula Barbieri's sports utility vehicle *was* stolen on January 24, 1994, while Paula Barbieri was having her hair done. William Benson Wasz *was* arrested on January 31, 1994 in possession of that vehicle. In that vehicle *was* found a notebook which detailed Wasz's stalking Nicole Brown Simpson on January 6th and 7th, 1994.

In an interview with L.A.P.D. detectives on August 23, 1994—after Nicole had been murdered on June 12, 1994—Wasz confirmed for detectives that the notebook and notes were his, that he did follow Nicole and record her activities on January 6th and 7th, 1994. The report says, "Mr. Wasz was asked about the stolen vehicle he was apprehended in. He replied the people whom he was working for called him by telephone and informed him he had only 30 minutes to get that particular vehicle. They told him where the vehicle was and told him the keys would be in the vehicle. He got a ride to the location, saw the vehicle parked, the keys were in the ignition. He got in the vehicle and drove off. He kept the vehicle until he was apprehended. Mr. Wasz was asked about robbing the people he worked for. Mr. Wasz's reply was, when he felt he was going to jail, he would burn all of the bridges before he got apprehended."

If William Benson Wasz was looking for his fifteen minutes of fame, it was his for the taking on August 23, 1994. If he was looking to cut a deal for less prison time, that deal was staring him in the face in that meeting with the L.A.P.D. detectives. If he was going to fabricate a story about being hired to murder Nicole

Brown Simpson, the opportunity for him to do so was on August 23, 1994 in that meeting with L.A.P.D. detectives—not after O.J. Simpson was acquitted and the prosecution's main target was off the bargaining table. All he had to do was name O.J. Simpson as the person who'd hired him back in January, and Marcia Clark would have offered him immunity and a reduced sentence so fast his head would have spun.

If William Benson Wasz had only been hired to stalk Nicole and take pictures of her on January 6th and 7th, 1994, then why did he steal Paula Barbieri's sports utility vehicle on January 24, 1994—seventeen days later? If he was inclined to stalk Paula Barbieri as he had previously stalked Nicole, then why are there only notes of stalking Nicole, and no notes of him stalking Paula? And if he wasn't stalking Paula, then how would he come to be stealing her vehicle?

William Benson Wasz's words are consistent not only with the physical evidence that was taken into evidence by police on January 31, 1994 when he was arrested, but they are also logically consistent with the story he tells. It is difficult to come up with a plausible alternative explanation of why he would be stalking Nicole and take careful notes of it, and subsequently steal Paula Barbieri's vehicle, where the notebook was recovered by police. Wasz can not have altered that notebook since the murder of Nicole, since it has not been in his possession since January 31, 1994—five months before Nicole's murder.

So we come to another key question: if Wasz is telling the truth, then was O.J. Simpson involved in a January, 1994 conspiracy to murder Nicole?

In January, 1994, O.J. Simpson and Nicole were still romantically involved—still within the one year reconciliation attempt that Nicole had begged O.J. for.

If O.J. Simpson had some reason to want Nicole dead in January 1994, and that reason still existed five months later, then O.J. Simpson did not need to murder Nicole himself on June 12,

1994. He could easily have found a replacement for William Benson Wasz to commit the murder for him. In which case, if O.J. did not personally commit the murders but hired someone else to do it, then why did the trail of forensic clues lead directly back to O.J. Simpson and his Brentwood estate on Rockingham? And if the point of a proxy murderer is to be somewhere else during the murder, then why did the murder occur when O.J. was within a five-minute drive of the murder scene and had no alibi?

Further, if O.J. Simpson was part of a conspiracy to murder Nicole in January 1994, then why is the plan for the murderer to steal his other girlfriend's sports utility vehicle and murder Nicole using a small caliber pistol at O.J.'s own home? As one writer in a Usenet news group wrote upon reading Whistle Blower's post, "Did O.J. make sure that Wasz had one of O.J.'s business cards to leave at the scene of the murder?"

William Benson Wasz, significant parts of his story, and corroborating physical evidence have been available to L.A.P.D. Detectives and the Los Angeles County District Attorney's office since before the criminal trial of O.J. Simpson. Yet they covered all this up during the Simpson trial, apparently with complicity of O.J. Simpson's own attorneys, whose primary professional duty was assuring acquittal of their client, which they knew they could accomplish by using a demographic artifact of the Los Angeles County jury-selection process which worked to their client's advantage.

It was left to Joe Bosco, a reporter of the old school, to convince William Benson Wasz to tell his story and bring it to the authorities by way of the lawyer the reporter got him, and it was the disgust of an invisible Internet whistleblower toward the laxity of the Los Angeles County District Attorney's office that we are finally in possession of William Benson Wasz's story.

Moreover, since it is apparently possible for this information to appear on the ubiquitous Internet without being pursued by a single major news organ in this, the land of the First Amendment, it is up to me to sound the trumpet for my friend Joe Bosco, and demand that the media pick up his story.

An accusation has been made, regardless of whether the Los Angeles District Attorney's office wants to investigate it or not. The source isn't credible enough to be believed on his own, but the evidence which backs up his story makes his story credible enough to be investigated.

The Brown-Goldman murder case needs to be re-opened, and we need to ask: if William Benson Wasz told the truth and is the one person we know couldn't have murdered Nicole Brown Simpson and Ronald Goldman ... then who replaced him ... and why do the details of Wasz's story point to a transparent frame-up of Orenthal James Simpson?

April 27, 1998

Simpson Friend Alleged to Have Lied About Knowledge of Murders

"Possible Accomplice," suggests L.A.P.D. Detective

Dear Mr. Schulman,

I am in receipt of your telephone message and Email. As I advanced the exact theories you have mentioned some two and a half years ago, along with the "key question" you would like to know, I am somewhat nonplussed as to how I might be of assistance to you...I was offered a small fortune at the time to publish my thoughts, however, out of respect for the individuals involved, I turned the offers down....Any involvement of mine must be held in the utmost of confidentiality."

Email from my source
September 11, 1997

The only friend of O.J. Simpson to testify for the prosecution in the Simpson criminal trial, ex-L.A.P.D. officer Ron Shipp, is being accused of lying under oath when he stated that he first learned of his friend Nicole's murder the following morning at 10:30 AM, while standing in a bank teller's line at the First Interstate Bank.

A source who wishes to remain anonymous, but who provided this information not only to this reporter but to the L.A. County Prosecutor's office, Simpson's attorneys, and Fred Goldman's attorney, Daniel Petrocelli, has stated categorically that he and his wife received a telephone call from Ron Shipp between 5:30 AM and 6:00 AM, Los Angeles time, the morning of June 13, 1994, in which Ron Shipp broke the news of Nicole's murder the previous night.

That is the time testified to during the Simpson trial that De-

tectives Phillips, Fuhrman, Lange, and Vannatter were first entering O.J. Simpson's Rockingham estate, before they had first
awakened Kato Kaelin or Arnelle Simpson, before O.J.'s personal
assistant, Cathy Randa, had been telephoned to help locate
Simpson, and before a detective telephoned O.J. Simpson at his
hotel room in Chicago to notify him about the murders.

No news stories about the murders had appeared in any media at that hour.

The source, who is close to principals in the Simpson case and
had both personal and business contacts with Ron Shipp prior to
the Brown-Goldman murders, also stated in an interview with
this reporter that he would be willing to testify that Ron Shipp
had "bragged about snuffing people while on the L.A.P.D.." He
also told this reporter that he had witnessed Shipp, attending a
1980's party of O.J. Simpson's while wearing the L.A.P.D. uniform, nodding to acknowledge that he was the one who had
brought a "softball-sized" amount of cocaine powder to the party;
that he had observed Shipp, while working for him as a private
detective and bodyguard, wearing a black commando suit which
Shipp referred to as "my SWAT outfit"; and that Shipp had once
invented a threat against him in order to extend his employ-
ment.

One of the two telephone conversations made by Shipp to this
source was tape-recorded, and a copy of the tape handed to
Simpson investigator, Bill Pavelic, in a June 29, 1994 meeting at
the Carriage Inn in Van Nuys.

October 21, 1997

<u>ATTENTION:</u>

William Pavelic

Dear Bill,

    I am faxing to ask that you might make a copy of the taped telephone conversation between myself and Ron Shipp that you have in your possession and give to a Mr. J. Neil Schulman at the earliest opportunity.
    I thank you in advance for any prompt attention you can give to this matter.
    It is to be hoped my note finds you and your lovely family in best of health and spirits.

Kind regards,

Attention: SKIP TAFT

Dec-04-97 10:12A FROM LAW OFFICES   310 820 0094   P.02

LAW OFFICES
LEROY B. TAFT
A PROFESSIONAL LAW CORPORATION

LEROY SKIP TAFT

BRENTWOOD SQUARE · SUITE 600
11661 SAN VICENTE BOULEVARD
LOS ANGELES, CALIFORNIA 90049
TELEPHONE (310) 820-6767
TELECOPIER (310) 820-0094

December 3, 1997

VIA FAX TRANSMISSION

J. Neil Schulman
10736 Jefferson Boulevard, No. 775
Culver City, CA 90230-4969

Dear Neil:

I received your fax communication of December 1, 1997. I have written to Attorney Carl Douglas and requested a copy of the taped telephone conversation between █████ and Shipp.

As soon as Carl gets back to me I will let you know what his response is.

Sincerely,

LEROY B. TAFT

LBT:jk

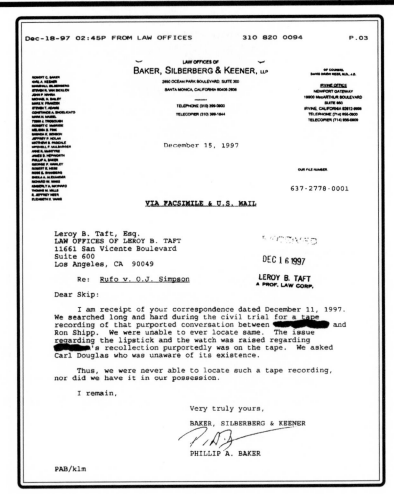

Dec-18-97 02:45P FROM LAW OFFICES   310 820 0094   P.03

LAW OFFICES OF
BAKER, SILBERBERG & KEENER, LLP

2950 OCEAN PARK BOULEVARD, SUITE 300
SANTA MONICA, CALIFORNIA 90405-2936

TELEPHONE (310) 399-0900
TELECOPIER (310) 399-1644

December 15, 1997

OUR FILE NUMBER

637-2778-0001

VIA FACSIMILE & U.S. MAIL

Leroy B. Taft, Esq.
LAW OFFICES OF LEROY B. TAFT
11661 San Vicente Boulevard
Suite 600
Los Angeles, CA 90049

DEC 16 1997

LEROY B. TAFT
A PROF. LAW CORP.

     Re: Rufo v. O.J. Simpson

Dear Skip:

     I am receipt of your correspondence dated December 11, 1997.
We searched long and hard during the civil trial for a tape
recording of that purported conversation between ████████ and
Ron Shipp. We were unable to ever locate same. The issue
regarding the lipstick and the watch was raised regarding
████████'s recollection purportedly was on the tape. We asked
Carl Douglas who was unaware of its existence.

     Thus, we were never able to locate such a tape recording,
nor did we have it in our possession.

     I remain,

                              Very truly yours,

                              BAKER, SILBERBERG & KEENER

                              PHILLIP A. BAKER

PAB/klm

Pavelic claims to have passed his only copy of that tape recording on during the criminal trial to Simpson attorney Carl Douglas at Johnnie Cochran's law firm. However, a December 15, 1997 letter from Simpson civil attorney, Phillip A. Baker, to Simpson business manager, Leroy "Skip" Taft, states that "we searched long and hard during the civil trial" for the tape recording in question, but "We were unable to ever locate same. ... We asked Carl Douglas, who was unaware of its existence."

Simpson investigator, Pat McKenna, stated in a May 13, 1998 interview that Pavelic did not tell him nor any of Simpson's attorneys during the criminal trial of the existence of the tape recording nor that Shipp was aware of the murders that early. "It would have raised a red flag if we had known about this," McKenna stated.

In his February 1, 1995 direct examination by prosecutor, Christopher Darden, Shipp was asked, "You told us that you heard on Monday, June 13, that Nicole Brown was dead; is that right?"

Shipp answers, "Yes, I did."

"And where were you when you heard the news?"

"I was in a bank, the First Interstate Bank."

Simpson attorney Carl Douglas asks in later cross examination, "You first called the Simpson home on June 13th sometime that morning; is that correct?"

Shipp replies: "Yes, I did."

Douglas: "And that was sometime about 10 o'clock in the morning; wasn't it?"

Shipp: "Yeah, my mom paged me at around, about 10, 10:30."

Shipp goes on to describe his phone call to Simpson's house, in which he reached L.A.P.D. Detective Mark Fuhrman, and asked him if Nicole was really dead and if O.J. had killed her.

In a May 6, 1998 telephone interview with this reporter, L.A.P.D. Robbery/Homicide Detective Vic Pietrantoni, who has been assigned to replace retired detectives Philip Vannatter and Tom Lange for all Simpson-case related investigation, stated that this information could mean that Shipp had either some "guilty knowledge" of the crime, or even that Shipp was an "accomplice" to it.

Detective Pietrantoni declined to admit the possibility that Shipp might, himself, be considered a suspect for the murders, repeating a statement he had first made in a March 21, 1997 telephone interview with this reporter that "I know that Simpson committed these murders because Simpson confessed to it."

In that March, 1997 interview, Detective Pietrantoni had represented to this reporter that one of Simpson's attorneys was working with the L.A.P.D. and had revealed to them after

Simpson's acquittal that Simpson had confessed. Pressed to reveal who this Simpson attorney was, Pietrantoni had declined to do so, but stated at that time that he expected Simpson to make his confession public shortly. To date, over a year from that representation, Simpson is still maintaining his innocence.

Asked to reaffirm his statement in a second May 6, 1998 telephone conversation, Pietrantoni repudiated his earlier statement to this reporter regarding a Simpson attorney bringing Simpson's confession to the L.A.P.D., and stated that he merely "believed" that Simpson had confessed.

Ron Shipp was the fourth prosecution witness against O.J. Simpson, on February 1st and 2nd, 1995, a black ex-L.A.P.D. officer with 15 years on the force. He testified that he had been a friend of O.J.'s for 26 years at the time of his testimony, and had met Nicole in 1979 or 1980 and was close friends with her until her June 12, 1994 death.

In addition to testifying to details of the January 1, 1989 domestic violence incident for which O.J. Simpson pled no contest, Shipp testified in the Simpson criminal trial that on the night of June 13, 1994, O.J. Simpson had invited him into his bedroom for a private conversation. Shipp testified that in this alleged conversation Simpson asked him about how long it would take DNA evidence to come back. Because of trial rules that forbid references to lie-detectors, Shipp could not testify on the stand to statements he'd made to prosecutors that in that same conversation O.J. had allegedly expressed worry about taking a lie detector test, but Shipp did testify that O.J. had told him, "To be honest, Shipp ... I've had some dreams of killing her."

Shipp's testimony with respect to this bedroom conversation with Simpson was contradicted by trial testimony from Simpson's daughter, Arnelle, and his sister, Shirley Baker. Both denied that O.J. had ever been left alone in his bedroom, or that Ron Shipp had ever left his bar stool in O.J.'s living room that night. After the trial, Shirley and her husband, Benny Baker, told reporters that they made sure O.J. was never alone that night because they were afraid he might attempt suicide.

The allegations that Shipp knew about the murders early that morning, and lied about it under oath, call into question the reasons for Shipp's incriminating testimony against Simpson, a man about whom he testified, "I still love the guy."

On May 13, 1997 this reporter provided Ron Shipp an advance draft of the manuscript for this reporter's book, *The Frame of The Century?*. The book, published May 21, 1997 on the World Wide Web, outlines a theory that Ron Shipp could have obtained a sample of blood containing the genetic markers of O.J. Simpson, and could have planted it at the crime scenes the night of June 12, 1994 to implicate Simpson in the murders.

Ron Shipp has subsequently claimed, in a June 12, 1997 interview on *Larry King Live*, and again in a call-in to KABC Radio's Larry Elder on January 16, 1998, that he was at home at the time of the Brown-Goldman murders, but there has never been any investigation of this claim.

Shipp had an intimate knowledge of the Simpson estate, having repeatedly brought L.A.P.D. officers over to the house to play tennis, often in Simpson's absence. Marc Eliot's book, *Kato Kaelin: The Whole Truth*, quotes a taped interview with Kaelin on page 239: "Shipp got to know the ins and outs of the house. He discovered, for example, that the Ashford gate had a latch that could be opened from the outside."

Shipp was also, uninvited, at Simpson's house late at night approximately a week before the Brown-Goldman murders.

This reporter provided a final draft of *The Frame of the Century?* to Shipp on May 18, 1997, and to Shipp's attorney, Robert McNeill, on May 19, 1997. Cover letters invited Shipp or his attorney to respond to any of the facts or theories presented in the book before publication, but they declined to do so, and still have not responded in any way, even though over 9,000 copies of the book have been downloaded from this reporter's World Wide

Web site since its first publication on May 21, 1997.

In that book, this reporter published the following as facts:

Like O.J. Simpson, Ron Shipp wears size-12 shoes—the size of the bloody Bruno Magli shoe prints found on Nicole's Bundy Drive walkway.

According to Sheila Weller, who interviewed Shipp extensively, Shipp, "had a good working knowledge of criminal forensics."

When Marcia Clark and Philip Vannatter interviewed Shipp before the Simpson criminal trial, Vannatter asked Ron Shipp if he thought O.J. did it. Shipp answered, "Whoever did this did a heck of a job framing him."

May 15, 1998

A Letter to Daniel Petrocelli

Fred Goldman's attorney in his successful civil suit against O.J. Simpson, Daniel Petrocelli, has been all over television recently, promoting his new book on the Simpson case. His two talking points for most of the talk shows were the same: O.J. Simpson murdered Nicole because she had resumed her affair with Marcus Allen; and the fact that the alarm that Kato Kaelin had set in O.J.'s house was off again when Arnelle let the L.A.P.D. detectives in "proved" that someone close to Simpson had "cleaned up" the house.

I decided to show him why simple logic proved him wrong on this second point. I emailed him, on May 14, 1998:

Dear Mr. Petrocelli,

I believe you're already familiar with my book, *The Frame of the Century?*. In that book, as you have done in yours, I discuss the fact that the alarm in O.J.'s house was mysteriously off when Arnelle took the L.A.P.D. detectives in. I also discuss how the laundry room at Rockingham could have been used for a clean up.

The only difference between us is that I'm suggesting that these are indications that someone came to O.J.'s after the murders in order to plant evidence, and you're suggesting that someone came to O.J.'s after the murders in order to clean up evidence.

So my question is: if you're right, and I'm wrong, then why didn't the clean up guy clean up O.J.'s blood drops in the front foyer? (Unless he was the guy who dropped them there from the supply of O.J.'s blood obtained earlier from the autologous blood bank on the fourth floor of Cedars Sinai Hospital, where O.J. had left his blood for knee surgery.)

Oops?

Best regards,

J. Neil Schulman

Mr. Petrocelli did not reply.

I subsequently read Petrocelli's book *Triumph of Justice: The Final Judgment on the Simpson Saga*. On page 279 of his book, Petrocelli writes,

[Simpson] made at least one phone call—to Kato— just before board-
ing his plane from a pay phone at the gate. He could have made other
phone calls then, or even when he landed at O'Hare. ...Who might
Simpson call? Who were the people closest to him? Who could he trust?
Cowlings had returned from a party and was at home alone. Arnelle
was in her room alone. Cathy Randa was at her home alone. All were
familiar with Simpson's home and property.

Whoever he might have called, he or she or they gained access and
turned off the alarm system when they entered. They would not have
risked turning on the lights; Kato was in his room, neighbors might
notice, some stray motorist might remember lights blazing in the man-
sion late at night. So they picked up whatever they could find, and wiped
up the rest. It's not impossible to surmise that, in the dark, they might
have missed the few small blood drops that were still there when the
police entered early in the morning, or dropped something, like socks
on a carpet.

Well, there are several problems with that scenario.

From *Evidence Dismissed* by Detective Tom Lange and Detective Philip Vannatter, page 20, describing their decision to enter
Simpson's estate:

"Vannatter then turns to the others and says, 'Let's add this up:
We have lights on in the house and cars parked in the driveway.
Simpson and his live-in maid are supposed to be home, but no
one is answering either the intercom or the phone.'"

In the next paragraph, also on page 20, "Lange weighs in with
his opinion. 'Something's wrong. Lights on. Cars everywhere.
No one's answering. What if Simpson and his maid are in trouble
in there?"

So, the lights in the house were *on* when the detectives arrived at Simpson's house that morning. The lights being on provides one of the reasons they say they went in. This refutes
Petrocelli's assertion that someone "cleaning up" the house
would have missed blood drops in the foyer, or socks on the bedroom floor because the lights were off.

But it's perfectly consistent with my alternative explanation of
the alarm being off when Arnelle took the detectives into the

house: that someone came into the house after Kaelin set the alarm to *plant* evidence such as the blood drops and the socks.

But Petrocelli fails to answer an even more basic question about his scenario. If O.J. Simpson was going to telephone someone to come and clean up his house, why would he phone Kato Kaelin to turn his alarm system on in the first place? Just to make it more likely that his alarm would be accidentally set off and Westec security would arrive to catch the clean up?

Counselor, these sorts of items are what *I* call impeachment.

An *Editor's* Query Letter

A science-fiction editor I've worked with in the past, Beth Meacham, apparently reads the alt.true-crime news group on Usenet, where I posted a copy of my recent article on the Shipp allegations. Beth posted the following message query: "All very well, Neil, but how does this theory account for Ron Goldman's blood in O.J.'s Bronco?"

I replied:

The presence of Ron Goldman's blood in the Bronco can be accounted for in two ways, one of which supports my theory, and the other of which is neutral to it.

The neutral way, first: cross-contamination. I believe the same L.A.P.D. officer who was in contact with Nicole's Akita, which had Bundy-crime-scene blood on its paws, was later involved in towing the Bronco from in front of the Rockingham estate. I also believe it's been demonstrated that the Bronco was opened before it was towed to release the hand brake, providing an opportunity for transferring Bundy crime-scene blood to the Bronco.

My own theory, discussed in *The Frame of the Century?* is that Shipp easily could have grabbed the Bronco at Rockingham, driven it to Bundy, committed the murders (or been an accomplice to them), then returned the Bronco to Rockingham. The particular reason I discuss this scenario was the light bulb that had been removed from the Bronco's ceiling and placed under the seat, where it was later found by Detective Lange. Lange comments in his book with Vannatter, *Evidence Dismissed*, that this is a procedure used by L.A.P.D. patrol officers in their cruisers to prevent officers from being silhouetted when they open their car doors at night. Shipp had been an L.A.P.D. patrol officer for 8 years, and would have been in that habit.

A Correspondent's Questions About Simpson

Recurring questions in letters I get from readers of *The Frame of the Century?* are not about my investigation or theories of what happened, but how given O.J. Simpson's statements and demeanor he could possibly be innocent of the murders.

One correspondent named David asked me, as did Larry Elder, what I thought the motive could be for someone other than O.J. to murder Nicole.

I'd answered,

The question of motivation for the murders of Nicole Brown Simpson and Ronald Goldman asks for speculation, whether one regards the murderer as O.J. Simpson or—as I ask—Ron Shipp. Marcia Clark and Christopher Darden, in their prosecution of Simpson, went to a great deal of effort to establish a pattern of domestic abuse and stalking in their attempt to prove that Simpson had a likely intent to murder Nicole, but even they were never able to come up with more than the barest speculations about what might have been going through O.J.'s mind that would have led him to commit murder.

Our correspondence went back and forth over several days. Here are the highlights:

David:
You dwell, at great length, on motivation. Your analysis is based largely on speculation and a bunch of psycho-babble. You seem to be ignoring the far more compelling issue of *physical evidence* when comes to determining the real killer. And, in that regard, there can be little doubt that the perpetrator was none other than Orenthal James Simpson. To believe otherwise is simply illogical because it accepts the silly notion that everything—literally everything!—is planted, contaminated, concocted, misinterpreted, or manufactured.

JNS:

Logic can't tell you what happened. Logic can only eliminate what didn't happen. And exploring a possible and not yet eliminated explanation for known facts is never silly.

If I have learned one thing in looking into the circumstances of the Brown-Goldman murders, there is nothing simple or obvious about them.

David:

I guess we're just going to have to disagree on this matter. My life's experience has shown me that whenever there are *many* indicators of a particular scenario—more than likely the obvious, logical, and simplest explanation turns out to be the *fact* of the matter.

JNS:

If you replace "whenever" if the above sentence with "usually," I'll agree. I wrote, and believe, that the alternative scenario I'm exploring would be a rare set of circumstances.

David:

Have you ever read the transcript of Simpson's direct examination by Daniel Petrocelli during the civil trial? It's absolutely pitiful! He is not only unconvincing, evasive, and self-serving to the extreme *but* he is caught in such substantive lies that it begs the question, "Why is he lying if he's innocent?"

JNS:

That's interesting that we have this difference in perception. I don't find it at all obvious that Simpson is directly lying. I do see him having tunnel vision on a number of things, though.

David:

Let me ask you this: Why did Simpson lie about having received his messages from Paula Barbieri?

JNS:

We are talking about one message, not multiple messages, that he is supposedly lying about, and even Paula isn't convinced that Simpson received that particular message. But if he received it, Simpson's perception of it may be different from an objective observer's, because he may not have perceived it as being a "final break up message" since Paula was *always* leaving him "final break-up" messages. And, we have a proof of this because Paula rushed to his side again and even after his arrest.

David:

He got caught red-handed with this lie when confronted with his previous statements and telephone records.

JNS:

I went back and re-read the transcript of Simpson's civil trial testimony on this point. I don't think there's much doubt that he retrieved the message; but whether he listened to more than a few seconds of it—perhaps before getting distracted by something else—is an open question. I agree with you that Simpson is being obstinately wrong on this point.

David:

Naturally, Simpson didn't want it known that Barbieri terminated their relationship and that fact came to his attention on the June 12th. If he was truly innocent, why would he feel the need to lie about something like that?

JNS:
Pride?

David:
How convenient. How about *narcissism*?

JNS:
That's perhaps two ways of saying the same thing.

David:
True.

JNS:
But that Simpson lied isn't proof that he committed these murders. I'll agree that it shows consciousness of something he feels he needs to cover up, though. Precisely of what is something I'm still not sure of, given other events.

David:
Actually, the *physical* evidence is the prove that he committed the murders. It is very difficult to come up with an explanation on why Ron Goldman's blood would be in Simpson's Bronco. Wouldn't you say? But the fact that Simpson lies about material matters speaks volumes.

JNS:
You are correct so far as it goes. It is difficult to imagine, in the ordinary course of an investigation, that when a man with a history of domestic abuse is vague and prevaricates about material facts in a case where forensic evidence inculpates him for a capital murder of his ex-wife, that he could be innocent. This is just not a typical case. The Simpson case is an iceberg, with only the top 10% showing.

David:
I can certainly understand how there can be more to something than what meets the eye. In this case, however, there doesn't seem to be any evidence that there's more to this "iceberg."

JNS:
I know of some.

David:
At every turn, each piece of testimony and evidence only serves to

further corroborate each other.

JNS:

Yes, that's called a "case" in which one side presents evidence that inculpates and the other side presents evidence that exculpates. The Simpson defense would have had to know who and how a frame-up occurred in order to present an effective "Perry Mason" defense which shows evidence pointing in another direction.

David:

It flows far too smoothly in one direction to conclude that, in fact, it is flowing in the opposite direction.

JNS:

That comes down to one of two possibilities. Either Simpson did it, or someone (or some "ones") had the means and reason to frame him.

If Simpson was framed, it was an inside job.

From "Guilty" to "Reasonable Doubt"

Another correspondent named Harold wrote:

Having followed O.J.'s trial and having read several books on the murders of Nicole Brown Simpson and Ronald Goldman, I was convinced of O.J.'s guilt. There seemed no other plausible explanation of who killed these two people, that is until I read your alternate theory. While it's possible that your fevered imagination did the same thing that happened to the police, prosecutors, defense team and the American public, i.e. finger the suspect and make the facts fit the conclusion, you obviously pursued this theory with resolute determination. The fact that you haven't yet come up with any evidence to eliminate Ron Shipp as the alleged assassin is very compelling.

Harold had some questions, which I replied to.

Harold:
1. What became of the extra piece of luggage that O.J. had with him when he left L.A. for Chicago, but didn't have upon his return?

JNS:
I don't think it's been established that there was an extra piece of luggage. The thing I find interesting is that Goldman's lawyer, Dan Petrocelli, tried to make so much out of O.J. retrieving his golf clubs from LAX. The fact is, however, if O.J. had hidden something incriminating in the golf bag, why would he have left it with the Hertz guy—out of his hands—in the first place?

Harold:
2. Have you considered the possibility that O.J. and Ron Shipp conspired to commit these murders for whatever reason?

JNS:

Yes.

Harold:
I personally thought O.J.'s demeanor was strangely inappropriate at times just after the murders and during the trial.

JNS:
Inappropriate by what standard? How are you supposed to act when you're on trial for a crime you didn't commit? Give me someone we *know* was innocent and on trial for comparison.

Harold:
His claims of innocence never really rang true for me. At one time I thought that while he may not have committed the crimes, he might have known the person who did (perhaps his son) and was merely attempting to protect that person.

JNS:
I've considered that he may *think* he knows who did it.

Harold:
3. I never saw enough of Ron Shipp to be able to know whether he was sharp enough and skilled enough to plan for and commit the murders.

JNS:
I have information that tells me that he was. And I haven't eliminated the possibility that Shipp wasn't working alone; I just don't require additional persons for my theory.

Harold:
4. What is the likelihood that O.J. has become aware of your theory?

JNS:
99%

Harold:

If he were innocent of the murders including any potential conspiracy, don't you think he would confront Ron Shipp?

JNS:

Not if he thought that someone else was the killer.

Harold:

I mean, if O.J.'s life were as dependent upon hero worship as you suggest, wouldn't he go after the man who "destroyed" his life?

JNS:

If he were sure, yes.

Harold:

5. I have read that Paula Barbieri thought that O.J. was still obsessed with Nicole which was why she broke up with him. Might that not argue against your argument that O.J. could have any woman he wanted. The fact remains that Nicole rejected O.J. and while his rational mind could eventually accept this, his "dark side" could not.

JNS:

Being still in love with one woman while dating others doesn't indicate the sort of obsession that leads to murder, in my view.

Harold:

Thanks for pursuing and presenting this theory. It sure does make a scenario other than the one the public has been fed entirely plausible.

JNS:

You're welcome!

Will No One Rid Me of This Meddlesome Priest?

A reader of the alt.true-crime news group wrote:

The obvious question I see is why would anyone else bother to kill these people and then spend time to frame O.J.? If it wasn't O.J., there are no other suspects. There was no need to frame O.J.. On the other hand would you kill two people to frame a person? Why not just kill the person?

I replied:

"If a suspect falls in the forest and there's no official investigation, is there a suspect?"

Ron Goldman was likely killed for no other reason than he had the bad luck to be in the wrong place at the wrong time. I also agree that Nicole would not have been murdered for no other reason than to frame O.J. Simpson.

Second, you're correct that "If it wasn't O.J., there are no other suspects." The prosecution never found another suspect. The defense during both the criminal and civil trials never offered up an alternate suspect.

But now we have William Benson Wasz's attorney proffering that Wasz claims he was hired by Robert Kardashian to shoot Nicole to death five months before Nicole was murdered—and Joe Bosco says he has corroborating evidence to prove Wasz is telling the truth. Moreover we have someone credible who says he can prove that Ron Shipp already knew about the murders early enough that either Shipp was a participant in the crime or was at the crime scene unreported by the L.A.P.D.—and lied about it under oath.

I wrote a book in which I recounted circumstantial evidence indicating that Ron Shipp needs to be investigated as a suspect in the murder of Nicole Brown Simpson and Ronald Goldman—

and if for no other reason, than that Shipp was never investigated and therefore has never been eliminated as a suspect. The
detective who's currently assigned to any continuing Brown-
Goldman murder investigation admits that Shipp could be if
nothing else an accomplice to the murders.

So do we have a suspect if a journalistic investigation puts one
forward and there is no official investigation of it? That's an interesting semantic question. As far as the liability-conscious
mainstream press is concerned, there are no suspects unless
someone is being officially investigated as a suspect ... because
if they name someone as a suspect who *isn't* being officially investigated, they can get sued for libel.

Ron Shipp has had since *The Frame of the Century?* was published on May 21, 1997 to sue me for libel, and hasn't done so.

So, I have another suspect, even if neither the authorities nor
O.J. Simpson himself do not.

Now you say, "The obvious question I see is why would anyone else bother to kill these people and then spend time to frame
O.J.?"

Well, the first usual reason a murderer frames someone is to
divert attention away from himself.

The second reason would be if you have it in for two people,
and want to murder one and get the other blamed for it. Two
birds with one stone.

A third reason?

*Let's say that Jack has brought his friend Fred into his illegal
business. Fred's wife, Mary, knows about the illegal business. Fred
and Mary ultimately split up and, as many divorces end up, there
is a desire by Fred and Mary to hurt each other. Mary mouths off
about how with what she knows about Fred and Jack's illegal
business, Fred better not do anything to piss her off.*

*Fred vents to Jack about how Mary is threatening to screw him.
Jack says to Fred, "We'd better whack the bitch."*

Fred says, "I'd like nothing better, but I got our kids to think about, so forget it."

But Jack doesn't forget it. He hires a guy to take pictures of Mary screwing around behind Fred's back, and shows Fred the pictures. Fred hits the ceiling, but still isn't willing to go along with Jack's plan to have his ex-wife killed. So, Jack goes ahead on his own and puts out a contract—but the guy he hires flakes out on him and ends up in prison before he can carry out the hit. Jack's plan was to create just enough evidence that Fred was behind the murder attempt to keep his mouth shut about it.

Things quiet down for the next few months until Fred and Mary have a big blow-out which leads to their final break-up. Fred threatens to turn Mary into the IRS for tax fraud. Mary retaliates by threatening to go to the cops and tell what she knows about Fred's illegal business dealings with Jack.

Fred vents to Jack one more time about how Mary is threatening them, but still won't go along with Jack's plan to have Mary killed. Jack tells Fred that it's no longer a question of Fred's relationship with Mary—if Mary follows through on her threats to go to the cops, it will splash back on Jack and expose his other illegal enterprises. When Fred still won't go along with it, Jack decides that Fred is as much of a loose cannon threatening him as Mary is ... and he needs to take immediate action.

Jack hires a replacement killer to murder Mary, only this time, Fred has to be framed to take the fall for it. So Jack hires an ex-cop with forensic expertise who can get both jobs done. This ex-cop has bragged in the past that he's already "snuffed" people.

Mary is murdered, along with a friend of hers who happened along at the wrong time, and the evidence is manipulated to make it look as if no one else but Fred could have done it.

When Fred is called to tell him that Mary has been murdered, he's not sure at first who's behind it, but soon realizes that Jack is behind it, and went ahead behind his back. He gets so angry he breaks a glass. But he doesn't realize until it's too late that part of

Jack's plan was to frame him for it—and by the time he figures this out, the forensic evidence has convinced the cops and prosecutors that he's guilty. At this point, the last thing he wants to do is implicate Jack in the murders—because he knows that it won't do any good. If Jack goes down, Jack will turn "state's evidence" and testify under immunity he arranged for the murder because Fred asked him to.

Now, I'm going to label this scenario as speculation at this point. We'll see if evidence ever appears to confirm or eliminate this possibility.

A Contradiction

In alt.true-crime, "DeeTigress" wrote, "This crime wasn't a hit. It wasn't done execution style. It was brutal and it was very, very *personal*. It was O.J., face it."

I replied:

The crime scene evidence has always indicated a contradiction. Evidence found at the Bundy crime scene speaks of premeditation and planning. The style of the killings speaks of a crime of passion.

Now, this by itself doesn't rule out O.J. Simpson as the killer. But it could also include someone else who both had a reason to premeditate a killing and went wild during the commission of it.

Nicole was involved with many men. Ron Shipp bragged of being one of them. So, including him on the list as a possible killer, without further examination, doesn't rule out either a premeditated killing or an "overkill" crime of passion. Just because it could have been both doesn't mean O.J. Simpson was the only person with a visceral reaction to Nicole.

A Friendlier Talk Show Host

On May 21, 1998, I received the following private email from Bryan Styble, who identified himself as the Detroit host of "The Pontiac Insomniac with Bryan Styble" on WPON 1460 kHz, Mon-Fri midnight-2am. He was responding to my follow-up messages posted on alt.true-crime.

Dear Mr. Schulman:
Initially, let me say your sober, dispassionate exposition of your ideas is a refreshing break from the juvenile retorts which litter this newsgroup. Your retort to the person who flamed one of your postings was on the mark.
I must say, I don't fully understand your thesis. Do you suspect that Shipp: did the killings at Simpson's request ("You just do what ya hafta do, Ron, I don't wanna know *nothin'*!" I can easily imagine him saying); assisted Simpson at the scene; assisted Simpson after the fact; committed the murders unbeknownst to Simpson but with his presumed approval or appreciation; or killed the fair specifically in an effort to frame Simpson, angered by some falling-out?
Thanks in advance for the clarification.

I replied:
Thanks for the good words! They're appreciated.
If O.J. Simpson did not personally knife Nicole and Ron Goldman to death, the presence of fresh blood drops on the Bundy walkway which scientifically identify as his is inexplicable unless the chain of evidence was corrupted—or unless it was planted by the murderer(s).
That's why I discount any theory which has O.J. as a behind-the-scenes instigator of Nicole's murder. He wouldn't participate in framing himself.
If Shipp or anyone else did the murders, it was logically not with O.J. Simpson's complicity.

Cuts

In alt.true-crime, "Glas" wrote, "Please explain to the class how a grown man could forget when he cut his hand.

I replied:

Please explain why a grown man who's cutting himself all the time would pay any attention to a particular cut at all enough to remember it the next day. It is only in retrospect that it became an issue, and the first time he was asked about it, O.J. was fatigued and likely in shock. We only remember things that are important enough to notice in the first place. And O.J.'s statements about when he cut his hand were tentative right from his first interview with Vannatter and Lange. The interview looks precisely as if O.J. was trying to remember and couldn't, so he was trying to guess.

It's that sort of attempt to please a cop interviewing you, by giving him what he's looking for, that causes lawyers to forbid clients to talking to cops without them there. If Howard Weitzman had been any sort of a lawyer, he would have sat next to O.J. during the interview and said, "O.J., if you don't know for sure, don't makes guesses." You can read this sort of lawyerly advice constantly during O.J.'s civil trial depositions.

"Glas" also asked, "While he's at it, perhaps he can also explain how a grown man could come up with three different explanations for where he was during the half hour that the limo driver was ringing the doorbell.

"I was in the shower."

"I was taking a nap."

"I was out chucking golf balls around the lawn in the dark."

I replied:

O.J. never testified he was taking a nap, and never said it in an interview. Kato suggested to Alan Park that O.J. might be taking a nap, and Park later adopted that statement and attributed it to

Simpson.

The other stuff was sequential, not simultaneous, and fits the time line with no problems.

From Hate Mail to Baseball

One correspondent started our by insulting me, and ending by commiserating with me about the Dodgers trading Piazza. Since he wishes to remain anonymous, I'll call him "Dodger."

Dodger:
Yes, it does sound far fetched. Much more far fetched that on the morning O.J. was, for the first time, without a woman who wanted him,

JNS:
And he was on the phone making a date with Gretchen Stockdale two hours before Nicole was murdered. Guys like O.J. have women throwing themselves at him. His infidelities were what broke up both his marriages.

Dodger:
O.J. cutting his hand and having a scar and admitting to the cops that he cut his hand the night the murders occurred is just a little coincidence.

JNS:
The transcript of O.J.'s conversation is fuzzier than that. O.J. appears to be *guessing* that he cut his hand that night. Vannatter and Lange tell O.J. that blood was found on his driveway and foyer, and that they have a problem with it. O.J. says *immediately*, "Take my blood test." That's a statement made by a man who doesn't expect the result to come back incriminating him. And, Pat McKenna says that when the results did come back incriminating him, O.J. was genuinely shocked. McKenna, who previous investigated about 500 homicides, has the background to make judgment calls like that.

Dodger:
And, of course he has no memory about the scar inducing cut. Has that

happened to you?

JNS:

Lots of time. I've found blood on my shirt, on papers I've been working with, on my pillow, and never had a clue what caused it.

Dodger:

You care nothing about Kato hearing O.J. come back from the murders when the glove was dropped.

JNS:

That testimony is not in the criminal trial, it's not in Kaelin's deposition, and it's not in the civil trial testimony. And no one knows when the glove was dropped, except we know it was there by around 6:30 A.M. when Fuhrman reported it to Vannatter and Lange.

Dodger:

The evidence shows that Kaelin heard the thumps. Obviously those sounds were made by O.J. coming back from the murder scene. What's your theory on the thumps? Oh, don't tell me. Let's use some more benefit of the doubt for O.J.. The framer made the sounds. Perfectly timed too. What with O.J. showing up outside moments later, according to Kato.

JNS:

I don't know what caused the thumps. It could have been a way of making sure someone went to look for the glove. But if O.J. wanted to sneak back onto his property, he would have come in through the Von Watt's property to the tennis courts, and never would have been behind the bungalows. Nobody, including the prosecution, was ever able to provide a single reason O.J. would be back there, coming from the Bronco parked out on Rockingham.

Dodger:

The diaries tell us he is a liar and wife beater. There's not much lower than beating up women.

JNS:

I'm not arguing that O.J. is always truthful, and I'm not arguing that he didn't beat up Nicole and I'm not arguing that wife-beating is morally acceptable. Simpson was convicted of abusing her on one occasion and served a court-ordered sentence on it. The incident happened 5-1/2 years earlier, and no one can document Simpson laying a hand on Nicole afterwards. Which doesn't surprise me because Simpson cut way back on cocaine after that.

None of this makes him a murderer. It would only work backwards in explaining why it happened if we knew for a fact that he was a murderer—and that's what you and I are debating. Using an explanation which works only if your conclusion is proved, as a premise to prove your conclusion, is a logical fallacy called "begging the question."

Dodger:

For you to say what O.J. would do, is so presumptuous. How do you know what's in his mind (re: how O.J. would get back to his property)? I thought it was very plausible that he would sneak back the way the prosecution said. But the thumps, we're perhaps the most incriminating evidence against O.J. Have you seen the property. It seems that he could have easily and logically went home the way they said.

JNS:

Well, I don't know what would have been on O.J.'s mind any more than Chris Darden did when he asserted that O.J. Simpson's motivation to kill Nicole was to control her, or Dan Petrocelli's assertion that it was out of jealousy of Marcus Allen.

But I spent a lot of time around Rockingham chatting up O.J.'s security guys and made friends with them; I also spoke to other people familiar with the estate.

When you own an estate, you know things about it that other people don't, and this gives him options that other people wouldn't have considered.

It just doesn't make any sense for him to come back from Bundy, park the Bronco on Rockingham knowing his limousine driver is just around the corner on Ashford, jump the gate, go behind the bungalows, pound three times on the air conditioner so hard that Kato thought it might be an earthquake, then be seen by Allan Park walking in the front door. It just doesn't work, especially since he was in the habit of using the back way onto his estate from the von Watt's, through the tennis courts, into the kitchen door. The house next to the Salinger's was empty and for sale; if he had an accomplice, he could have parked there and had someone move it later. But that still doesn't put him behind the bungalows for any possible reason.

The prosecution was always talking about two mutually exclusive things. One of them has O.J. parking the Bronco on Rockingham; the other is O.J. jumping the nine-foot gate between his estate and the Salinger's, next door on Rockingham, and knocking into the air conditioner in the dark. But there's no possible way he could have jumped that fence (not with his knees) and there's no reason for him to be back there anyway. It was blocked off and wouldn't get him anywhere. And he certainly didn't go back there to hide a glove while putting the rest of the bloody clothes somewhere else.

So, there's not a reason on earth for O.J. to be behind the bungalows, making the sound that scared Kaelin. That means, QED, someone else was, and the *three* knocks Kaelin heard and felt isn't anything casual or accidental.

Dodger:
And…if a witness lies once, you can assume he's lied about everything else. And…I do!

JNS:

The point is, he isn't lying about everything. O.J. has made assertion after assertion that I've been able to verify through independent investigation. Did you see the 160 minute interview that Ross Becker did with him—the video that some company paid O.J. a hefty sum for then lost their shirt when they couldn't buy advertising for it anywhere but on BET? I'd say it's 95% truthful.

Where O.J. has been less than truthful is in areas where I—in the position of an innocent man framed for a crime—might very well have tried the same lies. Situations where there would have been impossible-to-explain circumstances that he knows were part of the frame-up but couldn't prove. He's told by the cops that there's blood on his driveway and in his foyer, He's tired from being up for almost 24 hours so says casually, "Well, it must be my blood" and "Take my blood test." He's not figuring at that point that he's been framed and that there's another source of his blood than his finger—such as the autologous blood bank at Cedars Sinai hospital, where he left blood for knee surgery.

He's told the shoe prints were made by Bruno Magli shoes. Now, there's two possibilities other than the incriminating one. The first is that he simply forgot he owned the damned things. Might have worn them two or three times then threw them in the back of his closet among forty other pairs of shoes—where they were stolen by the person intending to frame him. By the time the pictures of him wearing the shoes show up, he's screwed himself up and can't backtrack without looking even worse. The second is that he knew he owned the shoes but knew they must have been stolen, but couldn't prove it. So he denies it then when the pictures show up, he's screwed again.

Another example is his explanation of why he parked the Bronco out on Rockingham, which everybody who knows him well says he never did. Suppose I'm right and O.J. knows that the Bronco had been moved out there by someone else. At first he doesn't know who would have moved it. Could it be it Jason or Arnelle? he might think. If he tells the police he didn't park it on Rockingham, is he possibly implicating one of his kids in Nicole's murder? By the time he finds out, it's too late, and he's stuck with his story.

Or maybe it's more complicated than that. This whole thing might have had to do with murdering one loose-cannon and getting the other loose cannon blamed for it. By the time O.J. has figured out who's behind Nicole's death and understands that he was the patsy, he's already innocently made incriminating statements that play right into the framed-up evidence.

Dodger:
O.J. reminds me of myself at my worst. His charisma is phony. Just like mine.

JNS:
Not according to close friends of his, who charmingly referred to him to his face alternately as "large head" and "asshole." Just about everybody who hung around the guy finds him likable. Hell, Petrocelli found him likable and he's convinced the guy murdered his client's son. O.J.'s demeanor of innocence is so strong that nobody can hang around the guy and believe that he's a murderer while they're in his presence. Even people who think he did it assert that "he doesn't know he did it"—which is nonsense. If he did it, he knows it, and he wouldn't be doing lots of the things I know for a fact he's doing.

Dodger:
Isn't it weird how O.J. chose to go all the way to LAX to get his golf clubs, instead of a messenger or American Airlines personnel, rather than see and comfort his children after their mother was just murdered?)

JNS:

Have you ever sat *shiva* for someone close to you? You do lots of things, anything, to distract yourself from the pain. Going to the airport to pick up golf clubs is exactly the sort of thing someone in pain would do after a death and before the funeral, just to have something ordinary to do.

Dodger:
Instead of comforting your children? Or even seeing them??

JNS:

I wouldn't have helicopters and hoards of shouting reporters following me everywhere I went, scaring the bejezus out of them, asking me whether I murdered their mother. You're missing the context.

Dodger:
There's nothing ordinary about O.J. going to LAX to pick up his golf clubs. This is a man that hires people to do that. Unless there's trace evidence he's concerned about.

JNS:

These facts are the basis for making inferences. They are not in and of themselves determinative. You're pointing out to me facts which can imply guilt. I'm point out that these same facts can have innocent explanations. Until we have proof one way or the other, we don't know which context to apply.

What Might Be "Wrong" With "Something Wrong"

Once in a while I even respond to a Usenet comment, myself.

Al Walker had written email to me concerning my book shortly after its publication. In a recent post he made in the news group alt.fan.oj-simpson, Al was arguing in favor of the Simpson defense team's contention that the "wet transfers" Dr. Henry Lee had found on the bindles of blood evidence indicated that evidence had been switched in the L.A.P.D. forensic laboratory.

I had come up with a different theory about "wet transfers."

Al Walker:

Henry Lee testified to some faint wet transfer stains on the bindles. There were also similar wet transfer stains in a bindle containing reference samples collected from a pool of Nicole's blood.

JNS:

Al, there is one other possibility with respect to the wet transfer on Bindle 47—the drop of blood from the Bundy walkway which was identified by PCR as O.J.'s blood.

If the blood was planted on the Bundy walkway from a supply of frozen autologous blood containing the preservative glycerol— which is an anti-drying agent—it would have dried more slowly than blood not so preserved. It would have been diluted with water when collected, but there might have been just enough glycerol left in the sample to account for the "something wrong" Dr. Lee was discussing.

A Hard-Won Grudging Respect

A correspondence on alt.true-crime that began with "I'm betting at least one room in your house is lined with aluminum foil" ended with "Good luck with your website, Neil. I'll be looking for you on the talk shows. Let us know if you ever get a booking."

My correspondent identified herself as "Maggie8097" and when we stopped talking past each other, the questions got good.

Maggie wrote: "Seems to me that you are concluding the guilt of Ron Shipp on a hell of a lot less evidence than that against O.J. In fact, you are concluding the guilt of Ron Shipp on the basis of *no evidence* at all. Nada. Nothing. Zippo."

I replied:

"I have never, not once, not ever, written that I have concluded the guilt of Ron Shipp. I have written that I have sufficient evidence that he needs to be investigated.

"I have a personal belief on the subject, but that carries no weight whatsoever. We need to find the truth based on investigation and analysis of the facts of the case.

"At the current time, I have found no factual evidence which has been used to conclude the guilt of O.J. Simpson which can not be explained by the alternative theory I have proposed."

Our correspondence continued, at length:

Maggie:
I love the part where Ron Shipp obtained a vial of O.J.'s blood at some point prior to the murders, but somehow O.J. forgot all about Shipp having some of his blood and neglected to use it in his defense.

JNS:
Your statement is intentionally obtuse. Obviously if you're going to steal someone's blood to frame him, you're not going to tell him about it.

Maggie:
Steal someone's blood? Now Ron Shipp is a vampire? How do you take someone's blood without his knowledge? (And you say my perfectly clear statement was obtuse!)

JNS:
I describe five methods in *The Frame of the Century?* that Ron Shipp, prior to the Brown Goldman murders, could have obtained the 40 or 50 drops of blood with O.J. Simpson's genetic markers that have linked Simpson to the crime. They are:

1. Obtaining of an autologous blood donation O.J. had made in preparation for knee surgery. Autologous donation is blood you donate to yourself for later surgical or emergency transfusion. It's standard protocol for the knee surgery O.J. had. I've researched this possibility and it's my strongest scenario at this moment.

2. Collection of O.J.'s dried blood from tissue, cloth, or bandage found in Simpson's bathroom, then reconstitution into liquid form using either saline solution or distilled water. Shipp had access to O.J.'s home.

3. Collection of still liquid or partly dried O.J.'s blood from where O.J. bled in the Bronco or in his foyer, the night of June 12, 1994—then reconstitution into liquid form. (This ties into a theory that Shipp was already observing O.J. that night in preparation for framing him for the murders, and obtaining O.J.'s blood was simply an unexpected opportunity.)

4. Use of a tranquilizer such as Rhohypnol (better known as the "Date Rape" drug), or a high dose of a sedative such as Xanax, in a drink given to O.J. Once unconscious, blood could be pulled with no problem and nothing more than a pinhole bruise, and Simpson could assume he simply fell asleep from the alcohol. This would require someone who could have a private drink with O.J. Shipp had that sort of personal access.

5. Manufacture of blood evidence, using any genetic sample of O.J. Simpson (mucous, hair from a hairbrush, etc.) then replicating the DNA using the PCR process. The replicated DNA could be "salted" into any DNA-sterilized blood sample containing the same conventional blood type and subtypes as O.J. Simpson. This could be done in any laboratory with a thermal cycler and a blood centrifuge, by any technician with a high-school diploma.

Maggie:
I'm also pretty fond of the stuff about Shipp framing O.J. to provide a "Black Man Kills White Woman" story for the media.

JNS:
Well, considering that Shipp, like O.J., married a white woman, maybe he didn't particularly care about race any more than O.J. did.

Maggie:
I suppose you believe your statement, above, is not obtuse. I doubt many would agree. Did marrying this white woman make Ron Shipp lose his blackness? ....make him hate all black men? .... necessarily lead to some alliance with the media?

JNS:
No. I merely suggest he wouldn't have been focusing on the media implications of framing Simpson—it wouldn't have been on his mind at all.

Maggie:
It's very easy to develop a "theory" when you refuse to address the difficult questions, simply glossing over the more ridiculous aspects ("Ron Shipp obtained a vial of O.J.'s blood......")

JNS:
The whole point to my investigation is that Shipp had the fo-

rensic skills to do this, and the access to Simpson necessary to do this. Now, with a credible witness alleging that Shipp lied about when he first knew about Nicole's murder, we have a reason to question Shipp's incriminating testimony against O.J.—and to examine what hostile motivations might have existed for him to damage his "friend."

Maggie:
You haven't shown that Shipp had the forensic skills to show up for jury duty, much less the technical expertise to manufacture blood from O.J.'s mucous.

JNS:
He was an L.A.P.D. officer for 15 years, a patrol officer for 8. I believe he tried out for detective before leaving the force. After leaving the force he worked as a private detective for about a year.

According to Sheila Weller, who interviewed Shipp extensively for her book on the Simpson case, Shipp, "had a good working knowledge of criminal forensics."

Maggie:
So now you're trying to tell us that anyone with "a good working knowledge of criminal forensics" can manufacture blood?

JNS:
No, a person with "a good working knowledge of criminal forensics" couldn't manufacture blood without the help of a lab technician. But a person with "a good working knowledge of criminal forensics" would know how to collect liquid blood, collect dried blood and liquefy it, or know where to find a lab technician to help in doing so. A person with 15 years on the L.A.P.D. and another year as a private detective would certainly know these things, in addition to doing covert surveillance (which Shipp did for L.A.P.D.), and would know how easy it would be to get

blood out of a hospital blood bank which has no security what-soever.

Maggie:
Yea, yea, yea. I'm sure it happens all the time.

JNS:
And there's the crux of our disagreement. You think that just because something happens rarely, it doesn't need to be considered as a serious hypothesis.

I start off my book by suggesting that if my theory is right, it is describing events so rare as to make the theory unbelievable to anyone used to working in the criminal justice system.

Maggie:
Here's an idea—maybe Ron Shipp was told of Nicole's death by one of his ex-coworkers in the police department and is protecting that person because it is against regulations for police officers to notify civilians of crimes except through official channels. ... Sure makes a lot more sense than Shipp reconstituting O.J.'s blood from an old Band-Aid.

JNS:
If that is the case, Shipp is free to tell me or Dominick Dunne or Larry King which officer called him that night and brought him out to the crime scene. Then he can explain why he per-jured himself about it on the stand during the criminal trial.

Maggie:
And you think Shipp's "hostile motivations" are suspicious? Which planet are you from? Where I live, decent people are enraged by murderers. It's certainly reasonable to think that as a former police officer and friend of Nicole, Shipp would be angry at the murderer. What's not reasonable is making ridiculous claims about Ron Shipp stealing blood from hospital blood banks to try to make a human animal like O.J. Simpson appear innocent of a crime he clearly committed.

JNS:

Your reasoning is circular. All you're saying is that Shipp couldn't have done what I suggest because you already know that O.J. is guilty. It's circular because you are using your assumption to prove your conclusion. That's a classical error in logic.

Maggie:

Can you explain, briefly please, how Ron Shipp, having reconstituted blood, stolen knives, borrowed Broncos and whatever else, could be assured that O.J. wasn't on the phone with the mayor, or having dinner at home with a few close friends, or dining at Mezzaluna while Shipp was on Bundy knifing Ron and Nicole while wearing O.J.'s shoes and gloves?

JNS:

Shipp knew O.J.'s estate like the back of his hand. He was always over there hanging with his cop buddies, playing tennis with them. He knew the secret back way into the estate from the von Watt's property. He knew how the gates worked, where the spare key O.J. hid was, where the spare Bronco key was kept in the kitchen. O.J. had used him for security stuff in the past, so he knew the security code for the house, too.

From the tennis courts, he could see up into O.J.'s bedroom. Also, he had a security background that included electronic surveillance. From the phone out near the pool, he could also know whether O.J. was using the phone. All he needed was to observe O.J. for a single thirty-minute span that O.J. was without a visitor or a phone call, and O.J. wouldn't have an alibi for the crime. It wouldn't matter that the crime was committed during another half hour. Whether it was O.J. doing the driving, or Shipp, Nicole's condo was only a five-minute drive each way.

Now, consider what would have happened, with Nicole expecting Ron Goldman to bring over her glasses, if Ron Shipp had got on Nicole's intercom and said, "Nicole, it's Ron."

She would have buzzed him in, thinking it was Goldman, and

come outside to meet him.

Maggie:
Right. Ron Shipp, who is apparently able to creep all around O.J.'s house at will, went over to murder Nicole without even a plan for how to get into her house. So he decided to just buzz her, not knowing if, say, she's on the phone telling the other person that "Ron" is at the door. Makes as much sense as all your other stuff.

JNS:
I never said he wouldn't have had a back-up plan. I think he had Nicole's house key, the one that disappeared from her kitchen counter a few days before the murders, that she used for jogging. I'm just saying he probably wouldn't have had to use it. "Nicole, it's Ron" would have gotten Nicole to open up her door, even if it was to tell Shipp that she was busy and couldn't invite him in right now. Her confusing "Ron" Shipp for "Ron" Goldman, however, might have speeded up the process.

Maggie:
Big problem with this. How does Shipp know, while he's somehow surveiling O.J. and knows he's doing nothing, with nobody (another one of your wild leaps, by the way), that Nicole isn't on the phone with her mom? And how does he know O.J. doesn't pick up the phone, or admit a friend to his house, or go out with someone right after the surveillance ends? The problem is that watching O.J. just isn't enough.

JNS:
Re-read the above paragraph I posted. That covers how he knows O.J. hasn't picked up the phone, or admitted a friend to his house. Shipp would also have to know that Simpson isn't going anywhere because Simpson's waiting for his limo for the trip to Chicago. (Yes, I can anticipate your next challenge. How can Shipp know Simpson's travel schedule? I can't answer that question in print because it involves a discussion with a principal in

the case who doesn't want to be quoted on the record yet.)

Your question about how he could know Nicole isn't on the phone is a reasonable one. One obvious answer would be electronic surveillance, as I mentioned above. I could walk into a store I know on Sunset Blvd. and, for about $200, today, I could buy a transmitter that could easily make it from 875 S. Bundy Drive to 360 North Rockingham. That same store carries listening devices and even tiny TV cameras to hook up to such a transmitter, that I could pick up for under $1000. There are also telephone bugs you can get that can send a signal when a phone is picked up. Ron Shipp worked in undercover surveillance for the L.A.P.D., then used his skills after he left the force as a private investigator. I'd love to get a look at his credit-card records and see how much of this sort of stuff he owned, if he even had to buy it himself.

But in any case, 875 S. Bundy Drive is only five minutes away from 360 North Rockingham. The murder wouldn't have to be coordinated to the exact minute since nobody, looking at the crime scene, could know exactly when it took place. Even today, it can't be pinned down for sure within more than about an hour and a half. It's only the assumption that Simpson is the murderer that narrows it down more than that.

Maggie:
It's easy to say that after the fact. But no one planning this murder to frame another person could be sure that the murder scene (meticulously planned and staged *outside*, according to your theory) wouldn't be discovered immediately after the crime. Face it, anyone doing this to frame O.J. wouldn't have executed his plan where the fruits of his efforts might me discovered so quickly.

JNS:
Now that's a fascinating statement. You're sure that O.J. Simpson committed these murders, all by his lonesome self. Going over to Nicole's, O.J. would have had no way of knowing

that Nicole wasn't on the phone and told her caller, "Hold on, that asshole ex-husband of mine is outside." Simpson would have had no way of knowing Sydney wasn't awake watching TV with a friend sleeping over (as was scheduled and canceled at the last minute). And, the celebrity O.J. Simpson would have had no way of knowing that any one of his or Nicole's Brentwood neighbors wouldn't see his world-famous face near Nicole's during the murder, wearing no more of a disguise than a watch cap, and yelled out, "Hey, Juice!"

Yet, Nicole Brown and Ronald Goldman were in fact murdered. If you're going to argue someone framing O.J. couldn't do it, then O.J. couldn't do it, either—and the news reports of Nicole Brown's and Ronald Goldman's murders must be in error.

Maggie:

I suspect you don't even know that you proved my point with your two paragraphs, above. This was clearly not a long-planned execution with intent to frame someone else. This was a crime of passion, perpetrated by the only person who would bother to knife Nicole Simpson some 30 or so times in the yard of her house and, at least for a time, not even care if he was seen or heard. This crime was committed by someone who would seriously contemplate suicide, even writing a suicide note, days after allowing his anger to overcome him. Just the manner of the crime should be enough to prove that it wasn't the result of a well-thought out plan complete with remote surveillance, stealing of keys and shoes and gloves and knives and manufacturing of blood. Only O.J. would have committed the crime the way he did. Anyone else wouldn't have the anger which caused him to risk so much.

JNS:

A crime of passion, eh? A crime of passion which would involve, at the very least, bringing a knife over, which means it was premeditated.

Well, maybe you subscribe to Mark Fuhrman's theory that it could have been done with a Swiss army knife. As if happens, I've seen the exact type of Swiss army knife that Fuhrman was talking about. O.J. gave one as a gift to my source, and we looked it over carefully. There's no blade longer than about 2-1/2"— and even with both sharp blades extended in opposite directions, there's no way you could get the sort of grip on it that could account for the type of wounds inflicted on Nicole Brown and Ron Goldman.

The killer brought a knife suitable for murder, so we're back to premeditation. Back to worrying about getting caught. Worrying about being seen, being overheard, being identified on the phone, being seen by the kids.

But, you know, we're beyond that sort of discussion now. The reason is the proffer of William Benson Wasz that in January of 1994, six months before Nicole was murdered, Robert Kardashian offered him $15,000 to shoot Nicole while she was staying at Rockingham after the Northridge earthquake.

I know, you're going to call Wasz a liar, too. After all, he's serving a 20 year sentence for multiple armed robberies. But crimewriter Joseph Bosco has found the following corroboration, according to an article posted Friday, May 22, 1998, on *WorldNetDaily*, written by David Bresnahan:

> This is not a just a case of one man's word against another. There are police records tying Wasz to the theft of the camera, gun, and car. Wasz says Kardashian ordered those thefts.
>
> "Every aspect of the story is backed up," explained Bosco. "In other words it can be shown that Wasz did do business with Kardashian, he did sell them cocaine, they did meet at the Roxbury, he did the surveillance of Nicole Brown Simpson on January 6 and 7, 1994. There's a witness to this. He did turn over two rolls of undeveloped film to Robert Kardashian, taking an envelope with cash in it. There's proof of that. He did move into the Saharan Motel after being given this assignment to steal Paula Barbieri's car. We have those records, we have the phone records. It leads right up to January 14, the day Wasz says all this other business they've been through is when Robert Kardashian told him, or gave him, or asked him, or solicited him, however you want to say it, to kill Nicole Brown Simpson. Now understand, there are only two people and God who heard that conversation."
>
> Because the crime of solicitation to commit murder is so difficult to prove, simply because there are rarely any witnesses, California has a

statute to deal with it, according to Longo. In such a case, the jury will be instructed to weigh the evidence surrounding the incident to determine who to believe in a situation where it is one man's word against another.

So, if there was a contract to kill Nicole Brown Simpson six months earlier, and she was murdered six months after the contract was first put out by someone else, we know, if nothing else, that we are *not* talking about a crime of passion. We're talking about something with long-term contemplation, if not detailed planning, involved.

And we're not talking about something as sloppy as just randomly meandering over to Nicole's house an hour before taking off on a business trip, when Nicole might be on the phone, when the kids might be awake, when a neighbor can recognize your world-famous face and world-famous voice.

Could we be talking about O.J. Simpson engaging in a conspiracy with Robert Kardashian to contract a murder of Nicole, with a replacement killer for the imprisoned William Wasz? No way. If O.J. didn't do the knifings himself, then why is O.J. Simpson's blood on the scene? If O.J. Simpson did not do the killings himself, his blood was planted there as part of a frame-up, as I've been discussing. I don't think that frame-up could have been done after the fact, by the L.A.P.D.. QED: it would done by the killer or killers to frame him.

We would be talking about Robert Kardashian hiring a replacement killer, and either by Kardashian's intent, or the solo intent of the replacement killer, framing O.J. as part of the events of the murder.

But a crime of passion? No. Murder, premeditated, and cold. At least Marcia Clark, by accident, got this part right.

Maggie:
You speak as if there are two polar opposite types of murder—crimes of passion that are committed with not one second of premeditation and

cold, calculated, premeditated murders that are entered into completely dispassionately. Of course this is horseshit, but perhaps it helps you advance your little Ron Shipp theory.

The truth is that there is a continuum here, and O.J.'s murder of Ron and Nicole was a very passionate premeditated murder (which, by the way, happens all the time among people who know each other—most of the time they feel great remorse at some point after the crime—just like O.J. did during that Bronco ride). The thing that *doesn't* happen is for a contract killer to act with passion and reckless abandon—that's one of the many reasons your theory just doesn't work.

JNS:

"The truth is that there is a continuum here, and O.J.'s murder of Ron and Nicole was a very passionate premeditated murder."

Okay, Maggie, let's take this apart and look at it.

I have written before this (though not, I believe, in this series of back-and-forth with you) that the Bundy crime scene evidence speaks of premeditation (a glove and watch cap left at the scene), and the knifings themselves speak of great rage. Marcia Clark's book summarizes the knifings pretty much as Nicole was killed brutally but fairly quickly—the coup de grace being the killer pulling her head back and cutting her throat back to the spinal cord—while Ron Goldman was fought with and taunted with the knife before he was finished off.

The point I'm making with respect to the issue of rage is that enormous rage is created merely by the fact that a knife was the murder method. And the choice of a knife, rather than a gun, speaks of the location of the crime—an upscale suburban neighborhood where gun shots might have fetched the police.

Simpson was phobic about blood, as I've pointed out. If he wanted to murder Nicole with his own hands, he wouldn't have knifed her to death; he would have strangled her to death. Any profiler will tell you strangling, or smothering, is the chosen method of murder for someone who is a neatness freak like O.J.

Simpson.

But, it's even less likely that Simpson would do the killings himself. If he wanted Nicole dead, he simply would have hired someone to kill Nicole when she was vacationing in Cabo, and the Mexican constabulary could have been bribed never to investigate.

Back to the question of demeanor following the killings. If O.J. had committed these killings, he would have been enormously adrenalized for hours afterwards. The prosecution argued that he was overheated, which is why he asked the for air conditioning in the limo to be turned up. But there is an innocent explanation for that: the hot shower which he had just taken. (And this shower isn't in controversy; even the prosecution would argue he needed a shower if he was the killer, to clean up.) Regardless of the reason for his shower, that would have left his pores open and sweating, unless he was in the habit of turning the faucet to ice cold to seal his pores. Most people find that uncomfortable and don't do it.

There was also discussion that while O.J. was on the airliner, he kept drinking water and going to the bathroom. This can only seem incriminating if you haven't looked at the video *O.J. Simpson Minimum Maintenance Fitness For Men* which Simpson recorded (obviously) before he was in jail for 16 months following the murders. In this video, O.J. has a section on airplane travel, in which he advises drinking lots of water to avoid dehydration, and getting up and walking around the airplane to avoid jet lag.

Pat McKenna did the demeanor investigation for Simpson's defense team. Pat is adamant that from the moment O.J. arrived at Los Angeles Airport to the time he checked into the hotel room in Chicago, Simpson was relaxed, jovial, his usual self, judging from the comments of the dozens of people who saw him. Then, from the moment he gets the call from L.A.P.D. telling him of Nicole's murder, Simpson is agitated and angry. It would be an extremely strange form of adrenalization that would *not* be present immediately after committing what you're characterizing as a passionate double murder, but would be present hours later when you're notified of the death.

But I'm not done. Maggie, Ron Shipp could both have been hired to kill Nicole *and* have engaged in a "passionate" rage killing of her. Shipp claimed to have had an affair with Nicole. In the weeks just prior to Nicole's murder, Nicole was phoning O.J. complaining that Shipp was coming around her place unwanted and phoning her excessively. (I have this from two independent sources; it's not in my book because I learned about it after it was published.) And, Shipp was clearly obsessed with both O.J. and Nicole; I discuss this at length in the book. Read my discussion of Shipp's uninvited visits to the Rockingham estate, one of them with a woman he demanded O.J. meet because she was "a blonde Nicole type." (I've seen the woman; she is.)

I already have an allegation that Ron Shipp lied about when he first knew about the murders. I am still looking for any witness who saw Ron Shipp the night of the murders to tell me what *his* demeanor was like that night, sometime after 11:00 PM, June 12, 1994.

Maggie:

It must be awfully lonely being a voice in the wilderness, speaking the truth, while everyone else just ignores you. Very frustrating, I'm sure. It probably leads you to believing that just because you say something, it must be true.

JNS:

What I say doesn't have to be true. I'm not even asserting that it *is* true. I'm asserting that it provides a reasonable alternative explanation of how the evidence against O.J. Simpson doesn't prove Simpson's guilt, and creates a moral necessity for investigating my theory to eliminate it or prove it true.

Maggie:
Now you get to decide moral necessities? Thank god that's not true.

JNS:
Well, it certainly decides them for me. That's why I'm still investigating.

And, by the way, I've had to spend about two hours every day responding to the messages and private email I've got from my article since I posted it. I hardly feel lonely.

Maggie:
And you think it's curious that Shipp doesn't dignify your accusations with a response?

JNS:
Do *I* find it curious? No, I don't think it's curious at all. I would have been more surprised if he *had* responded. The *only* reason he would have responded would have been if he could have gotten this writer—who previously has written for major newspapers and national magazines—off his back, by showing me he had a solid alibi.

By not responding, upwards of nine thousand people have read my book, which demands that he be investigated for participation in a double murder.

Maggie:
Actually, what I am doing is reasoning from the known facts: O.J. killed Nicole and Ron, therefore, Ron Shipp could not have killed Nicole and Ron.

JNS:
Again, you're declaring that the issue at hand is settled, and you're the winner. And participants in a discussion don't have that privilege.

This discussion ends when one of us pulls out, or one of us

convinces the other, or when the matter is resolved by some other means.

It would end if someone publicly confessed to the murders, or admitted to being an eyewitness and had solid corroborating proof of who did it.

It would end if someone figured out a reliable way to talk to the dear departed, and could ask Nicole and Ron who knifed them to death.

And it would end if the blood drops collected by Fung and Mazzolla from the Bundy walkway, to the left of the bloody shoe prints—blood drops which have previously been identified as O.J. Simpson's by PCR and RFLP analysis—were to be placed under a scanning electronic microscope to check for the presence of glycerol, a preservative and anti-drying agent used to preserve autologous frozen blood. A positive detection of glycerol in this collected blood evidence would tell us once and for all that O.J. Simpson had been framed.

Maggie:
UNCLE!!

You win. I'm flying out to California tonight to effect a citizens' arrest of Ron Shipp. He is the devil incarnate and we all owe O.J. a huge apology and one big group hug. Who's with me? (Actually I'm just trying to see if anyone other than Neil and I are reading this thread.)

Anyway—I give. It's over. Good luck with your website, Neil. I'll be looking for you on the talk shows. Let us know if you ever get a booking.

Maggie

Who is Irresponsible?

Dear Neil,
  We are not in any disagreement on time, dates, etc...
  [O]ne thing is certain: [my wife] and I are not wrong about the morning call of the murders from Shipp ...

Email from my source,
October 30, 1997

In an email I received from my source to the allegations about Ron Shipp (detailed in my article "Simpson Friend Alleged To Have Lied About Knowledge of Murders," earlier in this book) my source wrote me:

"Nor would I ever call you a 'headcase,' or preposterous in your assumptions but I may say I thought you were irresponsible in presenting your theories on Shipp without any proof ..."

I wrote back:

If you had asked me, two years ago, whether I would have thought it responsible to publish a book with a theory that a private individual committed a murder, I probably would have said no. But there is a context for everything.

Regardless of the ultimate truth, O.J. Simpson was acquitted of murder by a properly empaneled jury after a nine-month trial. Marcia Clark and Chris Darden can bitch all they want about the jury pool. The fact is, they accepted that jury and all the alternates. The jury was charged with doing away with all reasonable doubts in their minds, or acquitting, and they found reasonable doubt. O.J. Simpson is, legally, "not guilty" regardless of anyone's private opinion.

I'm a libertarian who understands that the idea of juries arose as a protection of the private individual from the power of the king, and later the secular state.

But in today's political and social climate, no process is final anymore. If the cops who were accused of beating up Rodney King are acquitted, it's perfectly acceptable for the President of the United States, the Governor of the State of California, and the Mayor of the City of Los Angeles *all* to go on TV within an hour of the verdict and declare the jury wrong. Their doing so, incidentally, caused three days of rioting, looting, and arson. Over 1000 buildings were torched, some of them within a mile of the apartment complex I was managing at the time.

The fifth amendment to the U.S. Constitution also precludes double jeopardy, precisely because once a jury says "not guilty," it's supposed to mean something. But nowadays, nobody gives a damn about protecting people from the unlimited powers of government anymore. If you can't convict someone in a state court, you go to a federal court. If you can't convict them in a criminal trial, you go after them in civil court.

When prosecutors lose a case, they're supposed to go out afterward and declare that the jury verdict has meaning. All responsible public officials are supposed to make a big show out of agreeing with the prosecutor that the jury verdict is the final word. Without that, there can never be a limit to the state's power to accuse an individual of a crime, and a "not guilty" verdict will always be inadequate to give an acquitted man his life back.

But, in the Simpson case, the prosecutors went on TV and declared that they were right and the jury was wrong. Afterwards, Larry Elder, Geraldo Rivera, Charles Grodin, Judith Regan, Jay Leno, the producers of *Saturday Night Live*, Bill Maher, and hundreds of other broadcasters used their TV and radio microphones day after day after day to declare, or make jokes which said, that the jury screwed up and set an obviously guilty man free.

This is what I call irresponsible. In a sane society, the public officials who did it would have been themselves charged with criminal sanctions, and the broadcasters would have been taken off the air.

I am outraged, morally, politically, and practically, that this did not happen.

In my view, double jeopardy means that a man should not twice be tried for the same crime. The civil trial should only have been allowed to proceed against Simpson if the plaintiffs could prove O.J.'s liability on a theory *other* than that he, himself, was the murderer. One jury in superior court had already ruled on that fact as a matter of law, and the civil trial, taking place in another California superior court, should have been bound by that first verdict.

I published my theory about Ron Shipp before I had ever heard of you or knew about Shipp's phone call to you, proving that he perjured himself to help convict his supposed friend. I was careful in my book to state that I was not accusing Ron Shipp of the crime, and I was meticulous in giving him every opportunity to prevent me from publishing my theory simply by proving that what I was theorizing about him about was impossible.

Shipp chose not to take me up on that offer, made both to him directly and through his attorney before publication. You and I know why he declined: because in offering an alibi against a theory that he murdered Nicole and framed O.J., he would have to account for his perjury. People can talk all they like about how he wouldn't want to give credence to my theory by responding to it, but the fact is, I have not unweighty publications in my resume. At the time I made my offer, Shipp had no way of knowing how or where I was going to publish. He had no way of knowing my story wouldn't be in the *Los Angeles Times* or *National Review* or *Orange County Register* 24 hours after he declined my offer.

Once I spoke to you, and learned from you that Ron Shipp was a perjurer, a rogue cop and a con man, I lost any moral qualms I had previously had about publishing.

If it's not irresponsible to declare that a man acquitted in an American court is guilty of the crime for which he was acquitted, I don't see how it can be irresponsible for a journalist to say that the jury's reasonable doubt is meaningless if there exists a person with probable cause to be investigated for the crime, and the authorities charged with doing so are obstructing justice by failing to investigate.

Meeting O.J. Simpson

On Monday, June 1, 1998, a mutual friend of myself and O.J. Simpson, a person with whom I'd been working on my investigation, invited me to the Knollwood Country Club, where O.J. Simpson regularly plays golf. We found O.J. in the golf-course parking lot, packing up his clubs, and my friend drove up to him in a sporty convertible. O.J. came over to us and my friend introduced us, reminding Simpson of previous references to me and my investigation.

I gave Mr. Simpson a copy of the manuscript of *The Frame of the Century?*, and we exchanged pleasantries. I autographed for Mr. Simpson a paperback copy of my novel *Alongside Night*. Mr. Simpson said the book came at the right time because he'd just finished reading one novel and needed another one for his bed table. Mr. Simpson autographed my copy of *I Want To Tell You*, in large, neatly drawn script:

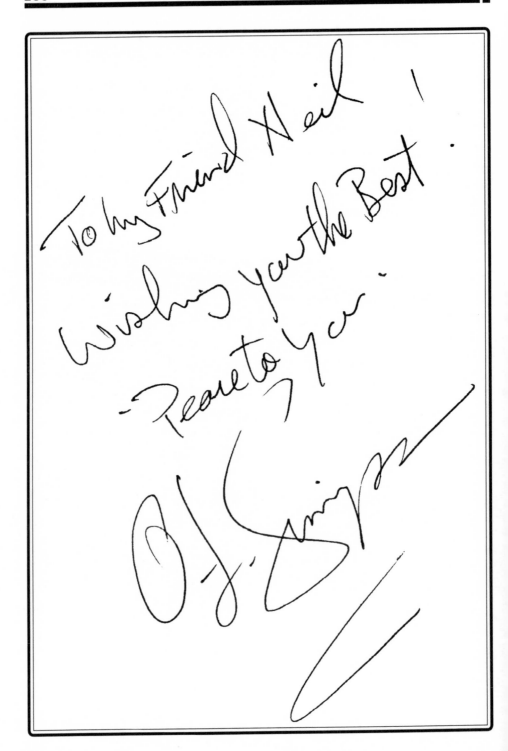

Before we drove off, Mr. Simpson told me that he'd be interested in talking with me later regarding my manuscript. I answered him, "Any time. Day or night."

However, a few days later I received a call from my friend, who'd received an angry phone call from Simpson's personal assistant, Cathy Randa. Cathy told my friend that book authors such as me had no actual interest in helping the investigation to bring out the truth but were only interested in exploiting Nicole's murder to sell books.

My friend was offended by Cathy's suggestion, and so was I. I responded to this relayed information by recording messages on both Mr. Simpson's and Cathy Randa's voice mail, then followed up with a fax to Simpson's business manager, Skip Taft.

I wrote in my fax pretty much what I also said in my messages: "If Mr. Simpson will grant me an interview to be used in _The Frame of the Century?_, in which he will freely answer my questions relating to my theory of the crime, I will commit to donating any advance and royalties I receive for the sale of the book to a charity of which he approves."

I did not receive any direct response from Mr. Simpson, Cathy Randa, or Skip Taft, leaving my offer as of this writing unanswered and declined. My friend, however, received a call from Cathy Randa the next day in which she said "We're working on this case every day." Cathy Randa told my friend (and presumably she was also speaking for Mr. Simpson) that there was nothing a book author such as myself could tell them that they hadn't already known or couldn't find out for themselves. In Cathy's words, relayed to me, "We've been burned too many times before. We won't be talking to any more writers until we're ready to reveal the results of our own investigation."

How Could Shipp Have Known?

You must understand, I did go public with my Shipp information—one day after the murders took place. Shipp contacted me in [deleted] and I taped the call. ... [We can discuss] that call and how it is impossible under the circumstances that he contact me, or be where he claimed he was when he called, Bundy Dr. with a detective...

I immediately flew to CA. and went to the D.A. Then to Skip Taft and his detectives after O.J. was arrested. I was politely hushed up after numerous meetings with Bill Pavelic, until Carl Douglas brought the matter up in court.... Quite some time after that, I was told O.J. did not want to pursue the issue. Then, surprisingly, during Carl Douglas's cross of Shipp, the matter was brought up... I was on the phone...and informed them Shipp was lying his head off. Nothing ever came of it....

Neil, you must understand, I knew Ron Shipp for twenty years, he was a loser with a capital L. A pathological liar, infatuated with Nicole, obsessed with O.J., fame and fortune, a druggie and alcoholic, a wife abuser and cheater, yet at the same time he had a dual personality that could charm the skin off a snake. But to all the inner group, he was a gopher and a wanna be. I had hired him for private detective work on numerous occasions, where I learned the real character and that he certainly had the knowledge, wherewithal and personality to murder someone...Did you know that Shipp had an outfit all in black, complete with watchcap, he called his "SWAT" outfit when he was P.I.ing at night? That he, as well as myself and others, were recipients of a multi-bladed Suisse Army knife given to us as presents by O.J. one Christmas. The very knife I have said from the day after the murders killed Nicole and Ron. Why did Ron Shipp seek out an attorney immediately after the murders? Why did he need one?

Email from my source,
September 17, 1997

On June 23, 1998, at about 5:50 P.M., I telephoned Detective Ron Phillips at the Los Angeles Police Department's West L.A. division.

Detective Phillips was the detective who, when the report of the murders at 875 South Bundy Drive first came in a little before 1:00 AM the morning of June 13, 1994, assigned Mark Fuhrman and Brad Roberts to investigate, and, along with Fuhrman, was one of the first two detectives to arrive at and walk through the Bundy crime scene, at 2:10 AM.

West L.A. division homicide detectives were responsible for investigating the Bundy Drive murders for only the next hour, until it was known that that one of the victims was a celebrity's ex-wife, then the case was reassigned to the L.A.P.D.'s elite Robbery/Homicide division at Parker Center, which handled high-profile investigations.

Detective Phillips was also one of the four detectives who left the Bundy crime scene about 4:55 AM to head over to O.J. Simpson's Rockingham estate. Phillips drove over with Mark Fuhrman, who knew the directions, with Detectives Vannatter and Lange following in the car behind them, and Phillips was one of the four detectives who entered Simpson's estate that morning. He was the first detective who Fuhrman took behind Kaelin's bungalow to see the glove. He was the detective who called O.J. in Chicago to tell him that Nicole had been killed.

Detective Phillips returned from Rockingham to the Bundy crime scene at about 7:15 AM.

As soon as Detective Phillips got on the phone with me, I gave him my name, identified myself as a journalist doing some fact-checking for my book on the Simpson case, then asked if he would answer a few questions. Phillips said I could ask but he wasn't promising that he'd answer.

I told Detective Phillips about the telephone call which my source and his wife received from Ron Shipp between 5:30 and 6:00 AM the morning of June 13, 1994, in which Shipp broke the news to them of Nicole Brown Simpson's murder. Then I asked Detective Phillips if he had any idea how Ron Shipp could have known about Nicole's murder that early. "Could an L.A.P.D. officer who knew Shipp was Simpson's friend have called Shipp when they found out that one of the victim's was O.J.'s ex wife? Would it have been against policy for one of the officers at Bundy to phone an ex-L.A.P.D. officer for information under these circumstances? Did Detective Phillips know of anyone who could have phoned Ron Shipp that early, or any other way that Shipp could have known? Was there any possibility that Shipp, himself, could have been at either the Bundy or Rockingham crime scenes with L.A.P.D. officers or detectives?"

Detective Phillips at first found it impossible to believe that Shipp could have known about the murders that early. "We were just getting to Rockingham at that time," Phillips told me. I told Phillips who my source was, but he said he'd never heard of him, and seemed inclined to dismiss my source's credibility until I told Phillips that the phone call had been recorded by my source, and that the time of Shipp's call was confirmed by my source's wife.

Detective Ron Phillips then answered my questions outright.

"I never heard about a 5:30 AM call that Ron Shipp made regarding the murder of Nicole Brown Simpson."

"I did not call Ron Shipp. I don't know of any police officer who called Ron Shipp."

"Ron Shipp was not at either the Bundy or Rockingham crime scenes that time of the morning with any L.A.P.D. officers."

"I don't have any idea how Ron Shipp could have known about Nicole's murder that early."

I read these quotes back to him and asked if I could quote him on them.

Detective Ron Phillips said yes.

Everything That Dan Petrocelli Had Against O.J. Simpson

I wrote the following review of Daniel Petrocelli's book as a customer review for Amazon.Com. It was posted on June 24, 1998.

Triumph of Justice: The Final Judgment on the Simpson Saga, by Daniel Petrocelli with Peter Knobler, is must reading for any Simpson case junkie. Even though it's over 600 pages long, I found it compelling, page-turning reading.

Petrocelli, who masterminded the civil case which won a 33.5 million judgment against Simpson for liability in the deaths of Ronald Goldman and Nicole Brown Simpson, shows us how he presented a tighter and more focused case than the criminal prosecution, and used his lawyerly skills to preempt a defense by Simpson first by excluding blacks from the civil jury by convincing the judge that they were biased, then by making motions upheld by the trial judge which prevented the defense from arguing that anyone else could have committed the murders or framed Simpson.

Petrocelli provides a wealth of circumstantial evidence against Simpson, even greater than in the criminal trial, and shows his committed advocacy to his client Fred Goldman by calling every witness who favored his side a truthful hero and every witness who favored the defense a liar and a bad guy.

He also makes the leap of faith that if O.J. Simpson lied about anything in the case, it must be because he was the murderer, and Petrocelli does not examine any other reasonable theories why an innocent man might lie. But the wealth of information Petrocelli developed through investigation and depositions manages to focus the primary question which I myself raised in my book *The Frame of the Century?* That question is: if O.J. Simpson did not commit the murders at Bundy, how could there be any possible reasonable explanation of how there could be so much credible evidence against him? Petrocelli's book may not be the final judgment on Simpson's guilt, but it does eliminate just about every other theory of the crime except the ones I examine in my own book. I endorse this book as the strongest possible case that can be made for O.J. Simpson's guilt.

Once you have read it, you'll understand why gaping holes are left which leave open the possibility that O.J. Simpson could only have been framed by someone with intimate access to him and Nicole, who also has a law enforcement background. That is the theory presented in *The Frame of the Century?*

Could O.J. Have Been Tricked into Framing Himself?

Daniel Petrocelli, in his book *Triumph of Justice*, repeatedly offers us the following syllogism: Innocent men don't lie. O.J. Simpson is lying. Therefore O.J. Simpson must be guilty of murdering Nicole Brown Simpson and Ronald Goldman.

I think the first premise of this syllogism is unproven, even if the second premise is true.

There are certain things that O.J. Simpson has testified to that I think he is probably not telling the truth about.

I think O.J. Simpson might have known that he owned the Bruno Magli shoes, but lied about it because he couldn't admit it without making himself look guilty, if he knew that the shoes had been stolen from his closet in order to frame him—or if he had walked in the blood at Bundy, wearing those shoes, in a scenario I'll get to shortly.

I also think O.J. Simpson probably did call Paula Barbieri from his Bronco at 10:03 PM the night of the murders, and retrieved his cell phone just before he left for the airport, but lied about it because his being in his Bronco near the time of the murders is extremely hard to explain. Even if we accept O.J.'s explanation that he'd driven the Bronco in the Ashford gate to retrieve golf clubs then drove out the Rockingham gate and parked there to avoid backing up through the Ashford gate, Allan Park's seeing the number 360 on the Rockingham curb, where the Bronco was found parked the morning of the 13th, would force us to assume that if O.J. was not out in the Bronco between 10:20 PM and his departure in the limousine at about 11:00 PM, someone else was.

That, and other clues, have caused me to consider that the Bronco might have been stolen at some time after 10:03 PM that night, to be used as part of the Simpson frame-up, and returned by 10:55 PM. This scenario is examined early in this book.

But I have also considered an alternative explanation: that O.J. Simpson was in his Bronco, away from Rockingham at the precise time of the murders, because drawing him away from Rockingham was part of the plan to frame him.

He might even have been at Nicole's, immediately after the murders.

And this might have left him plenty of reason to lie about where he was, what he was doing, and how he had come to leave his blood at the crime scene and track the victims' blood back to Rockingham.

Suppose at about 10:25 PM Simpson received a phone call from Nicole, calling him for help, just before she was killed. The call could have been made while the murderer was holding the knife to her throat. "Call O.J. or I go upstairs and kill your kids," the murderer could have said. There would be no billing records of such a free local call from Nicole to O.J., and Officer Robert Riske overwrote the last-call-redial on Nicole's downstairs phone when, after seeing O.J.'s photo in Nicole's apartment, he phoned in to report the murders rather than using his police radio, which might have alerted media who scan police frequencies regarding a celebrity-related murder.

A frantic phone call from Nicole would have brought Simpson to Nicole's condo within five or six minutes. In the time between Nicole's call and O.J.'s arrival, both Nicole and Ron Goldman could have been dead or dying—and O.J. Simpson might have walked into the middle of the blood on Nicole's Bundy walkway in his Bruno Magli shoes. The murderer might have gone out through the front gate within seconds after the murders, before the pool of blood had spread, and never stepped into the blood at all. The murderer doesn't leave a footprint. The patsy, called to the crime scene, does.

O.J. could have arrived with Nicole already dead, her head halfway cut off, and Ron Goldman dying but not dead. If Ron Goldman wasn't quite dead yet when Simpson arrived, Simpson bending over him could well explain why the dying Ron Goldman might have dug his fingernails into O.J.'s left hand, causing O.J.'s hand to start bleeding as he walked out the back gate, worried that he'd be seen. He might have turned briefly, considering going back for his kids, then heard something, lost his nerve, and ran.

The watchcap and gloves might have been the only items the murderer/framer would have had to have obtained before the murders in order to plant at Bundy and Rockingham in order to complete the frame-up-or maybe they were grabbed from a drawer in Nicole's condo while the murderer was inside with her.

Dropping Nicole's house key into O.J.'s travel bag would have been an easy enhancement to the frame-up, if the framer were Ron Shipp.

All the blood and fiber evidence linking Simpson to the Bundy crime scene would have been created by this simple expedient of forcing Nicole Brown Simpson to telephone O.J. to come over before killing her.

It could explain Jill Shively seeing O.J. in his Bronco, frantically trying to get back to his house before the limousine driver or Kato noticed his absence.

If this scenario were true, Simpson's hyperventilating escape from the bloody crime scene trailing blood and fiber evidence, and leaving Justin and Sydney alone upstairs, would brand him a cowardly lion who was thinking more about his reputation than his kids' welfare, and would certainly provide at least a hefty portion of any guilt he would have been feeling for the next week. It would also explain why he'd feel it necessary to lie about knowing about the murders.

If that's the only crime that O.J. Simpson is guilty of, then I think he has suffered way too much already.

But the question that I have been asked more than any other is: why? Why would anyone want Nicole murdered and O.J.

Simpson framed for it?

Let's consider that O.J. had some business dealings with some crime figure. It wouldn't be the first time that a sports figure or other celebrity was used by underworld figures for various purposes.

Let's also consider that if this were true, Nicole might very well know all about it. O.J. Simpson has a reputation of running off at the mouth.

So long as O.J. Simpson had "control" over Nicole, she represented no threat. But a break-up of their marriage, if Nicole knew too much, represented a threat to whatever underworld figures O.J. Simpson had been dealing with, whether it was drugs, or betting on point spreads of football games, or money laundering through a Pioneer Chicken franchise.

When O.J. Simpson sent Nicole the "I.R.S. letter," which disallowed her using Rockingham as her residence address and threatened her with a $90,000 capital gains tax liability for the sale of her condo in San Francisco, Nicole might have retaliated by threatening to "drop a dime"—call the police on them. A threat like this reaching the wrong ears could have sealed her fate— and O.J.'s fate, too.

Nicole might have been killed because she knew too much and was making threats to tell.

O.J. couldn't be killed, too, because the murder investigation of a celebrity of his stature wouldn't end until every business record, associate, and relationship had been followed up, and those trails might have led to the persons responsible for the murders.

O.J. couldn't just be left alone, because he probably would have dropped the dime on his unsavory associates himself, as revenge for Nicole's murder.

So O.J. would have to be discredited and coerced into silence.

Causing him to implicate himself in the murders by drawing him to the crime scene is one way.

But if O.J. didn't drive the Bronco to Nicole's—if he's been telling the truth that he didn't find out about the murders until he got to Chicago—here's another scenario that might have played out:

It had all gone so horribly wrong.

Nicole just didn't understand the sort of men he was dealing with—how her knowledge of them was a threat to their business, to their very lives. O.J. had been so naive to believe that they wouldn't kill her once it was clear that he'd lost control of her. He'd tried to reason with her, to tell her the dangerous game she was playing, but she just wouldn't listen. He'd tried to knock some sense into her at the last minute, but she was too pigheaded to understand his warning—to understand that he was trying to protect her, to keep her alive.

He'd promised them that he could control her, that if they simply frightened her enough, she'd understand the danger and promise to keep her mouth shut. That's all that was supposed to happen that Sunday night in June—a roughing up so she'd understand who she was dealing with. One last warning before things had progressed so far that even he couldn't protect her from the consequences of her threats.

So, he'd gotten on the plane to Chicago thinking that's all that had happened. She had been roughed up a little as a warning. It wasn't until Detective Phillips called him in Chicago that he knew he'd been double-crossed, that things had already passed the point of no return, that warning Nicole the night of June 12, 1994 was never the real plan, that silencing her forever was. "Nicole's killed? What do you mean she's been killed?" was all he could say into the phone when he was told of Nicole's death.

When he realized how he'd been deceived, double-crossed, how stupid he'd been, he lost it. That's when he broke the glass.

And when, a few days later, he realized that Nicole was dead because of his own naiveté, stupidity, greed, he lost it. Life was over. Things had caught up with him finally. There was no sense dragging it out. He didn't feel any goodness in himself anymore. He was the only one who'd deserved to get hurt! And there was no way that he was ever going to get the chance to tell Nicole how sorry he was.

But he still didn't realize that he was considered as much of a loose cannon as Nicole was. By trying to defend her to his "business associates," they'd lost confidence in him, doubted his resolve, doubted his willingness to place their interests above hers. It wasn't until he was in jail, and the blood from Bundy came back with his genetic markers, that he finally realized how much he'd been suckered. But by then it was too late.

He could never tell the truth about what he knew. He could never tell anyone what they had on him. He could never risk what they would do to his family if he didn't keep his mouth shut forever.

Could either of these two scenarios have happened?

Is O.J. Simpson lying about what he knows about the night of June 12, 1994 to protect his family from further threats—and himself from being seen as a dupe of organized crime figures and a cowardly lion?

I don't know. The earlier of these two final scenarios I'm offering up—O.J. being called to Bundy to arrive right after the murders—has an elegance of simplicity that all the other scenarios I've presented earlier in this book lack. Trust a novelist to complicate the plot more than he has to.

But if either of these scenarios is true, it could well explain why Orenthal James Simpson does not find it in his interest to discuss the murder of his ex-wife with an annoyingly persistent writer who, by trying to prove him innocent of that murder, just might expose him and his family to new dangers.

My only reply:

"The truth will out though the heavens fall."

—J. Neil Schulman, June 25. 1998

About J. Neil Schulman

J. Neil Schulman is the author of two Prometheus award-winning novels, *Alongside Night* and *The Rainbow Cadenza*, short fiction, nonfiction, and screenwritings, including the CBS *Twilight Zone* episode "Profile in Silver."

His first nonfiction book was *Stopping Power: Why 70 Million Americans Own Guns*, of which Charlton Heston said, "Mr. Schulman's book is the most cogent explanation of the gun issue I have yet read. He presents the assault on the Second Amendment in frighteningly clear terms. Even the extremists who would ban firearms will learn from his lucid prose."

Stopping Power was published in hardcover in June, 1994, by Synapse-Centurion, and sold out its first printing of 8,500 copies. It was quoted from by witnesses on both sides in the March, 1995 hearings on firearms before Congress's House Subcommittee on Crime. An updated edition with new material is being released by Pulpless.Com, Inc., in Spring, 1999.

Schulman's next book, *Self Control Not Gun Control*, picked up where *Stopping Power* left off with an exploration of the uses and abuses of both personal and political power.

Dr. Walter E. Williams, talk show host, newspaper columnist, and Chairman of the Department of Economics at George Mason University, says of *Self Control Not Gun Control*, "Schulman interestingly and insightfully raises a number of liberty-related issues that we ignore at the nation's peril. His ideas are precisely those that helped make our country the destination of those seeking liberty. The book's title says it all: personal responsibility, not laws and prohibitions, is the mark of a civil society."

Schulman's most-recent book is *The Robert Heinlein Interview and Other Heinleiniana*, just released by Pulpless.Com, Inc., which Virginia Heinlein calls "a book that should be on the shelves of everyone interested in science fiction."

Schulman has been published in the *Los Angeles Times* and other national newspapers, as well as *National Review*, *New Libertarian*, *Reason*, *Liberty*, and other magazines. His *L.A. Times* article "If Gun Laws Work, Why Are We Afraid?" won the James Madison Award from the Second Amendment Foundation; and in November, 1995, the 500,000-member Citizens Committee for the Right to Keep and Bear Arms awarded Schulman its Gun Rights Defender prize. Schulman's books have been praised by Nobel laureate Milton Friedman, Anthony Burgess, Robert A. Heinlein, Colin Wilson, and many other prominent individuals. His short story "The Repossessed" was the lead story in *Adventures in the Twilight Zone*, edited by Carol Serling; and his short story "Day of Atonement" appeared in the shared-world anthology *Free Space* edited by Brad Linaweaver and Ed Kramer, a Tor hardcover published in July, 1997.

Schulman is a popular speaker on a variety of topics, and a frequent talk show guest for such hosts as Dennis Prager, Michael Jackson, Oliver North, and Barry Farber. He was on ABC's *World News Tonight* as an expert on defensive use of firearms during the 1992 Los Angeles riots, and was chosen to debate Los Angeles County Sheriff Sherman Block on UPN Channel 13 News Los Angeles on the topic of the repeal of the federal "assault weapons" ban.

J. Neil Schulman is a pioneer in electronic publishing, having founded in 1987 the first company to distribute books by best-selling authors for download by modem. He is currently Chairman and Publisher of Pulpless.Com, Inc., which operates the Pulpless.Com web site—"Pulpless Fiction & Nonfiction, too!"—on the World Wide Web at www.pulpless.com, and his personal web site is at www.pulpless.com/jneil/. His internet address is jneil@pulpless.com.

All of Mr. Schulman's books are available for download from these web sites.

Lightning Source UK Ltd.
Milton Keynes UK
UKOW04f0627271015

261464UK00001B/24/P